THE FARM AT HOLSTEIN DIP

A BUR OAK BOOK

HOLLY CARVER, SERIES EDITOR

THE FARM

AT

HOLSTEIN DIP

AN IOWA BOYHOOD

Carroll Engelhardt

UNIVERSITY OF IOWA PRESS, IOWA CITY

University of Iowa Press, Iowa City 52242
Copyright © 2012 by Carroll Engelhardt
www.uiowapress.org
Printed in the United States of America
Design by April Leidig

The University of Iowa Press is a member of Green Press
Initiative and is committed to preserving natural resources.

Printed on acid-free paper

Engelhardt, Carroll L.
The farm at Holstein Dip: an Iowa boyhood /
by Carroll Engelhardt.
p. cm.—(A bur oak book)
Includes bibliographical references and index.
ISBN: 978-1-60938-117-2, 1-60938-117-3 (pbk)
ISBN: 978-1-60938-135-6, 1-60938-135-1 (ebook)
1. Engelhardt, Carroll L.—Childhood and youth. 2. Farm
life—Iowa—Clayton County. 3. Country life—Iowa—
Clayton County. 4. Clayton County (Iowa)—History—
20th century. 5. Clayton County (Iowa)—Social life and
customs. 6. Clayton County (Iowa)—Biography. I. Title.
F627.C56E64   2012
977.7'36—dc23   2012004387

CONTENTS

PREFACE AND ACKNOWLEDGMENTS

A CLASSMATE SAYS, "Elkader will always be a special place. It was a very good time to grow up." Writing about her Ames girlhood, Susan Allen Toth explains what made the forties and fifties special. We grew up "gradually and quietly" without drugs, poverty, racial tensions, crime, or violence. "Our adolescence . . . fermented in a kind of vacuum . . . [in which] nothing happened." We believed in perpetual youth until surprised by the onset of adulthood. We departed high school and home not knowing our hometown and young selves would stay with us forever.[1]

My life as a farm boy in northeastern Iowa differed from that of contemporaries reared in the college town of Ames; the predominantly Catholic, Democratic, and industrial city of Dubuque; and the onetime "Coal Capital" of Albia. My parents and other rural folk shared the world view of small-scale producers and owners in which work and thrift defined lives and success. They avoided waste, made do with less, and did it themselves. They did not buy what they did not need and avoided debt by paying cash. And they instilled these virtues in their children.[2]

The friendly moderation and civility of Iowa political culture to some degree shaped both town and farm kids. So did a national consumer society that targeted young people. Habits of thrift instilled by the Great Depression and limited family incomes checked our consumption, but we took part vicariously through the images and sounds of movies, radio, and eventually television. Popular media in these decades idealized small towns and the countryside as places filled with friendly folk who lived unchanging, secure lives. Meanwhile change registered even on my childhood consciousness as modernization and global events transformed farms, towns, and regions and forever altered the lives of their populations.[3]

Movies at midcentury shaped the thoughts and feelings of many people. Ten- and twenty-five-cent tickets made cinema a constant part of my upbringing. It elevated my appetites and left me dissatisfied with my dull life. It gave me models for manhood, womanhood, and hetero-sexual relations. Women appeared as large-busted wives and sex objects; a woman was good or bad depending on whether or not she obeyed her man and the moral rules. Screen romances portrayed prudishly with-out overt sex perpetuated my ignorance about the facts of life.[4] When movies and other media imparted values antithetical to church teach-ings, pundits, pastors, and parents voiced alarm about the pervasive and persuasive power of popular culture. Their warnings did not deter me and other kids from the siren call of seductive comic book covers, radio sounds, and cinematic images. Yet they did compel these industries to adopt self-regulatory codes.

Historian Joseph Amato—who believes that "people of every place and time deserve a history"—calls for reconstructing the everyday lives of ordinary citizens and their small communities.[5] This memoir of com-ing of age in Iowa at midcentury is offered as a modest contribution toward that end. It is a reminiscence of my boyhood, my hometown, and a vanished rural way of life. It is set within the context of the technologi-cal revolution of American agriculture, the Second World War, the cold war, and an emerging culture of affluence. Examining the lives of my family and our neighbors gives a fruitful perspective on these decades, which have been more often analyzed from an urban viewpoint.

My family, unfortunately, left behind no journals, diaries, or let-ters. I have relied on snapshots from my memory and those of surviv-ing relatives and schoolmates who took time to respond to what others likely regarded as bothersome questions. The *Clayton County Register*, the school newspaper and yearbooks, family photographs, histories of Clayton County, assorted public records, autobiographies, and histori-cal accounts of the time have supplied additional material. From these sources, I have reconstructed our family life at home and on the farm. In addition, I have described the town and assessed how it, family, popular culture, church, and school shaped me as a child. My account reflects my historical training by merging professional scholarship with personal recollections throughout.[6]

My title is taken from a scenic place of local renown located on our farm. Many had stories about the place, the people who went there, and their adventures. For me, Holstein Dip represented natural beauty, innocent childhood pleasures, and adult secrets. I spent my happiest hours swimming there on summer afternoons with my brother and dozens of other kids. A few adults came, too. They picnicked and sunbathed, seined minnows and caught chubs for bait, held midnight parties and had sex, judging by the used condoms we sometimes found.

SEVERAL PEOPLE and institutions assisted me with this book. Daughter Rachel Engelhardt long encouraged me to write about my childhood; her sister Kristen Gerlach offered support and suggested the title. Aunt Betty and brother Don Engelhardt, cousin Ron Gunderson, and former neighbor Elaine Felker Smith supplied family stories. Life partner Jo Engelhardt, as always, shared research trips and helped with photocopying, selecting pictures, and preparing the manuscript.

Several friends supplemented my imperfect mental record with memories of their own. Some completed a questionnaire or answered specific questions and volunteered information; others shared their recollections in *Memories, 1959–2009*, a booklet prepared for the fiftieth anniversary of our high school graduation. Their valuable contributions either confirmed my impressions or broadened them into a generational outlook. I am grateful for the assistance of classmates Janice (Carolan) Hamilton, Larry Dohrer, David Edwards, Janice (Lamker) Possehl, LeRoy Larson, Sandra (Lemka) Kramer, John Lenhart, Linda (Livingston) French, Eric Meisgeier, Diane (Schrody) Finley, Clarence Stahl, and Karen (Vigen) Bossard as well as schoolmates Glen Huebner, Patrick Keleher, Mary Niemeyer Harstad, John Niemeyer, and Ann (Oleson) Boultinghouse.

State Historical Society of Iowa staff enriched my visits to their Iowa City and Des Moines collections. Concordia College Interlibrary Loan Manager Leah Anderson obtained articles, books, and the *Clayton County Register* on microfilm. Fonda Dahling checked details for me at the

Elkader Public Library and librarian Carol Hauge located, photocopied, and mailed material on town history. Peace United Church of Christ secretary Kris Stark gave me access to baptismal and confirmation records and a copy of the 100th Anniversary History. Clayton County Recorder/ Registrar Sue Meyer furnished facts about my parents' farm and her staff photocopied the relevant property transfers.

Historian David B. Danbom, English professor James Coomber, and friend Eleanor Coomber carefully critiqued an earlier version. Colleague Vince Arnold rendered invaluable technical assistance. Clarence and Barbara Stahl shared photographs of Elkader at midcentury. University of Iowa Press editor Holly Carver improved the manuscript with judicious trimming and suggestions. Managing editor Charlotte Wright, copyeditor Alicia Chrest, and others at the Press guided me through publication and shaped the final product. The errors, of course, are all mine.

THE FARM AT HOLSTEIN DIP

⇒ INTRODUCTION ⇐

DURING THE mid-twentieth century, many Americans regarded the Middle West as "keeper of the nation's values." Rural rootedness of place gave meaning to the life of residents, which may be why columnist George F. Will says God is "at heart, a Middle Westerner." Iowa typifies the region in Grant Wood's paintings *Stone City* and *American Gothic*, Meredith Willson's reminiscences of Mason City in the *Music Man*, and Ding Darling's political cartoons.[1]

Historian Joseph Frazier Wall has asserted, "Iowa . . . is middle America." Located in the country's center between the Mississippi and Missouri river systems, it is bisected by the forty-second parallel, the approximate line of the first transcontinental railroad in the 1860s and an interstate highway nearly a century later. Its area, population, and personal income rank in the middle. Its political culture and parties tend toward moderation. Due to the economic dominance of Chicago, the state did not develop a regional metropolis of its own as a central place for the meeting of powerful, wealthy, and cultured elites. Iowans, famed for affability, tolerance, and hospitality, created a safe and sane place for coming of age by my contemporaries and me.[2]

Located in northeastern Iowa, an area untouched by the last Ice Age glacier, Clayton County had more forests than most of the state. Its scenic beauty of rugged, wooded hills and high limestone bluffs along streams as well as the fertile soil of the Garnavillo Prairie drew early settlers. Named in 1846 for Abd el Kader, who had been widely praised in the American press for leading the Algerian fight for freedom against French domination, Elkader had a store, a sawmill, a flourmill, and five hundred inhabitants within a decade. It waged a long "county seat war" with Garnavillo and Guttenberg before finally landing the prize.

Roman Catholic, Methodist, Universalist, and Congregational churches took root.[3]

John Thompson, an Elkader founder, also started Motor six miles downstream on the Turkey River. Using quarried limestone brought by cable car from the bluffs above, he built a six-story mill and other structures during the next two decades. The mill, which soon ceased operation, still stands as a testimony to skilled German stonemasons employed from nearby Communia. This secular socialist association of artisans, laborers, and tillers of the soil lasted a decade until ended by factional disputes.[4]

Nearly eight hundred incorporated places emerged in Iowa about every ten miles to provide farmers with access to goods, services, and markets for their crops. Towns depended upon proximity to railroads for their viability and prosperity, but hard times and natural disaster delayed rail service to Elkader until September 15, 1886. The Chicago, Milwaukee & St. Paul in 1864 bought controlling interest in the McGregor and Western, and extended its existing line northward to Minneapolis and westward into Dakota Territory. A local company began constructing a branch southward from the Milwaukee main line through Froelich, Farmersburg, and St. Olaf to Elkader, but high water on Pony Creek washed out the track and bankrupted the company. The Milwaukee took over the property and finally reached Elkader; it then denied a request by local boosters for an extension to Des Moines.[5]

The town incorporated in 1891, built a waterworks, and numbered 1,321 residents as the new century began. Within a decade, it had the brick Bayless Hotel adjoined by the Molumby Block, an electric power station, two banks, two livery stables, two lumberyards, seven saloons, and four newspapers. The *Nord Iowa Herald, Turn-Verein*—a social and gymnastic club, and Friedens Evangelical Church served a thriving German ethnic community. The jail, courthouse, and hospital for the incurably insane provided jobs, attracted trade, and ensured prosperity.[6]

Residents constructed three notable structures in these years. The twin-arch Keystone Arch Bridge—made from locally quarried limestone and acclaimed as the longest of its type west of the Mississippi—spanned the Turkey River in 1889. A decade later, Catholics dedicated the new St. Joseph's Church, designed in the popular Gothic style and built of limestone dug from the nearby hill. The first church remained in use as a parish hall. A new three-story Opera House opened in November 1903 with every seat filled for the play *Governor's Son* performed by the family of George M. Cohan. Headliner Ed Wynn also performed in what Elkader natives claimed was the best theater in northeast Iowa. Town boosters proudly publicized these structures and other symbols of small-town life with postcard images prepared by local photographers.[7]

In 1916, Realto E. Price compiled and published *History of Clayton County, Iowa* in two volumes. Among the first European Americans born in the area, he served as an attorney for fifty-seven years, remained influential in town and county affairs, and displayed his prominence by building an elegant Victorian brick mansion.[8]

Price's history lyrically described Elkader as lying "in the hollow of God's hand. Surrounded on every side by high majestic hills, with the river winding through it . . . with giant shade trees lining its streets . . . with hundreds of happy homes and handsome residences, it may surely come up to the ideal of the Peaceful Valley in many ways." He called the town "progressive" because it kept "its streets well cleaned and oiled," provided many municipal services, and offered substantial business houses of "brick or stone" in every line of retail trade. "An excellent moving picture theatre" complemented "a fine opera house." Opposite the courthouse, "the great stone mill rises impressively above the rock-lined walls of the river." The newly built "massive concrete dam" provides improved electric power, "affords fine boating above," and supplies "excellent fishing below."[9]

Exploding population and economic change pushed my ancestors from eastern Norway and Germany in the mid-nineteenth century; abundant, fertile land in the new state of Iowa pulled them to the United States. Finding what they came for in Clayton County, most of my great-great grandparents and three subsequent generations of their progeny stayed on as farmers.

Rich soil made Iowa famous. The state had twenty-six million acres of top-rated land, one-fourth of the national total. Iowans cultivated 98 percent of their fifty-six thousand square miles, the largest percentage of any state. The coming of immigrants, railroad entrepreneurs, and capital drew Iowa into the regional hinterland of Chicago, linked it to the global economy, and transformed its prairie landscape into corn, hogs, and feedlot cattle.[10]

Corn belt agriculture fueled Iowa's rapid population increase until the 1890 census showed a slowing of growth. The number of country dwellers receded as mechanization pushed many from farms, and factories drew them to cities. Clayton County, for example, peaked in 1880 at 28,829 people. It numbered 24,334 at about the time of my birth six decades later, and further decreased to 21,829 when I left for college. By that time, the state had recently become urban as 53 percent of its nearly 2.8 million people now lived in places larger than twenty-five hundred. Cedar Rapids, Dubuque, and other industrial cities boosted the Democratic Party. In 1932 and 1936, Franklin Roosevelt carried the state, which elected two Democratic senators who were not New Dealers. By the fifties, the Democrats threatened century-long Republican dominance.[11]

Germans and Norwegians settled through a three-stage chain migration, which preserved national customs. They moved initially to colonies of kin and neighbors. Later letters and remittances fostered further migration from their native region to these new American communities. Overcrowding prompted some to relocate further west where the process recurred. In the last stage newcomers came directly from the homeland to the new site. Resulting ethnic enclaves rarely interacted with Yankees and other groups. Residents conversed in their native language and founded newspapers as well as fraternal, cultural, and benevolent societies. Communal life centered on churches and pastoral leadership. Tightly knit congregations gave opportunities for social life as well as worship, and tended toward theological conservatism.[12]

Mother's paternal great-grandfather, Torkel Halstenson Groth, arrived in Clayton County from Norway in 1849. He joined the California gold rush without success. He returned, impregnated, and wed Anne Blakkestad, who soon gave birth to my great-grandmother, Rachel Halstenson. Pregnancy often preceded marriage among Norwegian peasants at that time. The couple had seven children when he died in a threshing accident in 1872 at age forty-six.[13]

In 1853, Mother's maternal great-grandparents, Endre and Brynhild Thorsdatter Wold, came with their children from eastern Norway to Wisconsin. After wintering there, they relocated to Iowa; Endre bought eighty acres from the government and soon added to it. His brother Thor settled nearby. Endre and Brynhild's oldest son Ole married Carrie Johnson Rodegarde; five sons and three daughters blessed the union. Ruth—their youngest daughter and my maternal grandmother—was born in Wagner Township on April 16, 1885. She recalled her younger brother, Ben, often being whipped with a leather strap. Yet other siblings remembered their father as "kind," charitable, and hospitable to guests.[14]

Mother's paternal great-grandparents, Ole Pederson Lerkerud and Anne Marie Iversdatter, married at Rakkestad Kirke in eastern Norway and had five children. While their daughter wed a tobacco merchant in the old country, four sons departed to Clayton County. When three relocated to the Red River Valley in North Dakota, Johan Christian Olson stayed in northeastern Iowa near his wife's family. He had married Rachel Halstenson, just four months before the birth of their first son Torkel (Tom). They had seven more children before Johan suffered a fatal heart attack at age forty-nine while chopping wood. His family found him in the timber sitting with his back against a tree. Adolph, my grandfather, was just five years old; his siblings ranged in age from fifteen years to nine months. Rachel found comfort in God during her forty-two years as a widow. After a stroke, she lived until death with her first-born son. Eight children, forty-three grandchildren, and sixteen great-grandchildren survived her.[15]

In 1862, Father's paternal great-grandparents, John and Mary Engelhardt, emigrated with their seven children from Anklam, Pomerania, to a farm near Garnavillo. The next year his grandfather, Rudolph, took a place close to St. Olaf where he gained "distinctive independence and substantial prosperity." He wed Marie Schmidt, who had been born in the same German area and whose family had immigrated to the same neighborhood as his had. She had borne eleven children and buried one before Rudolph died of a "ruptured blood vessel at the base of the brain" while threshing shortly after his fifty-second birthday. When he complained of not feeling well and lay down on sacks, his brother suggested taking medicine at home. Rudolph looked at him and said, "Charley, I'm past that now."[16]

Five years after her husband's death, Marie sold the farm to her son, John, and moved to the village of Farmersburg with her younger children, including my grandfather, Robert, who had been born on December 31, 1886. As a committed Lutheran, she angrily disowned her son, Lou, for marrying a Catholic. "You won't ever put your feet under my table again," she declared. Henceforth, she did all her business with him on the front porch. Upon her death, she had thirty-eight grandchildren and twenty-eight great-grandchildren.[17]

Father's maternal grandfather, John, was born in the north German state of Mecklenburg to Frederick and Kathrena Faber. He immigrated with his father, three brothers, and sister in 1865 after his mother's death. He married Isabelle Hulverson, who had emigrated from Norway as a child in 1859 with her parents Lars C. and Mary Hulverson. She and John settled on a farm in Farmersburg Township and later acquired eighty acres located seven miles north of Elkader on modern Highway 13. They lived here for thirty years until retiring to St. Olaf in 1918. Despite her Lutheranism, they attended the German United Brethren Church on the Gunder Road. Their three children included Ella, my grandmother.[18]

Ella married Robert Engelhardt just six months before the birth of their daughter Isabelle Frederica. The couple also had sons Curtis Rudolph, my father, and Allan Robert. Robert's slim physique and stern demeanor resembled his older brother, John. Ella had an infectious laugh, and at times irritated her serious husband. They farmed near Farmersburg until moving onto her father's place. They attended the Clayton Center Zion Lutheran Church. Isabelle, who married Melvin Peterson, suffered from a painful kidney infection when delivering her third son and soon died from hemorrhaging. Her husband, who could not bear her screams, left her in the care of others and fled to the barn until death silenced her.[19]

Adolph Olson was born on October 28, 1884, baptized and confirmed at the Marion Lutheran Church, and educated in a rural school and a Fayette business college. He married Ruth Wold on his birthday at the

Grandparents Robert Engelhardt and Ella Faber
on their wedding day, October 11, 1906.

recently dedicated brick Norway Lutheran Church, where she had been baptized and confirmed. He kept store in Gunder, rented the Thomas Peterson farm, and then resided thirty-five years on the Andrew Wold farm until Ruth's death. Ruth birthed two children: Kenneth (Kenny) and Ruby, my mother. Both were baptized at the Marion Lutheran Church, confirmed at the Norway Lutheran Church, and educated at the Glesne School. Kenny farmed; Mother boarded in Elkader, working as a housekeeper until she graduated from high school. She earned a Normal Certificate after two summer terms at Upper Iowa College, but the Great Depression limited her employment.[20]

After Father's parents relocated to the Faber farm, the Elkader Friedens Church pastor baptized him and his newborn brother. He finished eight grades in the country and then rode on horseback to high school. Town kids treated him as an awkward hayseed. He graduated and briefly

*Grandmother Ruth Wold Olson
and her son, Kenneth.*

attended junior college, withdrawing at the time of the stock market
crash that signaled the onset of the Great Depression. He scrambled for
work, selling axe handles and toiling on farms. Because rural Iowans had
a degree of security that urban workers did not, most did not leave the
land during the thirties. Father, who always had food and shelter, spoke
often about those hard times; fearing they would return, he would not
risk indebtedness.[21]

Father eventually took a job for room, board, and a small wage with
Charles and Elsa (Elsie) Felker, who belonged to the same neighborhood
card club as Adolph and Ruth Olson. Card parties may have sparked my
parents' romance. He moved with the Felkers to the Storbeck Farm on
the Old Volga Road. He carried on aiding daughters Elaine and Charldine with their homework until becoming a truck-driver for the Elkader
Bottling Works. After his confirmation at Friedens Evangelical, he wed

*Grandfather Adolph Olson
and his daughter, Ruby.*

Ruby Olson at the Norway Lutheran Church. They began married life in Elkader and then lived two years at Strawberry Point. They renewed their friendship with the Felkers in March 1937 when they rented an adjoining farm. The men shared labor at harvest time and the women helped one another fix meals. Each Saturday Mother waved Elaine and Charldine's hair.[22]

The Lutheran and pietistic faiths of my German and Norwegian ancestors sanctioned a strong work ethic that enabled them to occupy cheap land, establish farms, prosper, and assume membership in the old middle class. During the early years of settlement, their family-based households labored intensively to clear and fence fields as well as build houses, barns, and other buildings. Within the family, males and females of all ages worked. Men plowed, planted, harvested, tended livestock, handled legal issues, and directed capital investments. Women managed the

*When parents Curtis Engelhardt and Ruby Olson wed
on June 21, 1934, her brother, Kenneth, and cousin,
Marjorie Reierson, witnessed the ceremony.*

household; they cooked, cleaned, laundered, and reared children, instill-
ing moral standards. They also tended gardens, kept chickens, and made
butter. They sometimes helped men with their work; German women
toiled in fields, but Norwegian women did not. While wives did not have
equal rights, husbands valued their contributions to household wealth.[23]

Once my kinfolk attained prosperity, the women sought respectability through consuming manufactured goods. Sears Roebuck and Montgomery Ward mail order catalogs, rural free delivery, and improved roads
made shopping more important to farm families. Housewives emulated
German and Norwegian gentlefolk as well as American town women for
whom many had worked as servants. They purchased genteel dress and
furnishings as markers of middle-class status. Equating barnyard smells

with indecent behavior, they thoroughly cleaned homes and children, keeping them free from odor.[24]

My American-born grandparents and parents also learned middle-class values at the one-room rural schools they attended. Iowa Superintendent of Public Instruction Henry Sabin believed education secured social stability through training good citizens. Fearing the pernicious influence of foreign-born, ignorant, impoverished, and criminal Americans, Sabin mandated that teachers should be moral and Christian, have knowledge of the common branches, and be able to speak and write in English, which must be the language of instruction. He promoted flag ceremonies and gave out programs of special readings and music for observing Thanksgiving, Washington's Birthday, and Memorial Day. He recommended readers and histories that instilled religious, moral, and civic lessons.[25]

Work—a good thing in itself as Protestants believed—formed the core of middle-class morality in Iowa and elsewhere. It defined lives, determined individual success or failure, shaped local community prosperity, assured equality of opportunity, and sustained belief in a classless society. Churches, clubs, and lodges mirrored and sustained these communal ideals. Despite a growing number of clerks, wage-laborers, and tenants that exceeded farm owners in nearly 80 percent of Iowa counties by 1935, many Iowans aspired to independent proprietorship as farmers, shopkeepers, artisans, or professionals. When Mom and Pop owned the store or farm, they became their own boss as well as employee. Whatever wealth their labor produced belonged to themselves and their families. Agricultural cycles set workdays for farmers as well as town merchants, who kept long hours to better serve their rural patrons.[26]

The Second World War dramatically affected Iowa life. It advanced industrialization and urbanization with 154 new wartime plants. Geographical mobility increased; 24,000 left the state for defense work and 261,000 men as well as 4,000 women entered military service. Many embraced an American rather than an ethnic identity. Iowa women took jobs in larger numbers, which jumped 56 percent between 1940 and 1944. Many kept working in peacetime despite propaganda aimed at persuading them to return home. More wartime opportunities for Negroes later spawned the civil rights movement. Social change heightened personal insecurity and fostered the cult of domesticity with marriages at an earlier age, higher birth rates, and widespread fears of juvenile delinquency.[27]

The war-induced boom ended the Great Depression and furthered an emerging middle-class society. The less-well-paid-half of the population doubled their income. The backlog of consumer demand sustained peacetime economic expansion as well as employment, creating what came to be known as the affluent society. One-half of all Iowa families reported an income of at least five thousand dollars in 1959. Nationally, the number of middle-class families earning more than five thousand dollars after taxes expanded at the rate of 1.1 million annually and totaled 16.6 million at the end of 1956. No other country had ever enjoyed such abundance. As a consequence, most Americans experienced an increasingly uniform culture in which they had similar homes, appliances, furnishings, clothes, and amusements.[28]

MY FARM FAMILY shared in wartime prosperity and postwar affluence. We acquired tractors and tractor-powered machinery as well as electric home appliances that eased our labors and improved our quality of life. Yet we did not fully grasp how the war had further integrated towns and farms into national and regional economies or had advanced the agricultural production revolution. We did not foresee how quickly these trends would hasten the loss of diversified small farms, alter the lives of main street merchants, and encourage their children to depart.

While our parents lived by and instilled in my brother and me the work ethic and concern for respectability they had inherited from their German and Norwegian ancestors, they also participated in the emerging consumer society. We could hardly avoid awareness of national cultural trends and consumer goods widely publicized through newspapers, magazines, movies, and radio. Only our limited means kept us from acquiring all the material goods that we desired.

The urban class distinctions for youthful dress often blurred in our small-town high school. As farm kids, we wore Levis, flannel shirts, and even rebellious ducktail haircuts as well as chinos, button-down shirts, and flattops. Like our big city counterparts, we also tried to determine who we were in the times we spent alone with peers in cars and other places. Adults in Elkader—stirred by anxious talk nationwide about juvenile delinquency—took steps to control youthful behavior. The town council twice tried a teen center, created an ice-skating rink, and started a summertime recreation program. My church hired a youth pastor and sponsored activities. The public school kept teenagers occupied with extracurricular programs. The values imparted by this contradictory mix of national and local cultures shaped my coming of age.

HOME

ON MONDAY, September 15, 1941, Mother's labor began as she helped neighbor Elsie Felker serve the noon meal to silo fillers. She came home and summoned Dr. P. V. Hommel from Elkader just one mile away. Don, my brother-to-be, found an excited household when he returned from kindergarten. Sent to bed after supper without having his questions answered, he crept down the front stairs, entered the parlor, and peeped through the keyhole of the closed bedroom door. Unable to see anything, he went back to his room. At breakfast, he learned that his years as an only child had ended with my birth at 9:45 the previous evening.[1]

Pat Keleher, a boyhood friend, once asked in exasperation: "How many years must you live in Minnesota before you stop calling Elkader home?" I could not answer his question. Joseph Amato has since informed me what home means: "It is the source of first feelings and impressions . . . memories, and . . . passions. . . . [It is] the house into which one is born. . . . It embraces the environment, the historical era, and the temporal goods that fill it. . . . Home . . . prepares people for their encounter with the world."[2] My home encompassed a relatively new ideal of childhood, an emerging consumer society, and a rural neighborhood.

At that time, popular culture and public policy promoted childhood as a life stage devoted to play and devoid of adult tasks. Laws mandated compulsory school attendance, restricted child labor, and set a higher minimum age for marriage. All under age eighteen were now called "children" and "teenager" became a common term. After the Second World War, white middle-class suburban families adopted more relaxed child-rearing practices popularized by Dr. Benjamin Spock's best-selling *Baby and Child Care.* In the countryside my parents' generation still demanded obedience, courtesy, and diligence from their children. They also instilled habits of careful saving and smart spending. Yet even frugal folk embraced consumerism. They prepared their offspring for wise consumption by giving weekly allowances. They stepped out to dances and movies, and purchased brand name foods, furniture, radios, clothing, automobiles, and cigarettes.[3]

The cars men drove and the brands they smoked identified them. Ford or Chevy men like my father constituted a majority. Buicks or Chryslers denoted an acceptable symbol of success in our small town whereas driving a Cadillac or Lincoln seemed ostentatious. Males mostly bought unfiltered Camel, Lucky Strike, Chesterfield, or Pall Mall cigarettes. As these irritated Father's throat, he smoked Kool cigarettes, a menthol brand marketed to "sophisticated men," which he was not. He eventually turned to chain-smoking small Roi-Tan cigars known for "a hole in their head." Each came with a short plastic holder, enabling him to keep it in his mouth while working. Mother and most females did not smoke because it violated standards of respectability.[4]

We were one among eight families with seventeen sons and daughters that lived along a two-mile stretch of the Old Volga Road. Carl Ehrhardt owned the land he farmed while my father and Charles Felker rented theirs. Other neighbors toiled at the local dairy and hardware store or as a livestock/land dealer, butcher, and church custodian/gravedigger. As the youngest child but one, I learned early on about life's possibilities by observing the others graduate high school, take jobs locally or in a larger city, enter military service, attend college, and marry.

OUR SPACIOUS, white farmhouse had been erected sometime in the 1880s and enlarged later. Like many rural Iowa homes, it did not have indoor plumbing, electricity, or a furnace that worked.[5] All guests entered through a kitchen doorway from the screened-in porch. Mother locked this door at night and unlocked it the next day. She kept the porch entrance to the dining room bolted, opening it only when serving meals to threshing or haying crews. She did not secure the kitchen door that gave access to the back porch because the key had been lost. The family used this entry as we came and went for daily chores. The summertime sun warmed the screened porch mornings and trees shaded it afternoons, making it a pleasant place to play and read as a child.

Household life centered in the kitchen where we sat down to three meals daily. It had a table, chairs, cook stove, wood box, cupboards, and sink. A hand pump drew rainwater from a cistern in all seasons, but a drain to the septic field could be used only in frost-free months. At other times, Mother put a slop bucket under the enclosed sink and emptied it daily. White enameled wainscoting, curtains, wallpaper, and linoleum on the uneven floor brightened the room. Besides two entrances, four doorways opened to the rest of the house. One led to a pantry where a trapdoor covered the steep cellar stairway and a white porcelain pail for drinking water brought from the spring-fed outside well stood on a table. By the back entry, a door closed on the stairway landing where Father hung his work clothes.

Hooks for visitors' wraps and a telephone occupied walls on each side of the screened porch entry. An Aladdin Lamp by the dining room doorway gave some light to the adjoining space while illuminating the kitchen. Extra Aladdin Lamps, used only when hosting company, burned cleaner and brighter than the kerosene ones we had in our bedrooms. A battery-powered flashlight guided us through dark hallways to our beds.

Mother decorated the dining room with wallpaper, curtains, and linoleum. She kept its cherry woodwork shining and put a fern and other plants in front of a bay window lighted by the rising sun. She mended clothes or embroidered here while listening to afternoon soap operas on the consol radio. Other furnishings included a couch, an easy chair, and an oak dining room table with six chairs, one with arms in which Father always sat during holiday meals. Mother kept her silverware and best dishes in the matching buffet, a built-in china closet, and a freestanding cabinet with a curved glass door. An oil stove, erected here each winter, heated the house until 1948.

A doorway led to the bedroom where I was born. Mother, Father, and I slept here during my preschool years. Despite our close proximity, I did

not get the mumps when they did. The room had a window and an outside door with a decorative, frosted glass panel in which the red face of
the boogeyman appeared in one of my vivid dreams. He resembled Mr.
Pain of the Ben-Gay advertisements placed in the colored comic section
of the Sunday newspaper. Remodeling subsequently closed this entry.

Another door accessed the parlor, part of an addition to the original
house. Kept for company, this room had a carpet, comfortable furniture,
and two curtained windows looking out onto the well-kept lawn. Double sliding doors revealed the hallway between the dining room and an
unused front entrance. It had a hardwood floor, cherry woodwork, and
a closet, holding coats, Father's accordion that he never learned to play,
and Mother's ineffectively hidden Christmas presents. A pastel-colored
print of an idealized classical garden beside a mountain lake hung on
the lower landing of an open stairway. "Where is that place?" I often
wondered.

At the head of the stairs stood a foyer, bordered by a railing and well
lighted by two windows. Mother used her pedal-powered Singer sewing
machine in this space. It adjoined an attractive guest bedroom with two
windows, hardwood floor, and cherry woodwork. Furnishings consisted
of a double bed, dresser with mirror, cedar chest, and a small stand on
which Mother put a chamber pot, pitcher, bowl, towels, and washcloths.
A closet held additional clothing. Don stayed here when he returned
from the army as I did for the summer after my college graduation. In
this way Mother marked our passage to manhood.

An L-shaped hallway ran through the original house from the front
to the back stairway going down to the kitchen. From this passage doorways opened into two bedrooms, a closet, an attic, a playroom, and a
storeroom. Don slept in a bedroom heated through a floor vent by the
oil stove below. I joined him once I started school. Our parents relocated
here after putting in a new furnace, and we moved to the smaller room
over the kitchen. The storeroom held sacks of seed grain, crocks, jars,
and kettles; a closet for seldom-used garments such as Father's sheepskin
coat; and laundry baskets for our soiled clothes. The rafters and crannies
of the dimly lighted attic containing unused or damaged goods never
permitted total exploration by a curious child.

Three small windows admitted inadequate light to the dirt-floored, clammy basement. Opposite the potato bin beneath the stairway stood the hand-cranked cream separator. Adjoining the original cellar, the excavated area for the two-story addition held crocks of lard; myriad jars of home-canned vegetables, fruit, and meat; the furnace; and, with the coming of winter, piles of coal and wood. Mother dried frozen work clothes in this "dirty" place on frigid winter washdays and chilled food here before we acquired a refrigerator.

Two essential outbuildings sat near the back porch. A decrepit storage shed housed a kerosene barrel for fueling lanterns, lamps, and heater; a gasoline-engine-powered washing machine and washtubs; stacks of old newspapers; and barrels for collecting cans, jars, and other garbage. Rats resided under the rotting floor. Poison and Don's accuracy with a .22 caliber rifle controlled their numbers. We burned perishable waste by two rocks on the nearby creek bank, a chore I liked, having a youthful fascination with fire. We dumped the slop bucket and food scraps outside the yard fence and periodically hauled the remaining waste to the town dump.

Mother used a crude table attached to the outside shed wall for butchering roosters she raised from each year's batch of hatchery-bought chicks. She captured them with a long piece of heavy gauge wire that slipped over a bird's leg. She carried her victim to a sawed-off, bloodstained tree stump, laid its neck over the block, and sliced off its head with a corn knife. The decapitated chicken's death dance enthralled Don and me. Once its spasms ended, Mother dipped it in scalding water, plucked its feathers, and cleaned it.

A grape arbor screened from the road the weather-beaten privy located behind the shed. Like all others its door opened inward for ventilation and the privacy of users. Unlike others, it always contained real toilet paper. We did not discomfort our bottoms with corncobs or catalog pages. Flies in summer, stench in every season, and frost-covered holes on winter days made it an unpleasant place. Hence my brother and I used it only for defecation; he even tried to time his bowel movements for school hours. Otherwise, like all farm boys, we peed behind bushes, trees, or any inanimate object.[6] Beside these buildings stood the clothesline made of three heavy gauge wires strung on crossbars attached to four posts set firmly in the ground.

A large yard, enclosed by a woven wire fence to fend off livestock, surrounded the house. Mother loved flowers; she planted peonies, lilacs, and other flowering shrubs on the lawn and put a wild rose bush, irises, and other varieties in beds by the house and front gate. Three pines stood next to the county road; a bur oak, two elms, and three more pines shaded the house on the south and west. A huge, bountiful garden occupied the rest of the yard. Untended apple trees here and the nearby hillside yielded only stunted, wormy fruit.

Higher wartime income improved our material condition. Father and Grandpa Engelhardt built new steps to the screened porch and laid a cement walk from it to the farmyard and to the well. They constructed a new wooden back porch and a brick walkway to the shed and privy. The hard-surfaced walks diminished the tracking of mud into the kitchen, pleasing Mother, a fastidious housekeeper. Father eventually replaced decaying structures with a solidly built privy and a shed purchased at farm auctions. The white-painted outhouse better kept out wind, but its holes still gathered frost in winter.

Our parents restored central heating with a new furnace installed in 1948; they still did not heat the upstairs and only warmed the parlor for guests. A propane gas range replaced the old wood stove and box, making it easier for Mother to cook and keep the kitchen clean. Father tried several kerosene-powered refrigerators before obtaining a reliable model. After buying the farm, they got electricity. To save, many farmers limited electrical usage and kept older appliances until these wore out. They did without electric clocks, coffee makers, and other urban luxuries. Instead of buying new, Father rewired the battery-powered radio and substituted an electric motor for the gasoline one on Mother's washing machine. He built an electric fan but noise and vibration rendered it unusable. Like most rural wives, Mother preferred a gas to an electric range that cost more to buy and operate. Yet she bought an electric steam iron, refrigerator, mixer, and vacuum cleaner as quickly as her budget and tightfisted husband allowed.[7]

Despite the expense, many rural households installed indoor plumbing after the war. Fixtures, water heater, pump, and house renovations might cost over six hundred dollars.[8] Father feared additional fees for drilling a new well and excavating through limestone to install the septic system. This seemed so daunting that he refused to act. Living in the house for nearly four decades without running water, a water heater, and a modern bathroom inconvenienced Mother more than it did him.

From our house and yard, we heard typical farm sounds. Thunder signaled imminent storms. Wind rustled the trees, carrying the drone of tractors working in fields and the hum of highway traffic less than one mile away. Dogs barked when cars arrived. Chickens clucked and roosters crowed as they scratched in the farmyard. Outside the barn, newly fresh cows bellowed for their calves. Pigs snorted in eager expectation as Father called them from the hog pasture: "Sooouu . . . eeeeeee. . . . Soooouu . . . eeeeeeee. Here . . . pig-pig-pig-pig-pigggy." Birds chirped from their nests in trees or outbuildings. Pigeons flapped into the loft window of the barn while below swallows flitted in and out doorways to feed their young. A woodpecker beat a morning tattoo on the tin chimney flashing until Father killed it with a 12-gauge shotgun blast. When Mother objected he said, "Damn damage to the roof! That damn bird kept waking me up!"[9]

Poor insulation, drafty doors, lack of screens and storm windows for the second story, and no central heating rendered our house vulnerable to extremes of the midwestern continental climate. Iowa's average temperatures are moderate, but range from highs of one hundred in July and August to lows of minus forty in January. Weather ruled our conversations and lives. High temperatures and high humidity that produced hot, sultry days and uncomfortably warm evenings also grew bumper corn crops. Clayton County annually averaged thirty-some inches of precipitation; 70 percent fell from April through September typically during short-lived thunderstorms accompanied by strong winds and sometimes by hail and tornadoes. Iowa had dry years, but few widespread droughts. It had subfreezing winter temperatures yet infrequent extreme cold and blizzards.[10]

Thunderstorms frightened me as a child and sent some of our dogs cowering under the front porch. After a tornado destroyed buildings and livestock on eight farms north of Elkader, we drove to view the damage, elevating my anxiety about being swept away. A few years later, a tornado hit our farm without warning; it exploded the brooder house, ripped the roof from both the machine shed and old corncrib, and broke house windows. Father, having just walked from the barn, crouched behind our car in the garage. The same storm did $150,000 damage to Elkader's South Main business block, but did not kill or injure anyone.[11]

Heavy rains caused floods, affording us another tourist attraction and additional anxiety for me. Father monitored the nearby creek, having learned how quickly it came up while caught fixing fence during a sudden thunderstorm. The rapidly rising water reached hub-high on the tall wheels of his old wagon by the time he drove out of the streambed. The creek never overran our farmstead, but the Volga River swamped the villages of Volga, Littleport, Elkport, and Garber in June 1947. In 1951, the worst Mississippi River flood in seventy years inundated Marquette, McGregor, and Guttenberg.[12]

Even though heat waves and blizzards caused discomfort and inconvenience, they usually did not destroy lives or property. Ninety-degree temperatures might last a week or more, and at times the thermometer topped one hundred for as many as five days. When we could not sleep in our stifling second-story bedrooms, Mother opened all doors and windows and put our mattress on the floor of the living room or the front porch. We sometimes cooled down with a quart of ice cream purchased in town, eating it at the kitchen table with chocolate sauce and saltine crackers that Father preferred.[13]

On sub-zero mornings, ice formed on windows and edges of doors. Extra blankets, clothes, and the wood-fired cook stove kept us comfortable inside the house. To stay warm outside, we put on long underwear, two pairs of pants and gloves, sweaters, heavier coats, caps with earflaps, scarves, and four-buckle overshoes. Bulky garments made mobility and work difficult, but Father urged, "You got to keep moving to stay warm!" I moved most quickly getting inside by the kitchen stove.

Still, like others, we took perverse pride on those occasions when Elkader had the low for the state—or even nation. Local weatherman H. M. (Hank) Wolf actively campaigned for the honor. He reported lows annually ranging from minus eighteen to minus forty degrees, the record set on January 30, 1951. Our car did not start so we walked just over one mile to school and I got frostbite on two fingers. While running cold water over them at the water fountain, two concerned high school girls caused me to cry. Even though the water had solved my problem, the story later told on Main Street greatly exaggerated my injury.[14]

At least one major storm every winter yielded from eight to more than twenty inches of snow that stopped bus, car, truck, and train traffic. High winds drifted roads shut almost as fast as state and county plows opened them. Storms closed schools, businesses, and churches, but never farms. We still had to tend livestock, which called for shoveling feedlots, water tanks, and paths to the barn and other buildings.[15]

MOTHER'S CARE-WORN hands evidenced hard labor. She cooked, gardened, canned, laundered, and did other chores. As principal family caregiver, she enhanced our comfort and wealth. She welcomed overnight visits from relatives and nursed her ailing Aunt Mary and father during extended stays without modern plumbing. Despite arthritic hips and gastric distress, she expressed her love through serving others.

Mother prided herself in being an excellent housekeeper and cook, skills she had learned from her mother. Because farmers often toiled in mud and manure, wives expended much effort in keeping houses clean especially if they did not have electricity and running water. Mother regularly dusted, scrubbed, and swept. She painted, varnished, and wallpapered whenever a room looked shabby. An excellent baker, she often made cookies, bars, cakes, pies, donuts, caramel rolls, or frosted sweet rolls as well as fresh bread weekly. The house smelled wonderful on those days. Despite my frequent raids, the cookie jar never emptied completely. Although I loved the aroma of homemade bread, I preferred eating the store-bought product because its more uniform size and texture made better sandwiches. I most favored the sweet rolls she filled with strawberry and peach preserves. After I left home and married, Mother served them every time I brought my family for visits. Neither my wife nor two daughters ever appreciated these treats as much as me.

Mother daily prepared three abundant meals of common foods for the hearty appetites of her hardworking husband and growing sons. She always served bars or cookies because Father liked something sweet with his coffee. After milking, we sat down to a breakfast of fresh-squeezed orange juice and bacon, eggs, and toast; or pancakes, waffles, or French toast topped with copious amounts of syrup and butter; or cooked or cold cereal covered by thick cream and sugar. At noon, dinner consisted of boiled potatoes, meat, gravy, two or three vegetables, and dessert. After evening chores, we had a supper of fried potatoes sliced from boiled dinner leftovers, meat, vegetables, and dessert.

Mother occasionally substituted scrambled eggs and Spanish or glorified rice for another dish. She expanded servings of meatloaf, cream-style corn, and stewed tomatoes by mixing in crackers. She sometimes made vegetable beef stew or chicken noodle soup with dumplings. She fried fish if a neighborly angler had been lucky. She made Sunday dinners special by offering roast beef, roast pork, ham, or chicken with mashed potatoes and gravy. She overcooked steak, which remained tough even when tenderized by pounding with a special hammer.[16] Her hamburger, pork chops, and other meat dishes were better. For snacks, she let us have cookies, bars, or fresh fruit—apples, bananas, oranges, cherries, grapes, peaches, pears, and plums in season. Despite downing thousands of calories, Father's hard physical labor kept his weight at 170 pounds. Our active lives similarly spared Don and me from childhood obesity.

Mother toiled intensively in a large garden without much help from her men. Father plowed it for her in the spring. She drafted Don and me to push the hand cultivator between the rows, pull weeds, and dig potatoes with a silage fork. We invariably resisted, preferring to swim on sultry summer days and not appreciating our dependence upon garden produce. When I was about age five, we all harvested potatoes from the nearby bottom. Father hitched Belle and Dolly to the digger. We came behind, gathering tubers from the warm soil and putting them in old woven willow baskets for storage in the cool basement.[17]

Mother also grew beets, cabbage, cauliflower, cucumbers, eggplant, green and yellow beans, lettuce, onions, peas, radishes, squash, sweet corn, tomatoes, and other vegetables. She harvested rhubarb early and then strawberries from a large bed planted in the fifties. She picked buckets of gooseberries, black and red raspberries, blackberries, and elderberries, and later gathered wild plums, walnuts, and hickory nuts on mild, sunny autumn days in our or a neighbor's woodlot. She dried nuts on the grain binder platform and in the attic. She stripped the green outer coverings from walnuts by hammering them on a hard surface, wearing gloves to avoid staining her hands. She often shelled and picked nuts on winter nights.[18]

Canning extended summertime pleasures of vegetables and fruit throughout the year. To improve farm diets, extension home economists taught canning techniques. As a consequence, rural women widely used pressure canners by the twenties and thirties, and Iowa families during World War II preserved on average 120 quarts per season. Perspiration soaked Mother's dress and dripped from her face as she bent over boiling, pungently aromatic cauldrons of stewing tomatoes, berries, or other items in her kitchen. In addition to garden produce, she put up store-bought peaches, pears, and cherries. She made applesauce and many kinds of jams and jellies. Her legions of Kerr, Ball, and Mason jars created a rainbow of colors in the cellar. She canned meat and made sausage from slaughtered hogs or cattle until Lutz Locker in Elkader butchered and stored meat for us. After I left for college, she got a home freezer and preserved her bounty there. Homegrown vegetables, fruit, eggs, poultry, hogs, cattle, milk, and cream ensured a heavily laden table despite the modest earnings yielded by our small farm.[19]

Mother usually washed clothes on Mondays in all seasons. Without electricity and a hot water heater, it took a full day. We changed our work wear once each week and put it in the laundry basket after removing objects from pockets. Mother turned the pockets inside out and soaked the dirtiest overalls in a tub of cool water. She put the copper, oval-shaped boiler on the cook stove and filled it with rainwater pumped from the cistern because it is soft and forms suds better. Once it came to a boil, she carried buckets of steaming water outside to the washing machine in the shed. She filled and carried additional pails of cold water for rinsing.

Mother removed wet clothes from the washing machine with a wooden stick, put them through the hard rubber rollers of the hand-turned wringer, rinsed them in a tub of cold water, wrung them out again, and finally placed them on the line for drying. She pulled tight the edges of handkerchiefs, towels, sheets, and pillowcases to save ironing later. She turned colored items inside out to discourage fading. She hung shirts, blouses, and undershirts by the tails and pants and shorts from the top. She pinned socks in pairs by the toes. She put like items together. It irritated her years later when I did not hang correctly my sweat-soaked tennis clothes on her clothesline for drying.[20]

Once the washing had been hung, Mother carried the wastewater outside and dumped it over the yard fence. She assigned Don or me this chore if we were not in school. Since bedding and clothing froze stiff on cold winter days, Mother transferred them to temporary lines strung inside the house. As items thawed, a damp chill pervaded our home. In the evening Mother pressed clothes with flat irons heated on the top of the cook stove. Acquiring an electric iron eased her work. Mending socks, overalls, and other clothing followed. After Father moved the washing machine and tubs to the cellar, he rigged a pipe from the pantry, which enabled her to fill the machine without carrying buckets down steep stairs. He set up an electric pump and hose that emptied wastewater outside.

As family nurse, Mother applied Mercurochrome to small cuts, which did not sting like iodine. The antiseptic has since disappeared because it contained mercury. For colds, she had us drink hot lemonade and inhale melted Vicks vapors. She rubbed it or Mentholatum on our chests and necks, wrapping the latter with flannel cloth. For coughs, she gave us licorice-flavored Smith Brothers or triangular-shaped Vicks cough drops. If stricken with stomach flu, Mother emptied our chamber pot in the privy and rinsed it with scalding water for the next siege of nausea or diarrhea. She recommended milkweed sap for warts I had in early childhood and they disappeared. She applied damp heat and carbolic salve poultices to painful boils that plagued me in my teens. Relief came when these opened and drained large amounts of putrid matter.[21]

Father took daily spoonfuls of cod liver oil that Don and I refused. He and Mother rubbed liniment on their sore muscles gaining relief from its burning sensation. Except for being laid up with mumps and gall bladder surgery, our parents—no matter how ill they felt—

always did chores twice daily. In contrast, they granted Don and me "lay about" status when we were ill.[22]

"Doc" Hommel treated me for ringworm, whooping cough, and worms. He later prescribed drugs for pinkeye and an ear infection, but could do nothing for the chicken pox that children simply endured. When infected tonsils and enlarged adenoids troubled Don, an Oelwein doctor operated on both of us in 1949. My questions went unanswered about why his illness necessitated my treatment. Our bill for two operations and overnight hospital stays came to about sixty dollars. The same doctor diagnosed me with lazy eye a few years later—too late for the condition to be corrected. In annual visits to dentist "Doc" Meder, he fixed cavities with a slow drill and without Novocain until my high school years. Even though his scolding increased as decay advanced, my hygienic habits did not improve. No flossing and infrequent brushing has cost me thousands of dollars for root canals, crowns, and bridges. Still, modern dentistry saved my teeth; Grandpa Engelhardt long managed without any, and Mother got dentures at thirty-four.

Mother shopped for the household. "It's terrible," she said, when inflation pushed prices for a loaf of bread from eight to twenty cents between 1941 and 1959. She economized by clipping coupons, saving Gold Bond Stamps, and ordering from Montgomery Ward and Sears Roebuck catalogs. She also bought from the traveling Watkins Man, who sold vanilla extract, nectars, and spices at low prices. As the opening of school neared, we drove thirty miles to Oelwein, which had the nearest J. C. Penney and Sears stores where she bought us shoes, blue jeans, shirts, and underwear. Don and I liked watching the small cash box travel along a ceiling track from our clerk to the cashier. The Fluoroscope—a device used by shoe stores for X-raying feet to determine fit—attracted us and all other children. Mother always got orange slices and chocolate stars at the Woolworth's candy counter as a treat for our ride home.

Mother insisted that we put on clean clothes for going to town or visiting. She purchased attractive ties, dress shirts and pants, suits, and winter coats for us during sales at Theis Clothing, a local store. Lengthy conversations with manager Emmet Whalen preceded all transactions. She always dressed well herself, shopping at Phylls' Apparel for Women and Children. The elegant owner, Phyllis Patterson, had worked in smart shops in Miami Beach, Palm Springs, Hollywood, and Beverly Hills. She telephoned me years later to express her sympathy for Mother's death and to compliment her excellent fashion sense. Similarly the undertaker—a man who also knew something about presentation—told me: "Your mother always looked nice."[23]

Mother and Father instilled the Protestant work ethic in Don and me. They believed that the diligent application or willful neglect of its cardinal virtues explained the success or failure of every Iowa farm family. They labored most days from dawn to dusk. They expected us to do daily chores because it developed character and our sweat equity made up for lack of capital resources. They weighed every purchase for its necessity or utility. They drank alcohol in moderation, but sternly warned against excess, pointing to the hometown drunks, who had lost jobs, farms, wives, and children.

Habitual parsimony limited our participation in the postwar age of abundance and expanding consumer society. Mother and Father always paid cash. They rejected gasoline and other credit cards when these became available. They often made do with goods they already owned. When blond-finished furniture became popular, Mother sought fashion through industry rather than purchase. She spent winter evenings over a two- or three-year period laboriously refinishing the kitchen table and chairs, the dining room table and chairs, the buffet, the china cabinet, and the consul radio.

When Father decided to replace our 1934 Chevrolet sedan at the end of the Second World War, he put his name on a local dealer's list for a new car. During the lengthy waiting period created by the wartime suspension of automobile production, he bought a 1938 model. Even when new vehicles became available, he prudently avoided the large first-year depreciation by buying a succession of one- or two-year-old cars. He washed and waxed them regularly. His skill as an excellent "shade-tree mechanic" reaped additional savings. He replaced tubes, tires, batteries, plugs, points, filters, tailpipes, and mufflers. He purchased used farm machinery and kept it working with timely repairs.

Our parents also faced the challenge of rearing two rambunctious sons.

In Sunday clothes, I stand by Father's recently acquired secondhand Chevrolet.

Like many boys, Don and I abandoned any pretense to angelic behavior once adult backs were turned. We smoked cigarettes and cigars pilfered from Father. We gawked at photographs of nude women. We joked about masturbation, saying, "I will only do it until I need glasses," which I acquired in sixth grade without affecting my habits. We swore, saying "hell," "damn," and especially "shit," a predominant presence in our farm environment. We called one another "dumb shits" or "shit asses." We dismissed complaints with "tough shit." If angered by someone, we told him: "Stop giving me that shit!" "You are in my shit house!" "You are on my shit list!"[24]

We never said these things within earshot of our parents. Father had a reputation for being plainspoken and "particular about things." As a high school friend, Daryl Dahling, who worked at the Elkader Cooperative, recalled: "You always sort of knew where you stood with him." Descended from two Prussian immigrant grandfathers, he exercised patriarchal authority and expected our obedience. Mother backed his demands.

Our misbehavior seldom went uncorrected. Don once pushed me butt-first through the kitchen window while roughhousing on the porch.

Mother determined I had not been cut, then yelled at Don who took off running with her in hot pursuit. Failing to catch him, she threatened: "You will get it when your father comes home." Father gave me my last spanking at age four for messing my pants. The flat, pliable surface of a rubber-soled tennis shoe delivered a memorable sting. Our parents still gave, and we caught, "hell." Their scolding questioned our intelligence and moral worth. In theory, the shame instilled by such chastisement prevented future misdeeds.

Sometimes no retribution followed. At about age twelve, I helped myself to a shot of whiskey from the bottle Father kept in the pantry. Not satisfied with just one, I had another. Noting my pale demeanor and telltale breath at supper, my parents inquired, "How do you feel?" "Fine," I replied, unwilling ever to confess to anything. Nothing more was said. They assumed correctly that my experiment had taught me what I wanted to know about whiskey at that time. I never raided Father's liquor supply again, although in my late teens and early twenties I often overindulged to the point of sickness until I finally learned appropriate limits for my health.

After Don returned from the army and paid rent while living at home, he once stayed out all night. It had been too foggy to drive and he had not wanted to disturb us with a telephone call. Mother, anxious with worry, had not slept anyway. Upon Don's return the next morning, Father angrily rejected his story and grounded him for one week. This was hard for a twenty-two-year-old veteran to accept, but he submitted. Don soon found his own place to live, which Father welcomed as a sign of maturity.

At Father's death two decades later, Don remembered his authoritarianism with bitterness: "He had never been anywhere! He had never done anything! But he always thought he knew everything!" I understood his anger, but my struggles in parenting two daughters made me more charitable. Our parents raised us in the best way they could based on what they knew and had experienced from their own parents. They did not physically display affection with hugs, kisses, or even pats on the back. They did not praise us for good deeds or work well done. They simply expected us to do and behave our best. Their harsh criticisms left us both

Don and me with Uncle Kenny
at his parents' farm home.

with resentments and scars. Yet their provision for our material needs, practical instruction, and moral discipline expressed their deep love for us. Every childhood ought to be similarly blessed by such priorities.

IN AN OLD PHOTOGRAPH Uncle Kenneth Olson, nine-year-old Don, and three-year-old me stand in front of our maternal grandparents' stone farm home. With a meerschaum pipe in his mouth, Kenny is nattily attired in a jauntily cocked hat, tie, leather jacket, and dress pants. His belt has a monogrammed buckle. Don stands beside him, dressed in slacks and a short-sleeved shirt with his arms straight at his sides. I am in front, looking somewhat rumpled, wearing a jacket and short pants, and holding a flower in my left hand. Kenny sometimes played cornet duets with Don while I tapped along in time, convincing him I would become a drummer. A hard worker, he farmed with his parents. Mother attributed his bachelorhood to an eye discolored by a childhood accident. Father blamed alcohol: "He won't look at a woman until he is liquored-up, and then no woman will look at him."

After wartime production restrictions ended, Kenny bought a stylish 1948 Studebaker Champion coupe. Don and I were excited to ride with our grandparents in his new car to Oelwein. Kenny, who had gone to a tavern while his mother shopped, scared us on the trip home by driving too fast. As he ignored our tearful entreaties to slow down, Don insisted that we be allowed to walk the one-half mile to our farm from where the Old Volga Road intersected Highway 13. Our parents, seeing us on foot and upset, pressed for details that we could not provide. Grandma Olson soon telephoned with an explanation.

Alcohol made Kenny belligerent. He once scuffled with Father to the dismay of Mother and Grandma Olson. It ended with Father perched on his chest; Kenny never challenged him again. On other occasions, he fought with his father and perhaps his mother. She said falling down the stairs had bruised her. As a child, I accepted her story and often humorously recounted her fall: "Crash! Bang! Boom! Uff-da!"

An active, nervous, and slender woman, Grandma Olson cooked well and kept a clean house. To keep it cool on hot days, she served meals in the summer kitchen. She helped Mother can meat and make sausage. Mother aided her in feeding threshers, while I waited at the windmill for the "water boy" who drove the tank wagon for refilling the steam engine boiler. She attended church faithfully as evidenced by her well-worn Lutheran book of worship. She fretted that a bee sting made my swollen face unpresentable at the Elkader Fair, but she bathed me in a tin tub and took me there anyway. She teased me about "your girl friend Sheila Clark," my classmate and her neighbors' granddaughter. She gave me unlimited access to the player piano in her parlor. Pumping with my feet, I'd run through roll after roll of popular music that hardly enhanced my refinement, but gave me the pleasure that piano makers promised farm families.[25] She shot baskets with me with her hair in curlers and a towel draped over her shoulders during a home permanent given by Mother.

A few months later, she suffered a cerebral hemorrhage while preparing supper. As she lay comatose on the living room couch, Don and I sat on the stairs listening to the family talk about her medical condition.

Kenny adamantly insisted, "She is my Ma! I want her taken to the hospital!"

"Nei! Nei!" Grandpa Olson replied. "The doctor says nothing more can be done."

Father took us home and Mother sat with her through the night. She died early the next morning. When Mother lay on her deathbed forty-seven years later, she insisted that one of us stay with her as she had done with both her mother and husband. As it happened, her pastor, my brother, my wife, and myself were in the hospital at her side when she passed away.

Grandpa Olson somewhat resembled John Wayne in photographs taken of them at a similar age. A tall man, who spoke with a Norwegian accent, he could wiggle his ears, a fascinating skill for entertaining his grandsons. Once I swallowed a penny he had given me. He promptly dislodged it by turning me upside down and slapping me on the back. After losing a farm in the economic downturn following World War I, he rented two hundred acres from his brother-in-law, Andrew Wold. He kept a stud horse and a smokehouse for curing meat that made him well known over a wide area. As machine man for his threshing ring, he tended both the steam engine and separator. One day he gave me a pulsating ride on the antique tractor as he moved it slowly from one field to another. Without his dead wife's careful household management, his economic fortunes declined. He and Kenny bought a small, hilly place that Father called "a goat ranch." They sold it after a few years and relocated to a little house in Clermont. To qualify for social security, Adolph found a job while Kenny worked construction.

Grandparents Robert and Ella Engelhardt's house on the Faber farm did not have indoor plumbing or electricity. They had an old dog named Cap, Bantam hens and roosters, and equally combative geese that responded angrily to the curiosity of small boys. Uncle Allan, who had been born there, assisted his father until he married Betty Livingston in 1945 at the Evangelical and Reformed parsonage. His parents relocated to Elkader, and the newlyweds took over the farm. Twelve years younger and heavier than Father, Allan resembled his mother. His wife's friendly personality and gift of gab made her my favorite relative. They lived on the Faber farm until March 1950 when they moved to eighty acres Ella had purchased near St. Olaf. The property had a nice house with electricity and gravity feed from the cistern for washing in the basement, but no indoor toilet. They moved to Elkader in 1957, where Allan worked initially for Grau Lumber and then the Iowa State Highway Department.[26]

During initial visits to Grandma and Grandpa Engelhardt in town, Don and I slept in the same bed with Grandma. Since my restlessness kept everyone awake, she purchased a sofa-sleeper for us. A good-natured, roly-poly woman, she wore her long white hair in a bun. She relished quilting, and for weeks every winter the frame filled her dining room. She made many summer berry-picking expeditions and once got poison ivy much to Grandpa's irritation at her failure to see the danger. I liked staying with her; two school friends lived nearby and she kept a large set of tinker toys as well as a stereoscope—a handheld device for viewing pictures in three dimensions.

For reasons unknown to us, Grandpa Engelhardt slept separately upstairs. A slight, quiet man, he fretted so much about newly mown hay and harvesting other crops that he could not eat. In town he had a basement workshop and kept a large vegetable garden, vines of Concord grapes, and a strawberry bed. I much enjoyed these fruits of his labors. He frequently fished the Turkey River and shared his catch of suckers and sunfish with our family; the many bones of the former made his gift a mixed blessing. He once took Don and me fishing. After I tangled my line by fooling around, he never invited me again. He had me clean the chimney of his two-story house with a weighted sack attached to a rope. "He was like a cat on that roof," he told Father. At age fifteen, I did not yet fear heights.

Grandpa Engelhardt often came to our farm to dig thistles from the pasture or to help with other tasks. One day when we were removing rocks from a road leading to a hillside field, I commented, "I wish I had a nickel for every rock I've thrown this morning." He looked at me levelly and said, "You might as well wish for a dollar." This wisdom tersely delivered was typical. "He never said much, but when he said something you knew that he meant it," his sister Alma told us after his death. It isn't a bad credo to live by, I have often thought.

Like many families, ours gathered at Easter, Thanksgiving, and Christmas. Together with Uncle Allan and Aunt Betty we overflowed Grandma Engelhardt's small house. She added leaves to the table, covered it with a freshly laundered and ironed embroidered cloth, and set it with her best silverware and china. Mother and Betty contributed salads, pies, or other dishes to the feast. The women served the food, cleared the table, and washed the dishes. Men sat in the living room and talked about farm-related issues.[27] For Grandma Olson's dinners, she got up at 3:00 A.M. and put a thirty-five-pound turkey in the oven. The great-aunts and –uncles who gathered around her table spoke English or Norwegian, depending on what they thought children ought to hear.

When Grandma Olson died, the Thanksgiving meal she could not prepare is the first loss I experienced in her passing. Family, joined by friends and neighbors, still gathered that weekend at the wake held in her parlor. A memorial wreath on the front door greeted them. After mourners departed, Uncle Kenny let his German shepherd lie grieving beside her coffin. Mother, who could not understand "why she allowed that dog in her house," had nightmares about Grandma appearing and asking for her shoes. At her funeral, held at the country Norway Lutheran Church, six nephews served as her pallbearers as they would for her husband, son, son-in-law, and daughter when they passed.

After Grandma's death, Mother invited her father and brother as well as Father's parents to holiday dinners at our home. Wonderful odors filled the house long before she put the bountiful meal on the table. Although Mother served many of the same dishes, she fixed duck, goose, or chicken instead of a turkey, which was "too big and too dry." Mashed and sweet potatoes, gravy, stuffing with and without raisins, creamed corn and peas, squash, yams, and other vegetables, dinner rolls and lefse, pickles, pickled apples and beets, and glorified rice accompanied the meat course. After everyone had finished, coffee and dessert immediately followed. One learned at an early age that "eating one's fill" meant saving room for pie! Our choices included pumpkin and perhaps apple, cherry, peach, mincemeat, pecan, banana cream, or lemon meringue.

Mother and her mother-in-law then washed and dried the dishes in the kitchen while the men alternated between talking and dozing in the dining room. Father invariably proclaimed, "Days like this sitting around are hard for me. I'd rather be outside working." Socialized to regard industriousness as a good thing, no one regarded this as an inhospitable remark.

Mother prepared for Christmas by baking such traditional Norwegian treats as lefse, flat bread, sand cakes, rosettes, Krumkage, fruit soup, divinity, fudge, and several kinds of cookies. She decorated with seasonal runners, tablecloths, and center pieces. She dispatched Don and me to cut a tree from our timber. We invariably returned with a dried-out cedar. Some years we harvested one early and tried making it greener by placing it in water. The tree always looked festive once it had been decorated with tinsel, ornaments, and, after 1954, a string of lights. Before then, a lighted tree for us meant viewing it with a flashlight at night. I had my own Advent rituals. I studied Sears Roebuck and Montgomery Ward catalogs and gave Mother my list of toys not costing more than five dollars. As I waited impatiently for the magic day by listening to the many holiday programs on radio, I most enjoyed the annual broadcast of Charles Dickens' *A Christmas Carol*.

On Christmas Eve, we did chores early so that everyone could be bathed and dressed for the traditional Sunday School program at Friedens Evangelical and Reformed Church. For supper, Mother ordinarily prepared oyster stew, which she and Father enjoyed but Don and I did not. We made do by substituting crackers for the oysters in the tasty cream-based broth. After the service Father drove us about town so we could view the decorative lights displayed by residents. At home we ate cookies and drank cocoa, which only fueled our excitement.

Naturally, Don and I rose early on Christmas Day. I always garnered something from my wish list, but never everything. My parents routinely vetoed several items. Chemistry sets were too expensive and too dangerous. Erector sets contained numerous small, sharp-edged metal pieces that would be quickly lost or damage Mother's well-maintained woodwork. More Hardy Boy mysteries unnecessarily duplicated the three we possessed. Still, American Logs, American Bricks, and Lincoln Logs received at different times fulfilled my building urges. A windup locomotive that pulled five authentic looking railroad cars around an oval or figure-eight track entertained me for hours. One year, Grandma Olson gave me a watch with the Walt Disney character Daisy Duck on its face.

"Real boys don't wear girls' watches," I protested.

"The store did not have any more Donald Duck watches," she explained. I resigned myself to wearing her gift but clarified my plight to anyone who would listen.

For me, Christmas was more about getting than giving. Indifference, joined with lack of money, taste, and patience, made me a poor shopper. I gave Father a Zane Grey novel after Mother warned me that he would not have time to read it. Yet I did succeed once with her gift as an adolescent. She kept the hand-painted wooden plate on the kitchen wall until her death. "Happy is the Girl Who Learns to Cook, Either from Her Mother or from a Book" certainly expressed her credo in serving holiday and other meals to family and friends.

All too soon my parents and grandparents decided I was too big for toys and gave me more practical gifts such as clothes. Perhaps the communal nature of farm labor hastened turning kids into adults. The parental present of a watch formally marked this passage for me at age fourteen. Putting it on my wrist, I sat by the lighted tree in our living room and looked pensively into the Christmas Eve darkness as carols played on the radio. Noting my somber mood, Mother asked, "What's wrong?" I could not say, "I am not ready for adulthood."

Mother also hosted her father, brother, and in-laws at Easter Sunday dinners. At this less abundant but still ample feast, she often served ham accompanied by several of the main dishes featured at the other holiday meals. On that morning as children, Don and I searched the house for hidden Easter eggs and candy. One Easter Grandma Olson presented us with paper-mache rabbits filled with jelly beans and chocolate eggs.

Mother saved the bunnies and three decades later displayed them for her own granddaughters. I soon outgrew the Easter Bunny, aided by an older sibling who dispelled the Santa myth as well.

Farm kids did not participate in all holidays. On May Day town kids hung homemade paper baskets containing candy on doorknobs, rang the bell, and then fled to avoid being kissed by a member of the opposite sex. I envied them for this custom that did not lend itself to the conditions of rural life. Each Halloween when I pleaded for an opportunity to trick or treat with town kids, my parents refused, explaining, "It would be begging!" I did not take part in the annual Easter Egg Hunt sponsored by Elkader merchants for the same reason. I escaped their ban in 1953 when Halloween occurred on a Saturday night. While Mother shopped, I donned a black mask and went door-to-door accompanied by much more adorable small children. The night did not thrill me as I had anticipated when younger.[28]

RURAL IOWANS, like midwesterners generally, proficiently practiced neighborliness. They traded labor to complete large tasks. They did chores, planted, and harvested for those laid up by illness. They provided food and sympathetic support for bereaved families. They got together at card parties and dances. Their friendly conversations may have concealed true feelings, which seemed deceitful to urban dwellers. Yet it maintained goodwill among people who met together frequently.[29]

My parents knew their neighbors by name and visited with them if they met in town or someplace else. Yet they normally socialized only with farm families living along their road and beyond. They were among fifty guests at the wedding reception for Charldine Elsa Felker hosted by her parents in their home. They took part in wintertime card parties as well as birthday, anniversary, and retirement celebrations usually reported by the local newspaper. These events were often basket socials with each family bringing food to share. Guests arrived at about eight o'clock. They visited for a time and then played pinochle at portable card tables set up throughout the house. Laughter frequently punctuated conversation. Children amused themselves with games, ghost stories, or talk. At about eleven o'clock the hostess served sandwiches, Jell-O or macaroni salad, cookies or cake, and coffee or Kool-Aid.[30]

I liked lunch, thinking in those pre-Prilosec years that I slept better on a full stomach. Getting up for school the next day did not trouble me until my parents attended parties almost nightly over a two-week period; these honored a neighbor, who had terminal cancer. When asked what his friends might do for him, he said, "Play cards!"

"Pigeon fries" offered an exciting weekend variation in which men caught pigeons in barns and took them to one home where women cleaned them. The next evening everyone came back with dishes and deserts to complement the birds roasted by the hostess. The meat always tasted great, but it took several legs to achieve the pleasure afforded by a single chicken drumstick. Uncertain about the legality of these events, Mother told me not to talk about them at school. While animal rights activists certainly would object, farmers regarded pigeons as pests that deserved extermination.

The coming of television pretty much ended such large parties by the mid-fifties. As set numbers and per capita viewing hours grew over time, TV privatized leisure for most Americans who now amused themselves at home.[31] Mother and Father still played pinochle or five hundred with another couple while serving beer or mixed drinks. Lunch still ended the evening before midnight. I might sit in for a hand or two while Mother prepared food, but as an angst-ridden teenager I withdrew from these get-togethers.

The last large gathering at our home took place in August 1963 at a shivaree hosted by my parents for my bride and me. We had wed in her hometown. Few neighbors had traveled two hundred miles to the dry Methodist wedding. Father complained, "I couldn't even give a drink away!" Cars overflowed our farmyard with horns blowing and cowbells ringing. People filled the house, talking, drinking ice-cold beer, and eating lunch. All reminisced about the days when such events occurred more often.

Both Mother and Father had many aunts, uncles, and cousins. Relatives commonly went for Sunday drives and dropped in on one another or less frequently hosted family dinners. Such visits routinely prompted my query, "Do they have any kids?" If Mother answered "yes," I anticipated a fun-filled day. "No" implied a boring, interminable afternoon spent alone with adults. After a suitable time visiting, hospitality dictated offering company coffee and food. Guests accepted while saying, "You shouldn't go to any trouble." For farmers, anxious to depart by four o'clock for chores, lunch terminated the call. My grandparents often stopped more briefly without refreshments. On one such occasion when Grandma and Grandpa Engelhardt sat passing an idyllic summer evening on our screened-in porch, I recall thinking, "This must be what heaven is like."

Mother's Uncle Theodore Wold, an energetic septuagenarian widower, sometimes stayed overnight in our upstairs guest room. He won the hearts of his grandnephews by dancing a jig, eating peas with a knife, drinking coffee from a saucer where he had poured it to cool, playing cards, and giving us a dollar on our birthdays. Mother similarly hosted two servicemen from Michigan with whom Don had ridden when he returned home on leave from their base at Fort Lewis, Washington.

The most memorable visit occurred when Father's nephew came from Denver, Colorado, with his Mexican American wife and their three children—a dark-haired son and blond, identical twin girls. Mother, who had no knowledge of Mexican cookery, wanted to fix something culturally suitable. She therefore served Spanish rice and spaghetti with meatballs and tomato sauce. Rose graciously appreciated Mother's heartfelt and half-correct hospitality. My parents also took them to Pikes Peak State Park, overlooking the Mississippi River, and to the Bily Clocks Museum at Spillville, a Czech town.

"Your father was such a good dancer," a neighbor once told me. The many dances he and Mother attended with friends gave him plenty of practice. Dance halls ranged from respectable to raucous, with open bars selling 3.2 beer and pop as a mixer for those who brought bottles of liquor. Live "western swing" bands of five to ten men playing some mix of an accordion, fiddle, banjo, guitars, clarinet, trumpet, bass, and drums presented songs and instrumentals of varied quality. As a kid, I sometimes accompanied my parents to Communia Hall, site of a failed utopian settlement. Mother's cousin and his band, Ray Alto and His Cowboy Serenaders, often played there. "Don't run," she would say as I whizzed by with other children, competing to slide farthest on the sanded floor. The next day at play in the kitchen, I recreated the evening by building a trumpet from tinker toys and a stage with blocks.[32]

My parents had an opportunity at Lakeside Ballroom in Gutten-berg to "Dance to the Champagne Music of Lawrence Welk and his orchestra—Coming Direct from the Famous Roosevelt Hotel in New York City." They often went to the Elkader Vet's Club, where the Mississippi Nite Hawks played modern and old time music.[33] If I did not stay with grandparents, I slept in a locked automobile parked on Main Street that the town constable kept an eye on. I stayed alone at home after turning a trustworthy thirteen.

Like most farm families in the forties, ours spent many evenings gathered around the radio except during summer when the batteries on our set died and Father believed his sons should be outdoors. In the less clement months, listening lessened our isolation, stimulated our imagi-nations, and created a national identity that we shared with ethnically and socially diverse urban and country dwellers.[34]

While Father read his newspaper or farm journals and Mother mended clothes, Don and I listened to several Sunday night comedi-ans. We loved it when stingy Jack Benny visited his underground vault. We looked forward to the many voices of Mel Blanc, who played Jack's French violin teacher, the hard-to-start engine of his antique Maxwell, and a little Mexican. We liked how Charlie McCarthy mocked Edgar Bergen and rejected every lesson he tried to teach. We marveled at Mor-timer Snerd's stupidity. When told that he is considered ignorant, Mor-timer responds: "Awww, you're just saying that to make me feel good." The southern Senator Claghorn, who appeared with other regional and ethnic types on Fred Allen's "Alley," amused me most. He attended "CCNY—Charleston, Chattanooga, Natchez, and Yazoo, . . . graduated 'magnolia cum laude,' [and] his class voted him most likely to secede."[35]

Everything I knew as a child about African Americans came from *Amos 'n' Andy*, a popular show created by white actors Freeman Gos-den and Charles Correll. By the time I became a fan, the program had shifted to a thirty-minute spot on Sunday night and George "Kingfish" Stevens displaced Amos, leading me and other youngsters to wonder why the program was not called *Kingfish 'n' Andy*. Yet the humor still derived from characters, situations, black dialect, and misused words as the Kingfish regularly duped Andy with get-rich schemes. Despite its racial ventriloquism, many African Americans liked *Amos 'n' Andy* for portraying black characters in human terms. Yet the National Association for the Advancement of Colored People (NAACP) denounced its racial stereotypes of Negroes as uneducated, lazy, and slow, and eventually drove it from the air. As a child, it did not matter to me that white actors depicted blacks. I listened because the program was funny; the mistakes and misstatements of African Americans seemed a lot like those of whites on other shows.[36]

Stereotyping women did not trouble me, either. Kingfish's wife Sapphire and Wallace Wimple's wife "Sweetie Face" on *Fibber McGee and Molly* best embodied the shrew—a stereotype most often heard. Many comedians relied on mother-in-law jokes for almost certain laughs. *My Friend Irma* featured Marie Wilson as radio's dumbest blond, weekly helped out of self-induced troubles by her brighter roommate. In contrast, Eve Arden played a smart, independent, well-respected high school English teacher on *Our Miss Brooks*.[37]

While Don and I preferred comedies, Mother favored *Dr. Christian*, a medical serial that ran from 1937 to 1953. Danish actor Jean Hersholt played a dedicated doctor who tended the residents of River's End. Each show opened with nurse Judy Price (Rosemary De Camp) pleasantly answering the telephone: "Dr. Christian's office!" She also did the commercials for Vaseline, 100 percent pure petroleum jelly. We all liked mysteries. *Mr. and Mrs. North* aired on CBS from 1942 until 1954, eventually reaching twenty million listeners. Witty Jerry and Pam North lived in Greenwich Village and weekly solved crimes the police could not. The theme song, "Someday I'll Find You," introduced *Mr. Keen, Tracer of Lost Persons*, which ran longer than other detective series despite its mediocrity. The famous creaking door on the *Inner Sanctum* sounded scarier on the radio than it ever appeared on television. Listening to these tales in our darkened living room frightened me so much that I never tuned in unless accompanied by my older brother.[38]

During late winter, Mother popped corn as we listened to broadcasts of basketball tournament games. The women's teams from nearby Monona and Garnavillo gave us a lot to cheer about as they competed for five state championships in the early fifties. We also rooted for tiny Roland, led by its star guard Gary Thompson, which lost the boys championship to Davenport Central, the largest high school in the state. I also followed major league baseball once local hero Jack Dittmer joined the Braves and the team relocated to Milwaukee. Three years later, I monitored Harry Carey's broadcasts of the St. Louis Cardinals on my bedroom radio. Come October, I tuned to the World Series. I mourned when the hated, perennial world champion New York Yankees beat the Brooklyn Dodgers and the New York Giants swept my beloved Cleveland Indians.

Grandpa Engelhardt, Father, and I were among the millions who confirmed their manhood by tuning to the championship fights waged by heavyweights Joe Louis, Ezzard Charles, Rocky Marciano, Jersey Joe Walcott, and others.[39] Nor did listening to mumble-mouthed Tait Cummins on WMT (Cedar Rapids) keep me from becoming a rabid, lifelong fan of Iowa Hawkeye football.

In the arrogance of our ignorance we did not understand why classical artists ever won on *Arthur Godfrey's Talent Scouts*, an evening variety show. When one did, we protested to the studio audience: "You don't know what's good!" We liked *Your Hit Parade*, which weekly ranked the top songs sung by a rotating cast that included Dinah Shore, Dick Haymes, Dorothy Collins, and Snooky Lanson among others. We enjoyed country music, but rarely tuned to *The Grand Ole Opry*, *The National Barn Dance*, and *Louisiana Hayride* that neighbors heard more frequently.[40]

During the primary grades, I hurried home for children's shows created by corporate advertisers to offset the Great Depression. On the recommendation of classmates, I tuned to *Jack Armstrong, The All American Boy*, *The Lone Ranger*, and *Challenge of the Yukon*, featuring courageous, clean-living heroes sponsored by General Mills and other cereal-makers.

On Saturday mornings, I enjoyed *Let's Pretend*, an award winning program funded by Cream of Wheat on CBS, which adapted *Cinderella* and other fairy tales.[41]

Programs boosted sales through premiums and clubs, offering a fantasy world of secret messages and requiring additional purchases. While a Jack Armstrong Dragon's Eye Ring and a Lone Ranger Deputy Badge fostered consumption, they also spawned disappointment by failing to meet youthful expectations. As minimal consumers, my parents spared me from disillusion. They always refused my entreaties, saying "No! We aren't wasting good money on junk!"[42]

Before I became old enough to share milking chores, I heard the morning and evening newscasts that framed Mother's listening day. Newsmen attracted large audiences and become well-paid personalities like other entertainers. I still recall their distinctive voices. Harvard-educated H. V. Kaltenborn delivered the NBC evening news in an abrupt, academic style. Lowell Thomas abandoned Kaltenborn's godlike sound by opening with an affable "Good evening, everybody." Despite global calamities, Gabriel Heatter always insisted, "There's good news tonight!"[43]

On vacation or sick days, I shared Mother's imaginative world of talk radio and dramatic serials. Like other rural housewives, she led a lonely life. She did not drive and remained at home while Father worked outside and her children attended school. She eased her solitude in the same ways as other farmwomen by conversing on the telephone, eavesdropping on the party line, and listening to the radio. She especially liked *Arthur Godfrey Time*, featuring the "Old Redhead" with "a "barefoot voice" according to comedian Fred Allen. The audience of middle-aged housewives imagined themselves in the maternal role of Godfrey's studio family. He talked like a trustworthy neighbor, making himself radio's most effective pitchman. His morning and evening programs at their peak generated 12 percent of the total CBS advertising revenue.[44]

Soap operas — named after their corporate sponsors — ran from late morning through the afternoon. Mother and other housewives averaged six or seven daily. Serials typically began with organ music, followed with a plot synopsis and the day's episode, and ended by posing a new question. Most stories dealt with marital discord because troubles sold more soap. Plots evolved so slowly that even by listening infrequently I could still follow the misadventures of *Stella Dallas*, *Back Stage Wife*, *Our Gal Sunday*, and *The Romance of Helen Trent*.[45]

Networks invested radio earnings in the new television technology, which quickly pervaded the countryside after the FCC ban on expansion ended in 1952. Farm households with sets grew from 2.4 percent (1950) to 36 percent (1954); those in the Midwest owned a higher percentage than other regions. Like radio, television aired talk and game shows in the morning, soap operas in the afternoon, and varied entertainment in the evening. The standard screen steadily expanded from nine to twenty-one inches; the number of homes with sets grew at the rate of five million each year throughout the fifties.[46]

My parents purchased a Zenith twenty-one-inch set in 1957. To ensure reception, Father acquired three surplus poles from the telephone company; he attached an antenna to one that he set in the middle of the closest hilltop field. He placed another on the fence line and the third on the other side of the creek at the base of the hill. The technician strung a few hundred feet of copper wire along a path I had cleared through the woods with an axe. "Snow" precluded watching the Cedar Rapids ABC station, but we got a clear picture from CBS there and NBC in Waterloo. Mother put the set in the living room so it could be viewed from the kitchen while she worked or we ate.

Television did not captivate me as much as radio. High school activities kept me from watching on most weeknights but not weekends. We finished Saturday evening chores in time to see *Perry Mason*, an hour-long mystery series in which Mason (Raymond Burr) saved his innocent clients from prison by defeating the hapless District Attorney Hamilton Burger in court. While my parents went to town, I watched three of the many westerns that flooded the airwaves. *Wanted Dead Or Alive* starred young Steve McQueen as a bounty hunter. In the literate *Have Gun–Will Travel*, one-time Shakespearean actor Richard Boone portrayed Paladin, a black-clad, cold-blooded hired gun who liked the finer things in life including women. The highly rated *Gunsmoke* featured a chaste Marshall Matt Dillon protecting Kitty, Doc, Chester, and other Dodge City residents.[47]

On Sunday evenings our family usually tuned to three top ten shows that enabled CBS ratings domination: *The Ed Sullivan Show*, *Alfred Hitchcock Presents*, and *What's My Line?* My parents insisted on watching the stiff Sullivan introduce and lead applause for the talented performers who appeared on his variety show. As Oscar Levant said, "Ed Sullivan will last as long as other people have talent." I preferred *The Steve Allen Show* on NBC for its regular "Man in the Street" sketches that made stars of comedians Louis Nye, Tom Poston, and Don Knotts. Allen beat Sullivan in the ratings for the first time on July 1, 1956, when tuxedo-clad Elvis Presley sang "Hound Dog" to a basset hound. Sullivan responded by signing Elvis for fifty thousand dollars to do three shows, assuring Americans that the singer did not threaten their moral standards.[48]

The scandal that drove the top-rated *$64,000 Question* from the air did not touch the small-money and Emmy winning *What's My Line?* Impeccably dressed and well-mannered host John Charles Daly and regular panelists columnist Dorothy Kilgallen, actress Anne Francis, and Random House publisher Bennett Cerf epitomized New York City sophistication for me.[49]

My participation in high school drama drew me to *Alfred Hitchcock Presents* and *Playhouse 90*, which made this the golden age of television for many. Situation comedies also appealed when I had time to view them. On Sunday nights, I might watch *The Jack Benny Program* or *Bachelor Father*, which shared a time slot. On Wednesday or Monday evenings, Emmy-winning *Father Knows Best* presented an idealized and comic version of suburban family life markedly different from my own experience. Father Jim Anderson (Robert Young) adjusted to male domesticity and companionate marriage with wife Margaret (Jane Wyatt). They never yelled in anger at each other or their three children and resolved every family crisis within twenty-four minutes.[50]

DURING THE twenties and thirties, childhood experts promoted play as essential for development. Parents responded by giving their offspring more freedom and store-bought toys. City kids took public transportation to baseball games, amusement parks, and skating rinks. Rural kids, who lacked such mass recreation, had more autonomy and opportunity for outdoor play in every season even though their parents toiled long hours and assigned them chores. For example, Don and I transformed the farm into a playground. We made pets of animals. We rearranged hay bales into forts and turned the mow into a battlefield. I imagined the corncrib as a ship, the corn sheller as its wheel, a length of two-inch pipe as a cannon, and corncobs as shells.[51]

Adults then stressed safety less than now. Boys played with BB guns, slingshots, knives, and fireworks. We rode horses, cattle, and bicycles without helmets. We engaged in pick-up games of basketball and other sports, cowboys and Indians, and army. We regarded hopscotch, rope jumping, dolls, and playing house as girls-only games that real men avoided. We never complained about having nothing to do because parents always suggested tasks to occupy our time.[52]

Our grandparents had purchased a newly available array of books, games, and toys for their children. Similarly, Mother and Father gave Don and me what they could afford, teaching us never to expect costly playthings or entertainments. They bought one secondhand BB gun and bicycle instead of two new items for each of us. We shared a war-surplus helmet liner, gas-mask bag, and a bolt-action wooden training rifle. Father made me a wooden tractor and built a sand box, putting us among the 58 percent of professional families that had one.[53]

Our farmstead sat near a creek on a level valley floor between two wooded hillsides. Forty acres of timber and pasture gave us an ample playground. Grazing cattle created well-worn paths for our woodland romps. Limestone formations and stone-filled gullies, carved by run-off from thunderstorms, offered appealing places to explore. We yelled like Tarzan of the Apes and swung on wild grapevines that hung from the limbs and intertwined the trunks of mature oaks. Each autumn the woods blazed with gold, red, and yellow until the leaves fell and carpeted the ground. Then the barren trees stood out starkly during drab winter months brightened occasionally by new-fallen snow on which we sledded down hills. Budding trees heralded the springtime rebirth, and summer once more clothed our landscape with inviting shades of green.

The rock-filled creek, bubbling along happily over the stones, could be easily crossed on most days. Heavy rains transformed it into a chocolate-colored torrent. Led by Don perched on the lead cow, our dairy cattle then waded the deluge to be milked in our barn. Dead trees usually destroyed the creek fence at the southern property line. Repairing it headed the job list on poststorm days.

Cranes, crayfish, dragonflies, frogs, minnows, snakes, tadpoles, turtles, and water spiders populated the creek. Its shallow pools and rapids invited playing with toy boats as well as constructing harbors, dams, and waterways or prospecting for precious stones. After a larger pool in front of our house froze in winter, Don and I removed snow from the surface and played ice hockey without skates, using a tin can as a puck and curved tree limbs as sticks. We harvested ice, crushing it for use in an antiquated, hand-cranked ice cream maker. Even on freezing days, we welcomed this deliciously rich treat.

Topography changed above a single-span bridge located about a quarter mile northwest of our house. A high bank punctuated by rock outcroppings ran beside a level streambed of limestone that dropped into a pool with a depth of five feet covering an area between the stone bridge abutments. Called Holstein Dip, it served as an Elkader municipal pool for the many kids who swam here until the town built one in 1955.

Older boys climbed under the bridge and dropped into the water about twenty feet below. After someone cut his head while diving, we learned to clear the bottom of rocks washed in by each flood. Removing these posed hazards; Don once lost his grip on a boulder that rolled back, ripping out two fingernails. Cattle excrement and urine polluted the water, but made no one ill until the big kids built a dam with rocks dredged from the bottom. While this raised the water level, it also prevented the cleansing of bacteria. Although Father ordered the dam removed, sickness ended swimming for the rest of that summer. In a deeper pool located upstream from Holstein Dip, two swimmers with an inner tube saved another from drowning.[54] A subsequent flood filled the hole and it never reappeared, disappointing us. We sometimes fished in this and in other spots. Our catch was always too small for eating, but we annually put two or three in the livestock water tank to keep it clean.

Swimming and fishing were just two activities that Don and I shared with Milt and Clyde Kramer, whose family farm adjoined ours. When

Mother or Anna Mae telephoned for playdates, we were always together before the women finished their conversation. Until I turned six they had run off, leading me to welcome the 1946 birth of their brother Bob by saying, "Now I will have someone to play with!"

"Army" pitted younger against older brothers and dominated our play in all seasons. War in winter consisted of each side hiding and tracking the other through the snow; or we built forts to protect ourselves as we engaged in snowball fights. In the spring we erected fortresses from an abandoned wagon box, scrap lumber, and sheets of tin roofing in their farmyard. Battles commenced by hurling clods gathered by the bucketful from a freshly worked nearby field. Combat usually ended with parental intervention after a well-thrown missile likely hurt me. In the summertime we favored "army in the creek." Dressed in old clothes and tennis shoes, we chased one another through the water. The aquatic setting enhanced the fun of being shot and falling. On a day when thunderstorms had transformed the normally clear stream, we emerged covered with a muddy film. Pigs in a wallow could not have been happier. Yet their mothers would not have been as displeased as ours, who insisted that we henceforth confine our military operations to land.

One time, when joined by others, someone introduced a BB gun as a weapon. "Aim low" and "one round" were the rules. It ended the incessant debates about whether someone had been shot, but we did not care for the pain and risk involved. We liked the smell of burnt powder from firing roll caps in our pistols while impersonating cowboys. Fireworks enthralled us even more with bigger bangs, startling Mother when we set them off.

Recreating scenes from popular movies stimulated our games of war. We loved the footage of actual combat in *Sands of Iwo Jima* and *Twelve O'Clock High*. In the former, we identified with John Wayne as hard-nosed Marine Sergeant John M. Stryker, and argued endlessly over whether or not the Japanese sniper had shot him in the back. In the latter, we disliked Gregory Peck as General Frank Savage because the film's portrayal of heroism was too realistic for our tastes. We especially liked James Whitmore as the tough, tobacco-chewing Sergeant Kinnie in *Battleground*. Despite his frostbitten feet, the Sergeant had led his men away in a thrilling marching cadence after beating the Nazis in the Battle of the Bulge. In *Stalag 17*, we laughed at barracks clown Stanislas "Animal" Kasava (Robert Strauss), hated the sadistic camp commandant (Otto Preminger), and puzzled over cynical Sefton (William Holden).[55]

Baseball games in pastures or farmyards risked getting cow and chicken shit on the ball, hitting it in the creek, or losing it in woods or cornfields. We prepared for tackle football by folding newspapers into hip and shoulder pads as well as using them inside the single leather helmet that we shared. Basketball took place in the spacious stairway landing of a closed-off section of the high-ceilinged Kramer home built in the 1860s. Our games ended when Don turned sixteen and began work. Left behind once more, I turned to the youngest Kramer as a playmate. When I later played high school football, Bob told his family, "He should do alright. We taught him everything he knows!"

Using whiffle balls, school friends and I tested our batting skills against sharp-breaking curves or dancing knucklers that none of us could throw otherwise. *The Adventures of Robin Hood* and other movie swashbucklers modified games of war. Equipped with spears of dried ragweed stalks that sailed marvelously and swords of sticks fitted with jar lids as a guard for our hands, we sallied forth to battle. School authorities soon banned our frenetic sword fights as too dangerous. For a few Wednesday and Saturday evenings one summer, I joined town kids in "the game" in which two teams hunted and caught each other in the back alleys of the business district. Property owner complaints to the town cop ended these exhilarating chases as well as our earlier fort building at the cement block plant.

Pete Meder, Larry Dohrer, and I amused ourselves at school by hiding under the buses and in the shrubs or chasing one another in winter along fox and geese paths on Molumby Athletic Field. We argued about the relative superiority of our fathers' Studebaker and Chevrolet automobiles. Pete's father had a cabin on the Mississippi River, and he sometimes invited me there. We boated, hunted turtles with a .22 caliber rifle, and went for early morning swims on a sandbar. We hiked along the railroad track and climbed up a gully to Pikes Peak State Park. We

My canine friend is one in a succession of several family pets.

put pennies on the rails and waited for the frequent freight trains to fuse them to the surface. I also played with John Lenhart and Dave Edwards, who lived near my grandparents in town. I especially enjoyed John's electric train elaborately laid out on a large table.

Almost six years younger than my sibling, I often roamed the woods alone with a dog that we kept for herding cattle and standing watch. Rusty, a collie-shepherd mix and my favorite, replaced two others whose early deaths traumatized me. At age four I watched our collie, Sport, die from being hit by one of the cars he loved to chase. Don, who witnessed Father confront the driver for his deliberate deed, reported that the man fled the tavern in shame. At age six, I found our shepherd dead from an infection after being spayed by the veterinarian.

Other pastimes included batting rocks from the gravel road or creek bed with a stick, catching a rubber ball bounced off the barn, pitching at a strike zone chalked on a wall, or shooting baskets at a hoop attached to the garage. I played army or cowboys and Indians with imaginary friends. I also waged war by building forts or ships with American Bricks and Lincoln Logs and then destroying my creations by bombardment. Outdoors in the sandbox or any patch of dirt, I built roads, laid out airstrips for planes, dug foxholes for soldiers, and fortified artillery emplacements. For all my childhood military play, I did not serve as an adult and even protested the Vietnam War.

I followed sports, rooting for the Cleveland Indians and Browns as well as the Minneapolis Lakers because images of Iowa-born pitcher Bob Feller, quarterback Otto Graham, and center George Miken appeared side by side on Wheaties cereal boxes. Mother gave me a monthly subscription to *Sport* magazine. I purchased *Baseball Digest* and preseason previews for college and professional football at the local newsstand. I carefully read the *Des Moines Sunday Register* Big Peach Sports Section that featured diagramed wire-photo pictures of big plays. I won a shaving kit in a Pigskin Picks contest several years before I needed it.

I collected both Bowman and Topps trading cards, featuring a player's image on one side and his vital statistics on the other. Five cents purchased a pack of seven with a flat piece of bubblegum that I threw away because it sailed so well. I opened each pack eagerly, hoping to discover Ted Williams, Willie Mays, Warren Spahn, or other stars. Never finding Stan Musial or Mickey Mantle frustrated me. Instead of preserving my baseball and football cards in plastic, I created teams for which I staged contests and kept statistics. The baseball board game consisted of a bat with which I flipped a marble onto an enclosed diamond. Where it landed on the field indicated balls, strikes, hits, and outs. Foto-Electric Football utilized twelve offensive plays, six defensive formations, a play-viewer, a chart, a scoreboard, and three dice. These activities entertained me for hours, honed record-keeping skills, and made me an indifferent student.

As a high school junior, I reluctantly abandoned card collecting as appropriate only for children. Returning home to repossess my collection when it became more acceptable for adults a decade later, I discovered that Mother had given my cards away. I still resent her betrayal and mourn my loss.

At about the time I started public school, I sat at a small desk one afternoon scribbling on scraps of unused wallpaper and told Mother, "I am writing a book!" What inspired me to put crayon to paper? Rural Iowa is remote from the world of letters. My parents and grandparents had little time for reading except for daily newspapers and magazines. Most of my teachers did not motivate me beyond textbook lessons. In such a setting, what stimulated my love of books and reading?[56]

Little Golden Books with Walt Disney versions of assorted tales, a subscription to *The Open Road for Boys*, and popular youth novels came to Don and me as birthday and Christmas gifts. *The Open Road* sold fantasies and a way of life. Its cover often displayed airplanes, athletic competition, wildlife, or other exciting scenes. It featured adventure fiction, articles about model airplane construction, and cartoon contests. When *The Open Road* ceased publication, I got *Boys' Life*, the monthly Boy Scouts' magazine similarly devoted to outdoor adventures.[57]

Our small home library included *The Mercer Boys' Cruise in the Lassie*, *The Tower Treasure* (the first Hardy Boys mystery), and *Dave Dawson with the RAF*, which imparted similar moral lessons as *The Open Road* and *Boys' Life*. In the popular Mercer Boys books, the brothers and their friend Terry Mackson had many adventures while cruising in their boat, exploring an island, encountering smugglers, and solving mysteries at Woodcrest Academy. The Hardy Boys—thoughtful sixteen-year-old Frank and impulsive fifteen-year-old Joe—similarly met danger in helping their detective father solve his cases. Robert Sidney Bowen's *Dave Dawson War Adventure Series* recounted how, Dave, an American RAF pilot, and his English friend Freddy Farmer battled Axis powers in Europe and the Pacific. All three series featured brave, smart, young men not frightened by danger. I envied their exciting adventures and emulated them at play.[58]

The Stratemeyer Syndicate introduced the Hardy Boys mysteries in 1927. Once marketing them to fourth- through sixth-grade boys proved profitable, Stratemeyer created the Nancy Drew series for girls featuring the privileged, assertive female sleuth whose competence compelled her lawyer father to sometimes request her advice. I borrowed a few titles from a neighborhood girl and enjoyed them as much as those about the Hardy and Mercer boys. I did not notice the implicit feminism or explicit racism these books contained. African Americans appeared as happy, ignorant, superstitious domestic servants or menial laborers who spoke in a humorous dialect. Other ethnic groups often turned up as criminals or suspicious persons.[59]

I also read country school textbooks that my parents had saved from their childhood. These imparted the work ethic; taught that good acts are rewarded and bad ones punished; and inculcated patriotism by recounting the virtuous lives of American heroes George Washington, Benjamin Franklin, and Abraham Lincoln. Unaware these texts had been written to Americanize my German and Norwegian immigrant ancestors, I embraced their portrayal of United States English origins and later wrote a doctoral dissertation about citizenship in Iowa common schools.[60]

The Elkader Public Library provided additional adventure tales about Tom Swift and Tarzan after I obtained my library card in about the fifth grade. Among the many sports books I read, John Tunis showed how athletics developed character and democratic spirit.[61] George Orwell's *1984* and *Animal Farm* and Ray Bradbury's *Martian Chronicles* and *Fahrenheit 451* stimulated me to read science fiction throughout high school. I also enjoyed comic novelist Max Shulman's *Barefoot Boy With Cheek* and *Rally 'Round The Flag, Boys!* When I mentioned this reading during an interview for a college dormitory position, the pompous director rudely dismissed it as "not very heavy stuff." Despite his rebuff, reading stirred my imagination as a child and fueled my desire to leave the farm and drew me to academe.

My love for reading initially developed from a passion for comic books. These first appeared in 1933 and prospered by 1939 when DC Comics started selling one million copies per issue of *Superman*. Competitors soon created and marketed the exploits of more than four hundred superheroes including Aquaman, Captain Marvel, Green Lantern, and others.[62] Before enrolling in school, I perused Don's collection. Neighbor Marie Ehrhardt, who said her daughters had outgrown them, gave me a large number about the time I entered first grade. I eagerly accepted her gift, soon traded them with friends, and kept on until I owned two hundred issues and quit the business as a sophomore.

Comics helped me pass the time on humid summer or stormy winter days when I had nothing else to do. I liked all kinds. My favorite western heroes ranged from the Durango Kid to Red Ryder. Tarzan similarly saved innocent jungle inhabitants from wicked intruders. Superheroes Batman, Superman, and Wonder Woman showed how valiant striving defeated evildoers everywhere. I also read the controversial *Tales from the Crypt*, *Crime SuspenStories*, and *Frontline Combat* until alarmed adults eventually banished them.[63] On the lighter side, Donald Duck, Mickey Mouse, and Bugs Bunny always appealed to me. Archie and his friends gave me a humorous preview of my high school years that I enjoyed more than my actual experiences.

Pundits attacked comics for advancing immigrant working-class culture and weakening Anglo-Saxon upper-class literary norms. Many adults feared that comic books would create semiliterates. Well-known psychiatrist Fredric Wertham's national crusade for banning them coincided with the formation of Senator Estes Kefauver's Subcommittee on Juvenile Delinquency.[64] Mother learned of this controversy from *Ladies Home Journal*, but did not stop my reading.

Criticism spawned culturally acceptable alternatives. *Classics Illustrated*, the most successful, sold one hundred million copies. I enjoyed illustrated versions of Jonathan Swift's *Gulliver's Travels*, Victor Hugo's *Les Misérables*, James Fenimore Cooper's *Last of the Mohicans*, and other titles. Preferring pictures to texts did me no harm and exposed me to literature I would not have read otherwise. To be sure, I did not act on the notice placed at the end of each issue: "NOW THAT YOU HAVE READ THE CLASSICS ILLUSTRATED EDITION DON'T MISS THE ADDED ENJOYMENT OF READING THE ORIGINAL OBTAINABLE AT YOUR SCHOOL OR PUBLIC LIBRARY." Yet in adulthood I acquired and read paperback editions of the many works I had read as comics.[65]

Although the 1954 Comics Code banished the erection-inducing silhouettes of female forms, popular culture soon fueled raging adolescent male hormones in other ways. We enjoyed the photographs of female nudes airbrushed to perfection in copies of *Playboy* that schoolmates purloined from fathers or older brothers. Even though we never read the high quality articles Hugh Hefner published, we vaguely understood that he signaled the decline of Puritanism in an increasingly affluent society. On our basketball team's trip to watch the state tournament in Des Moines, a teammate spent the entire day reading *Peyton Place* by Grace Metalious and shared the "best parts" with any of us who would listen. The novel topped the *New York Times* best-seller list for fifty-nine weeks.[66]

Mad Magazine, edited primarily by first- and second-generation immigrants with an outsider's view of America, influenced many youthful founders of the next decade's counterculture. For me as an adolescent, it provided information about sex, drugs, other religions or lifestyles, and the pretensions of artists, business executives, and politicians. Despite its recurring cartoon violence and overendowed females, the magazine did not attract the public criticism that comic books had. Its circulation reached one million by satirizing everyone from anti-Communists to beatniks.[67]

MY SOLITARY, often idyllic childhood gave me freedom to roam and amuse myself without adult control. Father had old baseball equipment, kept a shotgun in the back stairway, and stored several cane fishing poles in the garage. Yet he rarely played catch with me, went hunting only one time, and did not fish from the summer before I was born until after he retired. His lack of interest did not bother me because I thought that in the natural order of things parents toiled and children played. Rather than entering my world, Father expected me to join his; he believed teaching me how to work was the most important lesson he could impart. As I preferred leisure to labor, our contrasting agendas caused friction between us.

Soon after I married, Father told my wife, "I turned him loose in the woods one day. The next time I looked, he had grown up." What did he mean by this cryptic remark? Was he sad that a score and two years had passed so quickly? Did he regret that his dutiful industry had kept him from spending more time with his son? Was he warning her that he had failed to instill a work ethic into an irresponsible and still willful youth? Whatever he meant, the lessons he and Mother imparted at home shaped my adulthood. My wife came from a similar background; our shared belief in toil and thrift sustained our marriage and carried me through graduate school and a teaching career.

2

FARM

THE JINGLE OF harnesses hooked to singletrees awakened me from a nap in an upstairs bedroom on a sultry afternoon. I sat up and looked out onto the mostly red-painted buildings that dotted our farmyard. I watched Father and Grandpa Engelhardt guide their horse-drawn culti-vators across the dust-coated and partially shaded ground to a flat-roofed machine shed, where they unhitched. They watered the animals, led them to the barn, removed their harnesses, and fed them oats and hay. The barn also had a granary, ten stanchions for milk cows, a second-story haymow, and an attached shed for additional cattle. Other struc-tures included an unpainted corncrib, a chicken house, a garage, and three hog houses situated across the county road.

Mother and Father rented this place from my paternal grandfather, who bought it for about forty-five hundred dollars. They likely borrowed an additional thirty-five hundred dollars needed for start-up from their parents or a bank. The land had changed hands many times since Isaac Havens paid fifty dollars for forty acres and received the first government patent in 1848. John Stevenson acquired an adjoining eighty acres for serving in the Pennsylvania Militia during the War of 1812. His widow transferred this land to Horatio W. Sanford for just twenty dollars in 1855. The two parcels had been joined except for seven acres when John Rice paid William and Amelia Witt twenty-two hundred dollars for them in 1897. Charles and Emma Perry and John and Mary Ann Melary subsequently owned the farm before Benjamin Meyers purchased it in 1935. He disliked the steepness of some fields and soon sold it.[1]

Farming liberated Father from an oppressive six months spent managing a Gambles hardware and auto supply store at Strawberry Point. Yet his new situation did not appear promising. Depression still gripped the country; eight worn-out fields scattered among bottoms and hillsides totaled only sixty-some tillable acres. Nonetheless, my parents through careful management sustained themselves here for thirty-seven years while an ongoing technological revolution altered their agricultural way of life.

More than thirty million people left the land between 1929 and 1965 because machines, hybrids, and chemicals made them unnecessary. Farms steadily became larger and more capitalized, which enhanced productivity and enabled ever fewer farmers to feed ever more urban dwellers. By 1964, the biggest 10 percent of farms generated almost one-half of the total output while the smallest 20 percent produced just one-thirty-third of that amount. Although high production and prices inflated income by 156 percent during the Second World War, postwar conditions did not sustain these earnings in Iowa after 1953. Supply outpaced domestic and foreign market demand for produce while costs rose for seed, machinery, and chemicals. The resulting cost-price squeeze pushed many from the land, improving prospects for those who remained if they rejected small-scale diversified farming.[2]

SETTLERS EARLY brought corn belt agriculture to Iowa from older midwestern states. Railroads expanding from Chicago made it a meatpacking center and Iowa the leading hog producer by 1880. In Clayton County, where my parents lived, most diversified farms ranged between eighty and one hundred sixty acres. The hills afforded abundant pasture and hay for dairy cattle while bottomlands and prairies yielded bumper oat and corn crops. Farmers devoted most of their arable land to feeding livestock, their major income source, rather than growing a single cash crop. Their cattle, hogs, and chickens provided milk, meat, and eggs for subsistence and a surplus for market. Those with fewer acres shared similar values and ambitions with those who had more. Everyone utilized the labor and skills of every family member. They gladly embraced machines and techniques that eased their reliance on the muscle power of horses and humans. They sought wealth to sustain their way of life and secure their children's future. In 1948, 70 percent of Clayton County farmers had incomes above the United States average.[3]

Like their rural neighbors, Mother and Father embraced several tenets of the agrarian myth popularized by Thomas Jefferson. He deemed freehold farmers the backbone of American democracy. Daily communing with nature made them naturally virtuous and owning property made them honest, independent, and more reliable citizens than propertyless, immoral city dwellers. Although such pastoralist pieties survived into the twentieth century, farmers meanwhile had embraced the commercial realities of agriculture. Farm journals and the Farm Bureau Federation urged farmers to emulate businessmen. In Clayton County annual membership drives, the bureau advertised itself as "a hard hitting farm organization that understands the problems of agriculture and the government threat to freedom." County membership almost doubled between 1941 and 1958.[4]

The Farm Bureau grew in part through ties to the extension service established by the federal government in 1914. It hired and directed the work of county agents, who dispensed the latest information from the United States Department of Agriculture (USDA) about farming and home economics to rural couples. Its male leaders supervised the women's committees that directed female extension activities and reinforced the nuclear family ideal.[5] Mother benefited from their teachings about gardening, canning, and cooking. Father proudly displayed his membership sign beside the driveway and carefully read the *Farm Journal* and *Wallace's Farmer*, which furthered his business point of view. As someone who worked long hours for limited pay, he stated his objections about labor unions to every member he met. He believed their demands for higher wages and fewer hours raised his costs and diminished his profits.

My parents came of age in a time when telephones, radios, automobiles, electricity, and other technologies revolutionized rural life. Iowa's strong cooperative tradition put telephones on more than 70 percent of farms by 1920. Families used them for ordering supplies and checking on markets. They visited with neighbors and shared music over party lines. Listening-in became a pervasive and accepted practice. Rural folk used

Father called this unruly team "his broncos." The better natured
Belle and Dolly had replaced them by my early childhood.

cars for many tasks, which stimulated production of smaller, cheaper, and more versatile tractors; gasoline-powered washers; and small gasoline engines to operate pumps and other machines.[6]

Mother and Father grew up in homes without electricity and on farms without tractors, and they began farming in the same way. He loved horses and used them for planting, cultivating, haying, threshing, and picking corn even after he and his brother jointly purchased their first tractor for plowing in 1945. He gave his team oats, hay, and plenty of water when working them hard. He kept them shod and trimmed their hooves periodically because they walked on a gravel road between fields. As Father acquired more efficient tractors, his team could no longer justify their keep. After planting corn with Belle and Dolly in 1954, he reluctantly sold them to a horse trader, who promised he had a buyer that would treat them well. Horse traders ranked even below used-car salesmen for integrity, and Father did not believe what he had been told.[7] Tears filled his eyes as he loaded his last team on the stock truck and it drove away. I would not see similar emotion from him until he faced a terminal cancer diagnosis years later.

The Rural Electrification Association (REA) electrified the countryside. Created by President Roosevelt's executive order in May 1935, the REA made low-interest loans to cooperatives or private utilities for generating and distributing power to rural areas. Farmers might borrow to pay for electrification and appliances. The energizing of 150 miles of line in January 1940 gave electric light to many rural Clayton County homes and schools for the first time. Nearly two years later, a third county project built another two hundred miles. From 1945 to 1954, the percentage of electrified farms nationwide grew from 48 to 93 percent. Electrification eased the labor of poultry and dairy production and gave an economic stimulus to electricians, contractors, and retailers.[8]

Although an REA line had run along the Old Volga Road for several years, my parents and Grandfather could not agree about who should pay the six hundred dollar cost for connecting to it and wiring the farm. My parents resolved this issue after purchasing the place in 1954. They did not limit their use of electric power as much as some farmers did; they extended it to the house, barn, chicken house, and garage; over time, they acquired appliances, power tools, and a milking machine.

Other New Deal measures similarly benefited farmers. The Agricultural Adjustment Administration (AAA) and Commodity Credit Corporation (CCC) promoted prosperity by inflating farm prices and incomes. Although the Second World War ended the Great Depression, the powerful Farm Bureau lobby and the Farm Bloc in Congress maintained acreage limitations and commodity loans. The bureau helped defeat the Brannan Plan for reducing commodity surpluses and government payments by bettering the American diet through growing more fruits, vegetables, and other foods. The bureau also influenced local administration of policy through annually elected county committees of farmers.[9]

Stephen G. Donlon, a neighbor, chaired the Clayton County committee through a succession of presidential administrations that altered its name from AAA to PMA (Production Management Administration) and finally to ASC (Agricultural Stabilization and Conservation). He also headed the Clayton County Farm Bureau in 1945 and 1946. During the early forties, Donlon furthered conservation and soil-building practices such as applying fertilizer and limestone, planting legumes and grasses for permanent pasture, and seeding strip crops. He distributed govern-

ment payments to farmers who adopted conservation and acreage allotments. Fewer acres planted meant smaller harvests and higher market
prices in theory. Yet farmers grew more on less land with USDA developed
hybrid seed and fertilizer. Enlarged wartime demand temporarily absorbed this increased supply. At the same time, farmers faced rationing
quotas for machinery and lumber and restrictions on slaughtering animals and selling the meat to urban dwellers.[10]

Father often said, "government always helps the big guy and offers
nothing for the little guy." Yet even he prospered when World War II advanced the large-scale, mechanized commercial farming most rewarded
by New Deal policies. Iowans planted ten million acres in corn, account-
ing for 20 percent of the United States crop; they increased pork, beef,
poultry, egg, and dairy production. As both large and small midwestern
farmers grew these things, both benefited. The cash value of farm products doubled, and Iowa agricultural income reached its highest level ever
in 1945.[11]

After the coming of peace made materials available, Father funded
improvements with savings from his enhanced wartime income. He even
acquired a small cement mixer for the work he had in mind. He and his
father poured a feeding floor adjacent to the two largest hog houses and
enclosed it with a wood fence. They erected a corncrib and feed house
nearby on eight cement footings formed by nail kegs. They put a concrete
floor in the barn for the dairy cattle, which eased the tasks of feeding
and cleaning. Finally, they installed a cement floor and footings for an
additional machine shed.

Father also worked to restore his worn-out land to productivity and
eventually succeeded. He rotated crops and applied manure, lime, and
fertilizer. He dynamited and removed large tree stumps from two fields
to make them more usable. "It took a long time before this place would
grow anything," he once told me. In the meantime, he searched for ways
to earn extra income. He worked as Boardman Township Assessor for
a number of years and later became an Archer Oil sales representative,
traveling farm to farm with a sample kit showing different weights of oil
and grease. "Unfortunately," a former customer reported, "his product
was not very good even though your father always stood behind it."

Father got a better job with the ASC in the early fifties. Iowa again had corn surpluses, and the federal government once more sustained farm income through guaranteed prices and storage. The Clayton County ASC warehoused two hundred thousand bushels in aluminum storage bins at Guttenberg and Elkader. It also offered farmers low-cost loans for expanding corn storage capacity. It told them that retaining title and possession gave them a reserve against a poor crop and a hedge against higher feed prices. Father inspected, sealed, and resealed corn stored on farms. At the two Clayton County bin sites, he mowed the grounds, sprayed for insects, and turned shelled corn to prevent spoilage. For twenty-five years, he worked perhaps ten or more days each month at these tasks. His federal wages accumulated interest in a bank savings account. Traditional diversified farming provided much of our food and sale of the surplus paid our living expenses. Other small farmers similarly expanded their nonfarm revenues from 26 to 47 percent of their total income at this time.[12]

Father and Mother derived considerable satisfaction from improving their livelihood. In the American tradition of small producer capitalism, however, they wanted to become owners. They looked at several farms in 1954 before paying Grandfather seventy-five hundred dollars for the one on which they lived. Why did they decide to stay? They may have considered my feelings; the prospect of moving and changing schools disturbed me greatly. They may have decided that relocating to a larger, more productive farm did not suit them. Why risk assuming a large mortgage at their respective ages of forty-two and forty if their sons did not want to farm? Twenty years later they sold their place for thirty-five thousand dollars. Father considered this nearly fivefold increase an excellent return on his investment.

At the fiftieth anniversary celebration of her high school graduation, Mother recalled her farm life by saying, "It seemed like the work was never done." It never was. She and Father each averaged more than sixty hours weekly, including three or more on Sunday. They toiled longer in summer and somewhat less in winter. They took only two vacations, one week visiting relatives in eastern South Dakota and a shorter trip to western Wisconsin. They divided their work according to gender with

*Don photographed our farmstead after Father
and Mother purchased it from Grandfather.*

*From the left, Grandfather Robert, Father Curtis, Brother Don, and
me taken during Don's furlough from Fort Lewis, Washington.*

each contributing to the farm's economic viability. She managed the house, gardened, cared for the chickens, and helped with the milking (a task traditionally performed by Norwegian women). He tilled, planted, harvested, and tended the livestock. Animals increased hours of labor in feeding, milking, and hauling manure; in return they fertilized fields and provided food that saved on purchasing expensive chemicals and groceries. Don and I helped out as soon as we were able. I despaired at the unending repetition and envied town kids, who took vacations or had cabins on the Mississippi River.[13]

Father rose daily at 5:30 A.M. to milk ten Guernseys, which yielded high butterfat. In summer he might bring them from the pasture, but they often waited nearby. When he opened the barn door they walked to their stanchions, where he fed them ground corn kept in an old water tank next to the granary. Meanwhile, Don or me after age eleven carted the freshly washed pails and cans to the barn. It took us about an hour to milk by hand. We used the dry teat method, pressing the forefinger and thumb together at the top of the teat and progressively tightening the other fingers while pulling downward slightly. We emptied each pail through a strainer into a ten- or an additional eight-gallon can needed at the peak of production in early summer. Several cats, kept to hunt mice, mewed for their share.[14]

We carted the filled cans to the basement where we separated the cream with a hand-cranked separator. Don or I slowly turned the handle while Father poured milk into the tub on top. Cream ran from a small spout into a five-gallon stainless-steel can and skim milk spilled from a large spout into a ten-gallon can. We put the cream can in the cooling tank and set aside the skimmed milk for the hogs. After she served us a hearty breakfast, Mother disassembled the separator, scrubbed the cone-shaped metal disks and other parts in hot, soapy water, rinsed them, and stacked them to dry. Twelve hours later, we repeated these chores. She reassembled the separator that Father rinsed by running two pails of clean water through it after he finished separating at night.[15]

Milking at the same time each day maximized production. Father delivered cream to the Farmers Cooperative Creamery, which made butter. He received a bimonthly check of between fifty and ninety dollars that gave us a steady income. He paid me 10 percent of this amount when I reached my teens, hoping to teach me important lessons about work, wages, saving, and spending. Because their livelihood depended on it, my parents bought only butter and opposed a bill permitting the sale of yellow oleomargarine and repealing the five-cent tax on the product. It took one hundred days of debate in the 1953 General Assembly before urban interests triumphed and enacted the measure. Even when the local plant shifted to purchasing whole milk and manufacturing cheese, my parents persisted in using butter and cream. Not until well into her widowhood did Mother at last serve skim milk and colored margarine.[16]

A galvanized metal stock tank situated at the corner of the farmyard next to the pasture watered the livestock. A wood cover, kerosene heater, and packed straw insulation kept it from freezing. A smaller wooden tank cooled the cream and later whole milk until its delivery to town. Water pumped twice daily from the well by a small gasoline engine refilled the stock tank and kept the other cold. Father drained the latter in winter and stored cream in the chilly cellar. After filling the tank, Father disengaged the motor and put it under a tin cover he had fashioned to keep it dry. We then pumped water by hand for household use.

Farmwives considered caring for chickens as housework. Mother's "grocery-bill flock" of between one and two hundred hens earned enough to pay for groceries. Neighbors with semicommercial flocks of more than two hundred received revenues on par with those from dairy cattle. Every morning and evening Mother carried two five-gallon pails of water from the stock tank to the chicken house, where she refilled two small reservoirs. She then replenished their feed and gathered eggs. In the house, she washed the eggs, placed them in crates, and stored these in the basement until delivery to the Produce Company on Saturday evening.[17]

In April hatcheries advertised, "The Chick Season is here!" Bandow Brothers in Elkader turned out ten thousand weekly and nearly 130,000 annually. They assured customers the birds are "Bred to Pay" and that Pillsbury Best Chick Starter will "Give 'em a good start!" Patrons might choose from among White Leghorns, Austria Whites, Rhode Island Reds, White Wyandottes, White Rocks, New Hampshire Reds, and

Red Rocks. Mother preferred the White Rocks, which at four pounds were ideal fryers. She rejected Leghorns, the best laying hens, because they were too small for eating and roosted in trees.[18] I empathized; I loved fried chicken and hated herding hens back inside each spring evening after she allowed them to range freely outside.

Mother annually ordered about one hundred; the small, noisy, yellow downy puffs excited me as a child when she opened the large, perforated delivery boxes on the kitchen table. She kept them warm initially by the kitchen stove, and then moved them to a small, kerosene-heated brooder house located in the nearby pasture. Once they matured, and she had culled and sold older, unproductive hens, she transferred them to the chicken house. When the government stopped supporting egg prices after World War II, overproduction and the free market caused women to average losses of fifty-two cents per bird by 1954. Extension agents urged them to either keep smaller flocks or move to larger capital-intensive operations.[19] Mother stopped buying chicks and selling eggs in town. She retained fewer, older hens that supplied fresh eggs for our table and for those who stopped at our farm to purchase one or two dozen. Word of mouth assured her a steady supply of customers.

After breakfast Father loaded the cans of separated milk into the back of an old 1928 pickup that had been created from "the first Model-A Ford in Elkader." It had a large barrel sitting on a platform attached to the truck's passenger side. He filled this by dipping several pails of water from the stock tank. He drove across the farmyard and the county road to the hog yard; there he transferred the water by pail to a reservoir where the pigs drank. He dumped the previous night's milk into another barrel, added two- or three-bushel baskets of ground feed, and stirred. He filled troughs with pails of swill and opened a gate to the feeding floor for the shoving, squealing animals. Several scoop shovels of corn from the nearby crib completed their meal. He fed them again in the evening. In the sense of physical labor required, his farm seemed closer to the nineteenth century than it did to the twentieth. Years later, Father visited the automated cattle-feeding operation of my professorial colleague Hiram Drache at Sabin, Minnesota. "What would a man want with all of that stuff?" he asked me afterward.

Because swine generated more income than cattle, many farmers regarded them as "mortgage lifters." Every autumn Father marketed about
one hundred mixed Poland China and Chester White hogs each weighing nearly two hundred pounds. These lighter animals brought higher
prices and required less feed than those weighing more than four hundred pounds that his father had produced. The shift occurred during the
twenties when consumers started using vegetable oil rather than lard and
eating lean bacon instead of fat salt pork and heavy hams.[20]

After shipping his pigs, Father rented a boar for breeding. Farrowing
started in March. He spent several nights attending deliveries, saving
piglets from being crushed under sows, making sure none froze to death,
and ensuring all could nurse. More than one chilled newborn spent the
night in a box behind the kitchen stove. Mother lifted her ban on pets
in the house for any income-producing animal. Once pigs were at least
three weeks old, Father castrated them on wet days, which lessened the
danger of infection. He used alcohol, a jackknife, a sharpening stone, a
pan, a needle, and thread. I sat on a milk stool and held the subject on
my knees; Father disinfected the spot, cut the pig, and tossed the testi-
cles into the pan. If an animal ruptured, he pushed protruding intestines
back inside the abdominal cavity and sewed it shut. Pigs squealed loudly
under the knife, shook themselves when put on their feet, and walked
away. Father later clipped copper rings in their snouts to prevent them
from rooting in the hog pasture. As the smartest farm animal, pigs went
easily through or under fences.[21]

Nature set the seasonal fieldwork cycle that engaged Father about
eight months each year. April 23 and October 14 were the earliest and
latest average dates for a killing frost. Clayton County had a 160-day
growing season, boosting yields for corn that usually matured in 120
days. He readied his machinery in late March and finished corn harvest
and fall plowing by Thanksgiving. With few acres and only one team
or tractor, he did the preparation work himself. He usually put fifteen
acres in oats; twenty-five in alfalfa, clover, and timothy; and twenty-five
in corn. He followed a five-year crop-rotation cycle. He planted oats
the first year; hay the next two; and corn the last two. He extended the
cycle to seven years on bottoms by putting in more corn crops. Rotation

controlled diseases and pests, fertilized with green manure by plowing under hay, and afforded economic security with diversity.[22]

By mid-April, Father sowed oats, alfalfa, clover, and timothy, which germinated despite cold soil and snow. The grain grew faster than next season's hay crop that developed beneath. He prepared the ground by disking diagonally, disposing of cornstalks and ridges left by the cultivator. Leveling the field in this way eased later oat and hay harvests. Corn planting ended about one month later. Its three-step process of plowing, disking, and harrowing demanded extra effort. Father plowed in either the fall or spring with a two fourteen-inch bottom plow that covered a width of twenty-eight inches on each pass around the field. Fall plowing had certain advantages. He generally had more time then; the soil collected moisture while winter freezing and thawing broke down dirt clods. Yet wind and water erosion increased. Sharp-edged round metal disks further cut up clumps of dirt and vegetation. The harrow finished leveling and working the ground to a fine powder.[23]

Father then used a horse-drawn two-row mechanical planter. Two tapered, pointed shovels at the front opened the earth for the seed, and the two concave rear wheels covered it as they passed. Kernels dropped at forty-two-inch intervals triggered by knots on a thin wire stretched across the field. Planting in a checkerboard pattern enabled weed control by a two-row horse-drawn or tractor-mounted cultivator, which he used at least three times before "laying by" the corn in mid-July.[24]

Farming is a gamble and farmers worry about the odds. Will spring be too cold and wet or too hot and dry? Once planted, will crops grow and mature for harvest? Will rain arrive at the right time? Too little or too much moisture reduces yields. Heavy rains accompanied by strong winds might strip and flatten corn, oats, and hay. Hail can thresh oats in the field and damage corn leaves, keeping ears from filling out. Even worse, tornados can destroy barns and other buildings. Corn borers annually threatened yields. Although bad weather had held down the infestation in 1948, the next year witnessed the worst damage in Clayton County history. For control, extension agents recommended fall plowing, suitable hybrids, and planting dates appropriate for soil, climate, and seed selected. By the mid-1950s, they suggested an application of one and one-half pounds of DDT per acre between June 18 and June 25.[25] Ever more extensive spraying eventually eliminated the corn borer menace.

Even with bumper crops, surpluses threatened livelihoods. Federal loans boosted corn prices for those who had storage capacity on their farms. For others who fed cheap grain to swine, rising amounts of pork in cold storage depressed the hog market. By the fifties, an extension economist called the rural outlook "neither feast nor famine." Times were better than the thirties, but not as good as the forties. If agrarians took advantage of sales and costs dropped as expected, they might enjoy a bit better standard of living than city dwellers.[26]

Expanding use of hybrids, machines, and chemicals boosted agricultural productivity and ended the diversified farming that Father practiced. First marketed in 1932, hybrid corn yielded about 20 percent more than previous varieties. Even though hybrid seed had to be purchased every year, farmers planted it on 99.8 percent of Iowa cornfields by 1944 because they wanted more bushels from the fewer acres allowed by the AAA. The heavier stalks and uniform height of hybrids made mechanical corn pickers practical. Hybrid corn's dense growth more rapidly depleted the soil, forcing use of more chemical fertilizers, herbicides, and pesticides that boosted yields even more. For example, Clayton tied for third place among Iowa counties in 1940 when it averaged sixty-one bushels per acre; a Garnavillo farmer nearly doubled that output a decade later.[27]

Mechanization accelerated after World War II. Tractors expanded from only two for every five United States farms in 1945 to 1.6 per farm in 1970. Advances such as the power takeoff that powered other implements made tractors even more useful. Electricity automated milk production, doubling use of milking machines during the war while refrigeration stored dairy products for longer periods. Mechanical pickers evolved into efficient grain combines that picked eight rows, shelled ears of corn in the field, and blew out the chopped stalks and cobs. Combines accelerated harvesting, reduced required man-hours, and saved up to 10 percent of the crop previously lost. Farmers enlarged their fields, abandoned crop rotation, adopted continuous corn production, and sold on world grain markets. Expanding demand for corn syrup and feed grains to sustain meat consumption worldwide drove these changes.[28]

Father embraced mechanization as quickly as his small operation permitted. His smaller expenditures for secondhand implements that he often repaired himself did not exceed the productive capacity of his farm. His first tractor—a cumbersome McCormick Deering 1020—had steel wheels on the front and rear. Within a few years he acquired a 1938 wc Allis-Chalmers equipped with a two-row mounted cultivator. After another four years, he bought a more powerful self-starting 1946 WD Allis-Chalmers that he used until retiring. In the late fifties, he picked up a 1943 Farmall H. More versatile tractors enabled him to acquire other laborsaving implements. He bought secondhand a single-row corn picker, a manure loader, a manure spreader, a seven-foot hay mower, a four-bar hay rake, a weed sprayer, a two sixteen-inch mounted plow, and two triple wagon boxes with flareboards. After the threshing ring folded, he bought a small combine and a forty-foot elevator for putting oats in the granary, hay bales in the barn, and corn in the crib. By 1957 he got a secondhand milking machine and later an electric milk cooler.

Petroleum-based chemical anhydrous ammonia augmented production with nitrogen, allowing farmers to abandon crop rotation and plant corn more densely and continuously. As the thick stands made cultivation difficult, chemists supplied new pesticides and herbicides to control insects and weeds. DDT and 2, 4-D became available to farmers after the war. DDT killed so many pests that it appeared to be a cure-all. Yet its efficacy masked several negative effects. It eliminated desirable as well as undesirable insects before all built up resistance. It attacked the nervous system, damaging animal and human health. It led scientists to neglect research on more environmentally friendly methods of biological pest control. A growth hormone, 2, 4-D caused plants to grow themselves to death. Higher yields gained by laborsaving chemicals offset their expense even as they threatened long-range damage to soil and water supplies.[29]

Father and other Clayton County agrarians adopted better farming through chemistry as products became available. Iowa State College experts and extension agents assured the safety of 2, 4-D and DDT and promoted the latter for controlling flies. They demonstrated methods for spraying weeds and corn borers. They publicized how fertilizer increased yields. Under an AAA program for bettering soil, county farmers in 1947 applied twenty-five thousand tons of lime. Truckers contracted for spreading lime on fields and spraying thistles, weeds, and fruit trees.[30] Father used artificial fertilizer from the start, hired someone to apply lime, and later contracted for the application of anhydrous ammonia. He acquired his own tractor-mounted sprayer for controlling weeds, but still cultivated his corn as long as I lived at home.

NEIGHBORING FAMILIES necessarily worked together to complete harvests successfully within narrow time limits imposed by weather. Communal labor reached its highest development in threshing rings formed in the 1870s after the application of steam power to the separation of grain. Steam and shared labor enabled a shift from stack to shock threshing that put crops in granaries sooner with less grain loss and freed space in barns for storing hay. Rings had charters, annual meetings, and memberships of six to ten families. Members provided workers, who moved with the machine from farm to farm in a season lasting two to four weeks.[31]

In contrast to threshing, just two or three men could put up loose hay with less costly machinery. Haying started with a first cutting in early June and ended for us a few weeks later with a second crop that filled our haymow to capacity. Some harvested a third cutting, but Father used his hayfield as late-summer pasture. Alfalfa, red and white clover, and timothy comprised the hay that gave our dairy cows the most protein for milk production. As cows ate all the leaves and stems of hay that had been properly dried and stored, everyone raced against summer showers to complete the harvest. Unfortunately for Father, rain fell on his crop for twenty-three straight years. "If it weren't for bad luck, I would have no luck at all," he complained. Still, his crop was never completely ruined.[32]

Father initially put up loose hay, working with his father and brother. He could cut six acres in a ten-hour day with a horse-drawn two-wheeled mower and its four-foot sickle bar extended to the right. Triangular teeth of the reciprocating sickle cut at about two inches above the ground as pointed guards channeled grass to the blade for cutting and protected it from rocks. If the horses pulled too slowly, the mower broke off the stalks, and if they moved too fast, it clogged. He told Don and me tales of careless operators who had lost fingers when clearing a jammed bar. He changed the sickle twice daily and re-sharpened the dulled teeth later on a grindstone for the next day's work. He and others called the smell of newlycut clover or alfalfa their favorite rural fragrance.[33]

After the mown hay had cured one day, Father gathered it into flat, regular windrows with the long curved tongs of a horse-drawn side de-livery rake. In contrast to the uneven piles created by older dump rakes, uniform windrows allowed Father and Uncle Allan to use the labor-saving hay-loader. They hitched it behind a hayrack slowly pulled by horses straddling the windrow. Flexible teeth mounted on a succession of bars picked up hay from the ground and carried it up the sloping loader onto the wagon. Using three-tined pitchforks, they stacked it carefully so that the load remained in place during the jolting ride over steep hillside roads to the barn. Such hot, dusty work demanded drink-ing plenty of liquid. While Uncle Allan put ice water in a large thermos, Father filled a crock jug from our spring-fed well, wrapped it in a jacket, and placed it in a shady spot at the edge of the field.[34]

Lifting several tons of loose hay from the ground into a second-story hayloft required one horse, three humans, and mechanical equipment. Our barn and others had a hay carrier attached to a track that ran inside the crest of the roof. Ropes, threaded through a series of pulleys, were attached to the carrier, grab fork, and horse. Uncle Allan clamped the fork around some hay on the wagon, signaled my brother or me to start Belle across the dusty farmyard, which hoisted the hay up to the carrier that moved along the track until Father called for the load to be dropped. He then spread the hay evenly with a pitchfork. As this was the dirtiest, hardest, and hottest of all haymaking tasks, each brother worked in his own haymow. It may have been a sweatbox, but it preserved hay far bet-ter than stacking it outdoors. After Allan and Father had emptied the wagon, they always stopped for a drink at our well, using a weathered enamel cup that hung on the woven wire fence. Refreshed, they returned to the field for another load.[35]

Between 1940 and 1975, technology reduced the hours needed to pro-duce a ton of hay by more than two-thirds. Just one man equipped with a bale thrower, self-unloading wagon, vertical elevator, and mow conveyer could now bale, load, unload, and store the hay. Although Father did not benefit from such devices, he became more productive by switching to a tractor and baled hay. Farmers used mechanical balers more widely after the Second World War because they put up more in a one day than the old method, and this larger amount compacted into bales took up less hayloft space.[36]

Haymaking with motor-powered equipment did not alter long-established routines. Father converted his old mower and side-delivery rake from horse to tractor power. He later acquired a tractor mower with a seven-foot sickle bar that enabled him to mow his entire twenty-five-acre crop in a single day. Once the mown hay had cured, he raked it into windrows, which were baled after they felt dry to the touch.[37]

By the late 1940s, Father hired a custom baler for his second cutting while still putting up his first crop loose. As the machine dropped forty-pound bales on the ground, two or three men picked them up and put them onto a hayrack pulled slowly by a boy-driven tractor. Another man stacked them so that the load remained stable. Removing the side- and front-boards from the rack made it easier to load and unload. Substituting rubber tires for steel wheels ensured a smoother ride. Later, loading directly from the baler onto the wagon saved labor. A boy or woman drove the baler, and a man loaded the wagon. They switched to an empty rack and continued baling while another man hauled the full one to the barn. There, fork-loads of bales were pulled into the mow, dropped, and stacked into every inch of available space.[38] Before Father retired, he had an elevator that put hay into the loft more quickly than the now unnecessary hayfork and its driver.

My haying roles changed as I grew. At age nine or ten, I rode Belle on the hayfork for an entire afternoon as the foaming perspiration on her flanks soaked my jeans. Later, I drove a tractor on the fork and on the wagon in the field as men loaded bales. During one hot summer, they worked late five straight nights, waiting until the cool of the evening to gather what had been dropped during the day. At age fifteen or sixteen, I hired out to other farmers to load in the field or work in the haymow. On one extra-long day, another boy and I handled several hundred extremely heavy bales for a neighbor who usually put up his hay wet. No one ever understood why it never overheated and burned down his barn. After finishing at dark, I cleaned up and headed with a friend to a dance at Lakeside Ballroom in Guttenberg. Too tired to two-step, I ended up asleep in the car. Despite the demanding toil, I liked haying better than other farm work. I enjoyed the neighborliness of shared labor, hearty meals prepared by wives, and the satisfaction of laying in a food supply for the dairy herd that sustained our lives.

Harvesting oats occurred in late July or early August. Ripe grain must be cut when plants stop growing and kernels emerge from dry husks. If done too early, high moisture content reduced the crop's value. If taken too late, stalks might give way and be flattened by wind, rain, or hail. Father pulled the binder from the shed and parked it under a large oak. He greased every fitting and oiled every gear. He attached canvases to rollers on the platform and the inclined feeder to the binding mechanism.[39]

Hitching his tractor to the machine, he opened fields by cutting one swath near the fence line and another by driving in the opposite direction. I then took over and continued moving clockwise until the shrinking stand of grain vanished. Grandpa Engelhardt operated the binder, adjusting it to cut efficiently. The high, slatted, link-chain-powered reel pulled oat stems toward the reciprocating sickle in the cutter bar at nearly ground level. The reel pushed the cut stalks flat onto the canvas conveyor belt that carried them into the sheave-forming apparatus, bound them with twine, and pushed them out onto a claw-hand carrier. Once seven bundles had accumulated, Grandpa tripped the carrier and dropped them on the ground. Father followed along, slapping three pairs together, and spreading a seventh on top as a cap. Shocks protected his crop from thunderstorms during the week or two until threshers arrived. Meanwhile, he cleaned and patched his granary to bear scrutiny by the visiting crew.[40]

Development of small tractors that powered separators with takeoff pulleys ended the era of steam threshing. Itinerant rigs and crews disappeared, but otherwise the neighborhood groups did not change. In our small ring, the three who cooperatively owned the separator charged the others a small bushel fee for use of the machine; each member provided a tractor to power it while threshing at his place.[41]

Once harvesting had been completed, ring members and their families met. Males and females visited separately before the men eventually decided the threshing order, price per bushel, and any other procedural matters. Women then served lunch from baskets each had brought with coffee and Kool-Aid supplied by the host family. As a child, I looked forward to this meeting and an opportunity to play with other kids. When the sheet-metal separator arrived at our place, I eagerly explored it and watched the machine man place and prepare it the next day. Bundle teams pulled up to the feeder, and each man carefully pitched bundles singly into it headfirst. Straw and chaff blew onto the stack while the grain poured out a separate pipe into a waiting two-bushel sack held by one of the grain crew, who set it aside. Another man loaded the 130-pound bags onto a wagon that he drove to the granary and emptied, a physically demanding task.[42] I often rode along; at about age three I fell under the wagon, but avoided injury when one of the crew scooped me up.

Our ring had dwindled to six or seven by the time I became old enough to participate in 1952 until it dissolved in 1954. The machine man decided when threshing began and ended each day. He lubricated separator bearings and moving parts before the dew had dried at mid-morning and bundle haulers began loading. He unrolled the belt, made an extended figure eight, placed one end around the tractor's pulley, and attached the other end to the thresher's drive shaft. Once the machine started, knives cut the binder twine that held the bundles. The cylinder loosened the grain by knocking the heads while shaking and shifting the stalks. Shuttling sieve pans worked until the heavier kernels dropped into a pit where an auger lifted them up and out a spout into the waiting grain sack. Meanwhile, it heaved the straw through the blower pipe that the machine man adjusted to the wind and to the height of the growing pile.[43]

After threshing ended in late afternoon, the machine man detached the large drive belt from the tractor and separator, rolled it up tightly, and covered it with a tarpaulin for the night. He next removed smaller belts from secondary shafts and placed them inside the machine to protect them from the dew or rain. If a farmer's fields had been finished, he shortened the blower and rested it on top of the machine. He swung the grain spout around, put it in loops near the top edge, and secured it with a rope. He detached the feeder and fastened it to the rear end. He hitched a tractor to a tongue on the front and pulled the separator to another farm, where he left it overnight for the next day's threshing.[44]

Each farmer had the choice of stacking his own straw. Most simply blew it into a pile and baled some of it later if they wanted bedding for livestock. Father stacked his near the barn. The machine man placed the separator away from the wind so that chaff from the blower wouldn't settle on the crew. He extended the blower tube like a telescope toward where the stack would be built. One wheel controlled the left-right direction. Another determined the length of the tube, short at beginning the stack and all the way out when nearly finished. The rope-guided hood of the blower deflected the straw straight down, or allowed it to arch high in the air. The stacker indicated where he wanted the straw blown—left, right, nearer the machine, or farther from it. Despite the dirty task, Father enjoyed building the stack. If done properly, it kept most of the straw dry and eased the chore of removing it for bedding on cold winter days.[45]

At about age eleven after Don began working at Cheeseman's Garage, I drove for Father as he loaded bundles on the hayrack with its sides and front reattached. He skillfully laid row after row with bottoms out, and periodically anchored them by filling the hollow center of the rack. He accurately topped off his load by pitching the bundles in a wide arc over his shoulder and placing them exactly where he intended. Father then drove to the machine and took his turn unloading while I stayed in the field and drove for others, earning a few dollars from each at the end of the season. Father did not pay me extra for an expected family chore. As a crew member, my status improved to eating with the men as if my work mattered as much as theirs. Yet to them I remained a kid to be teased, especially about an appetite that exceeded my size. "He eats so much he gets thin carrying it around," one of them joked.[46]

Our operation shut down at noon. Wives did their best to fulfill the crew's expectations for substantial, well-cooked meals in clean, orderly dining rooms. Men drove their tractors and empty racks into the farmyard. No one needed to water and feed horses anymore. Wives set up washstands on the lawn with pails of hot and cold water, soap, towels, a mirror, a comb, and a brush. They opened doors and windows for ventilation on humid August days. They laid out dining-room tables with platters or bowls filled with fried chicken, ham, roast pork or beef; mashed potatoes and gravy; creamed corn, baked beans, fresh tomatoes, cucumbers, or other garden vegetables; bread and rolls, butter, jams, and jellies; homemade pickles; apple, peach, or cream pies and chocolate or other kinds of cake. They provided salmon or tuna on Fridays for Roman Catholics even though their priest may have given them a harvest dispensation. Stuffed with food, we rested briefly on the well-shaded lawn before resuming work.[47]

Friends or relatives assisted Mother and the other wives who worked from early morning on preparing dinner and the afternoon lunch. The women cheerfully greeted threshers and proudly displayed their culinary skill. They paused briefly to eat and to feed any children after the men had finished, washed and dried the dishes, and made lunch. It usually consisted of a milk can of lemonade clinking with an ice ring that had been frozen in a bunt cake mold; an enameled pot of coffee; cookies, cake, and sandwiches of well-buttered, store-bought white bread and thin slices of bologna or minced ham. They delivered it to the nearby threshing site in cloth-covered baskets hand-carried or put on a coaster wagon. Machine and crew barely paused as everyone ate and drank quickly with unwashed hands. Two more hours of threshing followed before the machine shut down at five o'clock so the crew could return home for chores.[48]

Threshing rings dissolved when members adopted combines that more efficiently merged reaping and threshing into a single operation performed by one man. Many had resisted change because the older technology seemed equal or superior to early versions of the new, which damaged the grain and reduced its market value. Father held out because he wanted a straw stack for the winter bedding his livestock required. Yet the loose straw that combines left in the field could be recovered. When Father and I threshed alone in 1955, we missed neighbors working and breaking bread together at elaborately laid harvest tables. Even Mother, relieved by easing her labor, lamented this death of rural community.[49] After Father bought a used combine, we harvested together until I graduated from college and left home. He ran the combine; I hauled grain from the field and shoveled it into a recently acquired secondhand elevator that carried it into our granary. Father then raked the straw into windrows and had it baled; we stacked the bales in the machine shed where the binder had once stood.

Picking corn by hand was more solitary, unpleasant, and time-consuming than the communal task of threshing. It started in late September and finished by Thanksgiving if weather permitted. Corn-picking vacation in country schools allowed older children to help throughout the twenties and thirties. During the Second World War, St. Joseph's Catholic School in Elkader dismissed classes, freeing forty boys for the corn harvest. Many likely eased the wartime labor shortage by absenting themselves from the public school as well.[50]

Mechanical corn pickers ended such tiresome toil. Father still picked by hand to open fields for the custom harvester and to fatten his hogs. Don and I helped on Saturdays, an offer we could not refuse. He hitched Belle and Dolly to an old wagon that had high iron-rimmed, wooden-spoked wheels and three additional "bang boards" on one side. He tied the reins to the wagon and commanded "giddap" and "whoa" for the trained team to move forward or stop. We picked from the left side. We wore jackets and double-thumbed cotton gloves to protect ourselves from the abrasive cornhusks and kernels. Early morning frost made it harder to break loose the ears than later in the day when the stalks had dried. Father wore a husking hook strapped to his right hand. He grabbed an ear with his left, ripped away the husks with the hook, snapped the uncovered ear from the stalk with his right, and threw it into the wagon. Don and I mimicked his motions unaided by the tool. We gained an idea of the length of eternity before yellow at last appeared above the sideboards and we joyfully could climb aboard.[51]

Father purchased a secondhand single row corn picker and a Farmall H on which to mount it in the late fifties. I helped him attach the picker to the tractor, straining to lift the heavy parts so they could be connected properly. He picked corn alone and did not keep me home from school to help. Despite plowing, planting, and harvesting very steep ground for almost four decades, he never had an accident. His neighbors, who had nervously navigated the hillsides in helping him, marveled that he had not had been killed or injured. His caution and skill at anticipating dangerous situations had kept him safe.

FARMERS EXPECTED children to be home from school for their assigned chores by 4:30. Little kids typically helped mothers while big kids aided fathers.[52] Every evening at about age six, I collected the corncobs that Mother used for starting fires in the cook stove. I restocked the kitchen woodbox by picking up pieces from the pile and hauling them in a coaster wagon to the house. I gathered ears of corn from the crib, put them through a hand-cranked sheller, and fed the kernels to the chickens. I then braved pecking hens and gathered eggs. At suppertime I brought a pail of fresh drinking water from the outside well. I dried the dishes that Mother washed while Father and Don milked. On Saturdays I filled baskets with hay chaff from the barn and carried them to the henhouse for feed. My slowness irritated Father; he would yell, causing me to jump and amusing Mother, who witnessed the scene from the house.

My chores grew with me. In summer I brought cows home from the pasture for milking in the evening. On winter afternoons I climbed an outside ladder into the hayloft and dropped ten bales down the chute. I stacked these for feeding the cattle and horses twice each day. I broke open bales by removing carefully the two pieces of twine and hanging them on a post so that livestock would not ingest the cord. Using a pitchfork to shake out the compacted chunks, I distributed hay evenly throughout the feed troughs. I carried five-gallon pails of water for heifers we kept in the shed. I fed recently born calves from a galvanized pail with a rubber teat attached. We trained them to drink by submerging our hand palm up in the milk and extending three fingers. As the calves sucked the digits, they took in milk. Within days, they drank directly from the pail.[53]

I started milking by hand at age eleven and continued until age sixteen when we obtained our first electric milker. Cows, which were confined in winter, often draped their urine and excrement soaked tails around our heads and shoulders as we sat by their flanks. As a consequence, we carried "barn smell" into the house. No wonder Mother always said "P-U" every winter evening and morning that we stepped into the kitchen.

Farm life placed us close to many animals. We fed and watered cattle, horses, chickens, and pigs. We rode, petted, and gave names to cows and horses. We excitedly welcomed all newborn kittens, puppies, piglets, calves, and chicks. Such attachments did not obscure the reality that our livelihood depended on the marketing and slaughter of livestock. Rural Iowans could not imagine or practice vegetarianism; we readily accepted killing an animal and eating its flesh at meals. Yet we viewed the death of marketable stock through accident or illness as a tragedy that deprived us of income. When a cow died, Father told Mother to call the rendering truck. It hauled away carcasses without charge for conversion into fertilizer and feed. I braved the lesser stench of chickens and pigs, burying them with a spade in a nearby cornfield.[54]

When livestock required treatment, we called "Doc" Crider, a loquacious veterinarian, who commented endlessly on current events as he worked. He kept on telling me why I needed an education even as he sawed horns off a heifer next to its scalp. The animal's terror, bellowing, and struggle to break free from the restraining ropes held by Father and me did not distract him from his message.[55]

Watching animals "do it" imparted sex education to me and other rural children. Our parents certainly did not discuss the topic with us, and our unmarried physical education instructors never mentioned it in our public school hygiene classes. We early learned that newborn kittens, puppies, and other creatures stemmed from the physical act of sex. We frequently witnessed a male and female dog stuck together after the deed was done. We saw roosters mount hens and the bull mount cows. When Don and I giggled in fascination at the length of the bull's penis as he pursued a cow, Father angrily sent us to the house. Dirty jokes and other misinformation shared with peers added to our knowledge without improving our understanding.[56]

As a high school senior I had a more frightening encounter with a bull. As I led him to water one November morning, he stopped before we got to the tank. When I attempted to pull him forward with the leather strap attached to his nose ring, he backed up, dragging me about thirty yards across the frozen farmyard. He then charged. I kept his head away from my body until he pushed me into the woven wire fence beside the house yard gate. My strap unhooked from his ring, he withdrew, and I slipped through the gate. What to do now? I was safe, but the bull was loose! I confined the angry animal to the farmyard by shutting the wire gate across the driveway. Fortunately, he quickly returned to his stall where I reattached his tether. Father appeared incredulous when I told him what had happened, but armed himself with a club the next time he watered the animal. He never asked me to perform that chore again, and I did not request a return engagement.

During the lull between threshing and corn picking, I helped Father with a variety of tasks. We cleaned out the manure that had accumulated around the barn and hog sheds. We spread it on the next season's corn ground. We mounted a large circle saw on the front of the tractor and cut firewood from logs he had gathered from our timber. We stored the wood in our basement and burned it with coal in the furnace until a natural gas line crossed our property in 1963.

We fixed fence, a tedious, unpleasant task inflicting scratches and snags as well as multiple bites from mosquitoes, gnats, and flies. The work never ended because our fences consisted of old, rusty wire strung between rotted posts overgrown with brush. Father often said, "We should tear it all out and start over with new." We never did. Lack of resources and time limited him to fixing only those parts that demanded immediate attention. We cleared away brush, posts, and rusted strands of barbed wire. We dug holes for new wooden posts, especially on corners, and along the line drove steel ones with a maul. We strung some new wire or reused the old if it could be salvaged and stretched it tight with a block and tackle. We sometimes installed an electric fence—a battery-powered current pushed through a single wire attached by insulators to steel posts, which allowed portions of a field to be used for pasturing cattle or hogs.[57]

Father waged an unending war on weeds. He applied chemicals to thistles initially with a portable hand sprayer and later with a tractor-mounted sprayer once he acquired one. He mowed the road banks, farm-yard, and accessible pasture land in late summer. He then used a scythe to cut along fence lines that his mower had not reached. He taught me how to swing this old haymaking tool, but I never learned to use it well. I either failed to cut all the standing grass and weeds or caught the blade in the woven wire.[58]

After the corn harvest, farm families traditionally butchered hogs and made soap. As a small child, I watched from the kitchen window as Father and others killed a hog and suspended it from an elm tree. I have no memories of the gristly process that followed. Nor do I recall Mother making soap even though I remember bars of it at home. After the war, cold storage lockers became popular. Our family annually took a hog and a heifer or two to Lutz Locker Plant, which slaughtered them, processed the meat, and put it in our rented locker. Paranoid patrons wondered whether or not they had received all of their meat, but as our neighbors had done the work, we kept our suspicions to ourselves. I liked retriev-ing meat from the frost-covered walk-in storage area on summer days. We kept meat there until Mother acquired a home freezer in the sixties.

In winter we cleaned the cow barn every other day. On Saturdays we did the hog houses and the pile accumulated from my regular clearing of the hog floor. For some, removing pig waste was the worst farm task because of its acrid stench or its smothering summertime dust. For me, all excrement smelled and I lacked the sophistication to distinguish the bouquet. Winter is the best time for spreading manure on fields. The tractor and spreader did not compact the frozen soil, and the manure seeped into the ground as it thawed. A canvas heat-house made this bone-chilling task bearable. We then gathered straw from the pile and put down fresh bedding for the hogs and cattle. Pigs, which kept most of their pen dry by dropping excrement and urine in one corner, appreci-ated the new straw and sometimes played in it. Because I never mastered the technique of removing large forkfuls from the stack, it took me a long time when Father sealed corn and I worked alone.[59]

Farm kids learned additional lessons from 4-H clubs. The parents of most club members belonged to the Farm Bureau, which utilized the ex-tension agent in carrying out its work. The agent took part in 4-H events and encouraged membership in the youth and adult bodies. Father joined during one of the bureau's enlistment drives; he served as co-leader of the Boardman Worthwhile 4-H Club after Don became eligible at age ten. Meetings at our farm opened with a recitation of the 4-H pledge that dedicated head, heart, hands, and health to club, community, country, and world. Too young for club business, I looked forward to collecting fireflies and playing with my friend, Bernard Bergan.[60]

As many as eighteen club members later gathered for meetings at the Elkader Farm Bureau Office, according to reporter Don Engelhardt. On one occasion, the group received twenty-five dollars for assisting with lunch at the annual Elkader Cooperative meeting. On another, veterinarian "Doc" Crider spoke on "Youth Growing Up." At other meetings, individuals gave talks about cattle judging or buying feed and demonstrations on calf stanchions or a pig brooder. One of the neighborhood women served lunch. Like most boys, Don raised and showed a heifer, "Princess," at the Elkader Fair for his project. Girls, who might join clubs with boys, had their own groups devoted to domestic tasks. Don soon withdrew from 4-H, and I never joined. Father knew my lack of aptitude for farming made me an unlikely member.[61]

Work defined our parents' lives. Long before I studied the Protestant ethic as a history graduate student at the University of Iowa, I had witnessed its daily application and had been socialized to its values. For Mother and Father, chores had been an apprenticeship for farming. Even though I did not follow their occupation and resisted their teachings when young, the lessons they taught stayed with me for a lifetime.

Doing chores always compelled our family to return home at about four o'clock. My feelings about this daily routine resembled those described by Iowa poet James Hearst: "I found myself irritable, stubborn, resentful of words of correction, of my share of the chores." Like him, I loved to read. His father often came to the house and asked, "Where's that boy?"[62] My father frequently told me, "You can't make your living from a book!" My disinterest and ineptitude frustrated him and his demands angered me. After one heated exchange, Mother sent me to gather eggs, and I relieved my frustration by yelling at the chickens. As

I turned to leave, I found him listening at the doorway. He exercised more patience for some time afterward. A few months before his death, Father may have had our battles in mind when he told me, "It is a good thing you did not become a farmer. You would have starved to death!"

When our parents started farming in the Great Depression, they dreamed of eventually owning land and giving Don and me a secure home. Yet they did not impose their dreams on us. As college graduates more than doubled during the forties and the GI Bill of Rights established it as an entitlement for some, Father urged Don to use his GI educational benefits. He did not, but their conversations stimulated me to enroll at Iowa State Teachers College nearly two years later. I covered my expenses with a loan from Father at 4 percent annual interest payable after graduation, a small scholarship, and my earnings. At school I bused dishes in the cafeteria and served as dormitory staff. During summers I toiled at construction, plumbing, cheese making, surveying, and farming. Father's help and his expectation of repayment reflected the values by which he had lived. I have tried to aid my daughters similarly.

At commencement I received awards for scholarship and extracurricular participation. Later that summer as we did the milking, I hinted my prizes indicated superior ability. Father quickly quashed my self-importance, saying, "You were lucky!" He perhaps feared conceit might keep me from the unremitting toil needed for survival. After my parents had passed away, a neighbor told me how proud they had been of my accomplishments. Of course, they never shared these feelings with me. Yet Father once revealed his pride in an exchange with an acquaintance from his corn-sealing days.

"What do you do?" the man inquired.

"I teach school," I humbly replied.

"You teach college," Father corrected and then added, "He spent a long time going to school to do that."

"That's fine if you can afford it," the man responded.

"He paid for it himself," Father proudly concluded.

My parents held their farm auction in October 1974 and retired to town in December. As practical, unsentimental individuals, did they experience sadness at seeing their memory-laden material possessions pass to others? If so, they did not tell me and talked instead about how much people paid for Aladdin Lamps and other goods of a bygone era. They received about fifty thousand dollars for their farmstead, land, livestock, machinery, and other goods.

This paltry sum seems insufficient to fund retirement. Yet they managed with the same frugality that had served them in the past. They had savings from Father's government job and small inheritances. They paid $14,500 for a small house in Elkader. A change in federal law in 1954 had made farmers eligible for Social Security. They obtained cards, began earning credits in 1955,[63] and drew benefits at age sixty-two. When Father died in 1979, their net worth amounted to one hundred thousand dollars plus the house. Mother's estate totaled three hundred thousand dollars upon her death eighteen years later. Good interest rates steadily enhanced the worth of her CDs as her house tripled in value. Good health allowed her to live on Social Security without drawing down savings. Mother's thrift enabled her upon passing to compensate Don and me for our youthful contributions to the family farm economy. When I had whined about doing chores, I had never expected to be rewarded later.

Father and Mother died in hospitals after surgery revealed and failed to stop the cancers that killed them. He lingered two weeks at La Crosse, Wisconsin. When his breathing became more labored, Mother pressed the call button and three nurses came and stood silently bearing witness as his life ended with a profound sigh. "What will I do now?" Mother cried. "It's alright," I said, holding her. "No it's not," she protested. Her widowhood ended at the Central Community Hospital in Elkader, where she had lingered nearly ten weeks. She insisted that I stay with her at the end as she had with her mother and husband. As it happened, Don and I were at her bedside when she passed away. Our parents died as stoically as they had lived, and we grieved in the same way. No one said a tearful good-bye; love remained unexpressed. The community in which they had spent lifetimes turned out to pay respects at their wakes and nearly filled Peace United Church of Christ at their funerals. They had done the same for the many family, friends, and neighbors who had gone before.

MOTHER AND FATHER retired during an agricultural boom that accelerated changes, ending small-scale diversified farming. As farm prices rose, Secretary of Agriculture Earl Butz advised, "Get bigger, get better, or get out." They got out and sold their land at an inflated price. Farmers paid annual interest rates of 15 percent or higher to buy ever-more expensive land. Many abandoned raising livestock, concentrated on growing corn, and adopted soybeans as a second cash crop, which paid more and required less work. Separating crop from livestock production limited the application of animal manure to only one Corn Belt acre in six and increased the use of chemical fertilizers. This and herbicides amplified worries about effects of chemicals on the environment and human health.[64]

The new owners of my parents' farm gutted and modernized the house. "They simply dumped the cherrywood molding and flooring beside the creek," Mother bitterly recalled. "It all had to be new," Father complained. The husband, a skilled cabinetmaker, remodeled the barn for use as his shop. He removed the hog houses as well as the oak corncrib and cement feeding floor that Father constructed after World War II. He terraced hillsides, and left so little topsoil the fields could no longer grow corn. After the couple divorced, the farmstead and land passed separately to new owners. Now the house and yard are poorly kept; the barn stands open to the weather; and other buildings are unused. The overgrown pasture no longer sustains livestock. The decay of what Father and Mother so carefully cared for and the tree farm on ground he worked so hard to clear would deeply sadden them both.

3

TOWN

EVERY SATURDAY EVENING, Mother heated water on the woodstove, put a galvanized tin tub on the kitchen floor, and bathed me until I grew old enough to wash myself mostly. Compelled by ingrained Norwegian American standards of cleanliness, she checked my ears and neck for a few more years. She sent me upstairs to dress, emptied the tub, and poured hot water for herself. She heated more for Don and Father, who took their turns when they had finished milking. Once everyone had put on clean clothes, we made our short trip to Elkader.

Saturday nights in town were a rural tradition.[1] In the summertime, well-lighted stores kept busy from seven until after ten o'clock. Early comers filled Main Street parking spaces, watched others amble by, and spoke with friends through rolled-down car windows. With falling darkness streetlights came on, drawing insect clouds. The aroma of freshly popped corn drifting on warm air attracted customers of every age who crowded around the stand. Sturdy men with bronzed faces and forearms set off by pale foreheads and biceps filled the four taverns, standing at the bar, shooting pool, or playing cards. Contrary to the hedonists who preferred many, Father insisted, "There is nothing wrong with drinking one beer!"

Stout perfumed, powdered, and rouged women filled the stores, purchasing groceries, clothing, dry goods, or other items from their carefully prepared lists. They paid with their weekly egg money received from the Produce Company. They paused in aisles or on sidewalks to speak with acquaintances. They might stop for a treat at one of three soda fountains. Talk did not halt commerce. Merchants rang up sales at their cash registers as customers exchanged complaints about the weather, government, and prices. Women still mingled inside stores that stayed busy in wintertime when the popcorn stand closed and crowds no longer gathered on sidewalks.

Kids had our own routines. We checked out comic books, looked at toys, and talked with friends. Don and I often saw B westerns on twin bills at the always-crowded Elkader Theatre. These formulaic, thrilling adventures typically featured chases, stampedes, robberies, fistfights, gun-battles, and murders in which heroes caught evildoers and saved innocent victims. Gene Autry and Roy Rogers sang too much to suit me. I also wondered how Gene could be at Melody Ranch on the radio and appear on the screen the same night. I favored less melodic cowboy stars like Charles Starrett (Durango Kid), Wild Bill Elliot (Red Ryder), Rod Cameron, Rory Calhoun, and Randolph Scott. While Scott at times married one of his buxom love interests, he more often departed alone on his attractive Palomino, "Stardust."[2]

At times B comedies appeared as a second Saturday feature. Don and I enjoyed the Bowery Boys led by "Slip" Mahony (Leo Gorcey), who spoke in a Brooklyn accent and delivered such malapropisms as "clever seduction" (for deduction) and "I regurgitate" (for reiterate). The slapstick comedic skills of Slip's main buddy "Sach" Jones (Huntz Hall) enlivened their detective work and get-rich schemes. Hillbilly characters Ma and Pa Kettle (Marjorie Main and Percy Kilbride) earned millions for Universal Studios in seven cheaply made pictures. Hardworking Ma, lazy Pa, and their rambunctious brood grew few crops on their run-down farm, but produced abundant cornball humor well suited to Iowans who packed the theater. Films with Abbott and Costello, America's most popular comedy team in the forties, often sold out, disappointing Don and me. We blamed Father for dawdling at chores because he disliked "their stupid antics." Stupid is what we liked, even though their meeting Frankenstein frightened me as a seven-year-old.[3]

Town joined home and farm as a third socializing agent for my coming of age. Living just one mile from the bank corner facilitated frequent trips. I attended the Evangelical and Reformed Sunday School and the

Elkader Public School from kindergarten through commencement. By the fifties, I played baseball in the summer recreation program, swam at the new municipal pool, took out books from the public library, and hung out at friends' homes. Frequent movie attendance fueled my fantasies about adventure, manliness, femininity, and sexuality. Films gave me my earliest notions about large American, Asian, and European cities as well as the exotic and sometimes menacing peoples who inhabited these faraway places.

Despite changes initiated by the Great Depression, Second World War, cold war, and postwar affluence, Elkader remained an insular community devoted to traditional Christian, patriotic, and capitalistic values. Families rarely traveled to foreign lands or even other regions of the United States. Europeans, Asians, and Africans seldom visited the town. Easterners, westerners, southerners, and urbanites appeared only a bit more frequently. Apart from military service, most folks had little personal contact with other nationalities, races, or faiths. Residents retained a sense of stability and community. Most persons passing on the street said hello and might pause to discuss the weather, inquire about each other's health, or exchange gossip. They strengthened communal bonds by softening negative remarks and emphasizing positive news about individual and town achievements.[4]

A shared conception that work determined personal worth also bound them together. Most families had modest incomes. They saved in passbook bank accounts or patriotically purchased war bonds and waited for them to mature. The few with wealth did not flaunt it or boast about their stock portfolios. Small towns regarded working men as good; deemed all worthy who provided for their families; demanded compliance with moral standards; and stigmatized as unworthy those who struggled with alcohol, mental illness, nonconformity, and other kinds of deviance. By stigmatizing unacceptable behaviors and by disparaging wageworkers for spending too much time in taverns, respectable folk identified an underclass that belied their claims that social classes did not exist in their community.[5]

As youngsters, we roamed the town and countryside without fear and with minimal supervision. Church and school reinforced lessons taught at home. We early sensed that we lived in a protected and better place. We often heard adults say, "There's no place I'd rather live. . . . There isn't a better place to raise a family. . . . This is the best little town in the whole country." Such feelings made Elkader a good place for children to grow up.[6]

SEEKING TRADE from a wide area, Elkader merchants opened on Wednesday as well as Saturday nights from May until September for the convenience of farmers. They advertised weekly specials in the *Clayton County Register*, which reported the crowds that flocked to shop in town. Every Wednesday, the movie theatre held "Bank Night" drawings that filled the auditorium for both shows. A lucky winner might receive five hundred dollars.

A typical Commercial Club promotion attended by twelve hundred people took place on an April Saturday in 1942. Aunt Jemima—a "colored" cook sent courtesy of Quaker Oats—hosted a free pancake feed from 11:00 A.M. to 4:30 P.M. in the Opera House basement. In a telegram to club president A. H. Johnson, she said: "Ah was shore tickled to get yo' invitation to come to Elkader next Satid'day." A Bink's Mercantile advertisement featured her endorsement: "Listen Folks—Whey yo' is full o' pancakes go down to Bink's. Dey got the finest line o' merchandise I ever seen." Her dialect represented how small-town whites expected Negroes to speak. After all, Elkader had only one African American resident until the Clayton County Draft Board ordered him to report for military service. Prior to his induction, "Babe" Baker had been a porter for several years at the Bayless Hotel where he had "kept county seat shoes spotless and shining."[7]

Such attitudes did not change during my childhood. I shared black dialect jokes with friends and enjoyed similar language on the popular *Amos 'n' Andy* radio program. The high school staged a black-faced minstrel show as a fund-raiser in 1956. A few years later, some residents criticized me for walking down Main Street with an African American groomsman from my wedding party. This irritated Mother, who did not appreciate anyone from her family being ridiculed for such associations.

On at least two Yuletide Saturday afternoons each year, the Commercial Club sponsored free movies and bags of treats from Santa himself for several hundred kids. In 1941, more than six thousand people came for a parade featuring the Queen's Float with the Johansen twins, an American flag float, a "God Bless America" float, and smaller ones depicting nursery rhymes that were drawn by Shetland ponies. Despite wartime shortages, stores promised shoppers ample goods to meet their needs. This was not entirely true. When I asked Don why we had not received any metal toys as gifts, he responded with the wisdom of his advanced years, "Don't you know there is a war on?" Even though Easter never rivaled Christmas as the biggest bonanza for retailers, annual egg hunts at the fairgrounds drew two or three hundred youngsters and their parents to town. H. M. (Hank) Wolf, a retired Central States Power executive and local weatherman, played Santa Claus and headed the Easter event for many years.[8]

Bounded by wooded hills of the Turkey River Valley, picturesque Elkader featured many large, two-story homes with well-tended flowers, lawns, and shrubs. Towering elms shaded the residences and streets. On each side of the slightly more than two-block Front Street (later renamed Main), businesses occupied the ground level of brick buildings built in the late nineteenth or early twentieth centuries. Upstairs apartments in these structures at one time housed more than one hundred fifty people. The large bank at one corner of the main intersection had professional offices and lodge meeting rooms on its second and third stories. The Bayless Hotel—located diagonally across from the bank—had a lobby, barbershop, restaurant, and Walgreen Drug on its first floor.[9]

Other businesses in 1941 numbered Oehring Drug and Schmidt's Rexall Drugs; a Ben Franklin variety store; Kleinpell Hardware Company and Glesne Brothers Coast to Coast; Bink's Mercantile—a department store and grocery—Frick's Market, Economy Market, and two other groceries; Quality Bakery; Mac's Clothing Store and the Fashion Shoppe; McTaggart & Sons Furniture; Bridge Coffee Shop and Checkerboard Café; Hagensick Electric Service; Elkader Dry Cleaners; four taverns; four automobile dealerships selling Buick, Pontiac, Chevrolet, Oldsmobile, Ford, Mercury, and Studebaker; four gas stations; several professional men; and assorted other companies that included

*North Front (later Main) Street in the early 1940s displays marquees of
the recently closed Rivola Theatre and the newly opened Elkader Theatre.
Courtesy Clarence and Barbara Stahl.*

the Production Credit Association, Interstate Finance, Central States
Power & Light, Hyde Beverage, Hyde Brothers Implement, Farmers'
Cooperative Creamery, Witherell Produce, Elkader Cooperative, and
J. F. Anderson Lumber.[10]

As the Clayton County seat, Elkader retained businesses while the
number of firms in other Iowa villages declined between 1939 and 1948.
Besides providing jobs for residents, the courthouse drew patrons who
tended to their legal matters and possibly stayed to shop. Such an advantage helped the town weather the Great Depression as well as the
competition brought by motor vehicles and the construction of hard-
surfaced roads. Increased automobile ownership placed 80 percent of the
American population within an hour's trip by car to cities numbering
at least twenty-five thousand residents. Improved highways gave every
farm family more shopping sites. Trucks enabled them to ship livestock
and produce to urban markets, which reduced the importance of country
towns as assembly points for such goods.[11]

Despite these challenges, several businesses modernized fronts in
1941. Low-interest loans backed by the Federal Housing Administration
aided them in a New Deal program aimed at curing the Depression

by stimulating construction and commerce. N. H. Niemeyer selected "two tones of green structural glass" for his building and leased space to a Gambles store. Avron Oleson, who modernized after he obtained a Ben Franklin franchise that made him competitive with large chains, selected a tan and red color scheme for the structural and plate glass exterior of his variety store. Bink's added a new front, and installed a self-serve system in its grocery department for the convenience of its customers.[12]

Harold Hall relocated the Rivola Theatre to the other side of Front Street in a building that also housed an abstractor, jeweler, and credit bureau. The enlarged and renamed movie house had a modernistic design, motor-drawn curtains, indirect lighting, four hundred body form seats installed on an incline in three sections, Western Electric sound equipment, Century projectors in a fireproof cubicle, and an island ticket booth where adults, students, and children under twelve paid thirty-five, twenty-five, and ten cents respectively. In the lobby, patrons might purchase freshly popped corn for ten cents a bag and enjoy the convenience of two modern restrooms.[13]

Some merchants may have resented complaining rural patrons, whom they believed the federal government unfairly funded. Some farmers in turn claimed that storekeepers cheated them with high prices and had never done honest labor. This mutual distrust obscured their shared small-capitalist values. Both (including Catholics) practiced work and thrift even if not everyone preached the Protestant ethic as my parents did. Each group wanted ownership. Each toiled extremely hard just to survive. Each sought profitability by substituting labor and cost cutting for investment. Everyone worked in Elkader and other Iowa small towns. Fathers had stores, businesses, professions, or other jobs. Mothers — responsible for the reproductive sphere like their rural counterparts — cooked, gardened, kept house, and taught moral duties to their children; they sometimes took jobs if their husbands drank, deserted, or died. Wives typically worked with their spouses in stores or helped at home by taking telephone orders and keeping the books. Small towns often depended upon the cheap or donated labor of women.[14]

While the urban middle class embraced the new ideal of nonproductive childhood, rural residents persisted in putting kids to work. Small-town retailers and farmers viewed offspring as economic assets and early socialized them to toil. Both eliminated an employee or two by having their children help out. A retailer's daughter, Ann Oleson, recalls that she and her siblings "all learned to work." As a fifth grader, she checked freight, stocked shelves, and swept floors at her father's Ben Franklin store. She progressed to doing the books three years later. She hated these tasks initially, but enjoyed giving youngsters maximum amounts for their nickels and dimes at the bulk candy counter. A grocer's son, John Niemeyer, moved boxes from basement to storeroom to shelves, waited on customers, and delivered telephone orders once he could drive. The Ben Franklin owner hoped one of his children might take over the store; the grocer did not, sensing that the day of the small retailer had passed.[15]

Parents also assigned progeny chores and urged part-time jobs. Sons mowed the lawn, raked leaves, cleared snow, and shoveled coal; daughters did dishes, cooked, cleaned, and gardened. Boys expanded their earnings by performing chores for others as well as by delivering newspapers, setting pins at the bowling alley, or by laboring at gas stations, auto shops, and area farms during harvest. Girls baby-sat, did housework, carhopped at the M & L Drive-in, clerked in stores, assisted in nursing homes, and substituted as telephone operators. By earning money, adolescents aided family finances; gained independence, parental approval, and job training; and took a work ethic with them when they left home for college or employment.[16]

Small-town Iowa businessmen tended to be Republican. For the next century after its 1856 formation, the party held most county, state, and federal offices. Main-street Republicans backed free enterprise, attacked labor unions, resisted big government, denounced state regulation, and rejected other forms of compulsion. They praised individualism and voluntary groups. Yet they expected all business and professional men to join the Chamber of Commerce, participate in service clubs, contribute to worthy causes, and display patriotism. Even Elkader merchants who were Democrats probably shared these views. Residents might inwardly groan but never refused when approached by Legion Auxiliary members selling poppies to commemorate those who had died for their country. On Decoration Day itself, businesses and government offices closed. Veterans and the high school band marched, pupils decorated graves, and a politician or pastor spoke on the courthouse lawn.[17]

After Hitler invaded Poland in September 1939, many Iowans shared the isolationism expressed by an editorial in the *Des Moines Register*: the United States should "stay out of the fighting." Yet seventy-two Iowa manufacturers had already begun preparations for war production, and within two years defense contracts totaling $132 million had helped restore prosperity to the state. The 1940 Selective Service Act established a draft board that soon registered nearly twenty-five hundred men from Clayton County between the ages of twenty-one and thirty-six. They formed a reserve of trained soldiers for national defense. The local newspaper carried a cartoon captioned "Scrape Off Those Barnacles," indicating concern that strikes, labor unions, businessmen's fears of overproduction, political red tape, delays, and confusion hindered the defense effort.[18]

Iowans sympathized with war victims. The Rivola Theatre sponsored a Greek War Relief benefit in March 1941 at which its owner urged everyone to "aid this small, heroic country." The Japanese attack on Pearl Harbor in December ended isolationism in the state. The Iowa congressional delegation all voted for war, agreeing with representative Ben Jensen who said, "We are compelled to fight."[19]

NOT QUITE four months old when President Roosevelt asked Congress for a declaration of war and not yet four years old on V-J Day, I have few memories of the Second World War. I recall sitting in our parked car on a Saturday night and watching Father take the ration book from the glove compartment and give it to Mother for her weekly shopping. On another occasion she bought me an airman playsuit on sale at Bink's Department Store. It made me anxious to walk by recruiting posters of a stern Uncle Sam pointing his finger and saying "I Want You!" To save wear on our cheaply made, rationed shoes, Don and I often went barefoot in summertime. Even so, nails worked their way into the inside and wounded our heels. We pounded down the points and cut innersoles from cardboard to protect our feet. Adults told stories about boys who died or who returned and never spoke of war or who boozed and did not resume normal lives.

Wartime mobilization and propaganda affected Don more than me. Movies, radio, and comic books stirred youthful patriotism and taught hatred of the enemy. Schoolchildren sang patriotic songs in music classes, gathered scrap, and sold bonds while the high school band staged war benefit concerts. Adults praised these character-building activities, claiming they set a good example for all citizens and reduced juvenile delinquency.[20]

The *Clayton County Register* mobilized the home front with stories about selective service, civilian defense, rationing, and multiple war-related drives. It reported the recall of soldiers who had been drafted, trained, and sent home after one year. It announced successive draft registrations that created a system of universal military service. It made known deferments for farmers, who soldiered in the food for victory campaign. High draft calls continued until August 1945 because the military wanted reinforcements for combatants and assumed that invading Japan would result in high casualties. Demobilization began only after the atomic bombing of Hiroshima and Nagasaki convinced Emperor Hirohito to surrender. Happy to have at last gained victory over a hated enemy, most Iowans did not question President Truman's use of horrific weapons on Asian civilians.[21]

After the attack on Pearl Harbor, the *Clayton County Register* informed readers that four Elkader natives were among twenty-one county boys in the Pacific Theater. "Service Corner" soon featured news and letters from military personnel. Captain John Hommel piloted a B-17 Flying Fortress for the 15th AAF. In a 1944 letter to his wife, he described his experience on the first shuttle raid to Russia from Italy: "What a wonderful country this is. . . . The people are exciting, tall, strong, and so immensely proud. . . . So clean, compared to Italy. . . . We are making history. . . . I'm so happy and lucky to be a member of this unit." Hommel earned a medal "for meritorious achievement." Unhappily, the air force reported him missing in action over southern Germany just days before his son was born in Cresco, where his wife lived with her parents. The government confirmed his death several months later. While training, the pilot had buzzed his hometown in a bomber, dipping its wings and waving to residents who could clearly see the crew's faces. The window-rattling flight brought Dr. Hommel from his office crying, "That's my boy! That's my boy!"[22]

The Roosevelt administration organized the home front based on United States experience in the First World War and Great Britain's practices in the Second World War. It emphasized the voluntary participation of citizens as it created bit by bit a system of economic controls. It restrained inflation by raising taxes, rationing, imposing price and wage ceilings, and selling war bonds. Tax rates never climbed too high; few ever paid more than 20 percent. Payroll withholding began; accountants capitalized on completing the new, complicated IRS forms. Most Americans submitted to controls, which benefited many. Military contracts guaranteed employment for workers and profits for businessmen. Wages rose, consumption doubled, and civilians felt good about aiding the war effort.[23]

The Elkader Civilian Defense Council formed by autumn 1942. The mayor named sixteen committees, including air raid wardens; auxiliary firemen and police; decontamination, demolition, and clearance workers; ambulance drivers and other emergency medical personnel; and electrical, water, telephone, and highway repairmen. On December 14, the town joined in a blackout of the Midwest when the fire siren signaled "lights out." Air raid wardens and block workers attained complete darkness within one minute, and the county newspaper headlined, "Test Blackout Is Huge Success." Efficiency proved difficult to sustain. A surprise drill caused much confusion as people slowly cleared streets and turned off lights. A daylight alert went more smoothly and kicked off the third county war loan drive. Civilian defense activities waned after that as the war went better for the United States.[24]

Rationing began with automobile tires at the end of 1941, and eventually expanded to include sugar, fuel oil, gasoline, coffee, meat, fats, oils, butter, cheese, and canned goods. It ceased for most items before the close of November 1945, for rubber tires on December 31, and for sugar on June 11, 1947. The *Clayton County Register* informed citizens about rationing requirements. It announced monthly county tire quotas; told everyone they must sell tires in excess of five for cars before receiving gasoline ration cards; advised they must declare all canned goods in their possession when registering for their second ration book; directed townspeople to the public school and rural folk to district schools to get their fourth books upon returning current ones; notified stove dealers to register with the local War Price and Rationing Board, report the number they had sold, and sell only to customers issued certificates by the board; and urged using the "Share-the-Ride Program."[25]

Compelled by inflationary pressure, the Office of Price Administration (OPA) imposed retail price controls in early 1942. Small-town editors protested this unfair burden on merchants and demanded caps on skyrocketing wages and farm prices. The OPA eventually limited wage hikes, but delayed farm price ceilings until the next year, indicating how wartime restraints usually aided agriculture. Farmers also received special allocations for petroleum, tires, machinery, and workers to sustain food production. To fight inflation, housewives promised local Civilian Defense Councils they would buy goods only with ration stamps at listed prices.[26]

The OPA achieved significant stabilization, holding the consumer price rise to just 31 percent—one-half that experienced during World War I. Despite patriotic intentions to ration goods fairly, an expanding black market indicated that many ignored the call for sacrifice. Black marketers even circulated Elkader at night, selling tires from the backs of trucks. To stop illegal sales, the OPA and the Iowa Petroleum Conservation Committee sponsored an August 1944 open meeting at the Elkader Opera House. The OPA soon mandated accurate record keeping for all gasoline delivered to farms. The date and amount of each bulk delivery in theory prevented diversion to highway driving by farmers and their friends. The OPA also verified conformity through tire compliance surveys. Yet investigations revealed that between 57 and 70 percent of businessmen nationally violated price controls. They were rarely prosecuted or stigmatized. Indeed, one-third of those polled said they would buy anything they needed on the black market.[27]

The Treasury Department began war bond sales on May 1, 1941, and intensified efforts after the United States entered the conflict. Citizens paid $18.75 for the twenty-five dollar "people's bond" that matured in ten years. They also purchased ten-cent stamps, collected them, and exchanged them for bonds. Iowans ranked high nationally in contributions per capita as more than 80 percent took part. The state easily topped its quota with purchases totaling more that $2.5 billion. Clayton County also exceeded its assigned quota in each of the eight campaigns, raising more than thirteen million dollars.[28]

Efforts began locally at the Commercial Club Christmas Party in 1941. First Congregational Pastor George M. Richter spoke, pointing out that United States privilege gave it "the greatest responsibility to all nations [and] we should lay ourselves upon the altar of all mankind." Guests responded by pledging nearly forty-five hundred dollars. Just days later, nine-year-old George Leonard bought a bond with nineteen hundred pennies at the Central State Bank. He patriotically promised to save more pennies and buy another. In coming months, all people with income were urged to buy bonds regularly. During July, Elkader retailers awarded seventy-six dollars in bonds as premiums and gave minuteman programs at Wednesday evening band concerts. By October, the county superintendent of schools—recently named to head the drive—urged all salaried persons to contribute 10 percent monthly as "a patriotic duty." The Schools at War program meanwhile transformed districts into sales territories, used teachers as motivators, and enlisted youth as buyers and door-to-door sellers.[29]

Slow sales moved the Treasury Department to more spirited, periodic crusades. In September 1943, the third campaign started depicting citizens as soldiers. Air raid drills kicked off the Clayton County drive and mayors proclaimed a War Bond Day for their towns. Businesses closed while Boy Scouts, minutemen, and other groups solicited door-to-door. The Elkader High School Band staged a concert devoted to the theme "America on the March." Publicity stressed bonds would win the war. Troops depended on the home front doing its part. Purchases kept down inflation, built nest eggs, insured peace, and cushioned postwar readjustment. Talk of peace and the postwar showed growing faith in inevitable United States victory.[30]

The fourth, fifth, and sixth campaigns propagandized more stridently to overcome 1944 "peace jitters" of an overconfident citizenry. Publicity depicted Japan's brutal conquest of the Philippines and caricatured Japanese soldiers as buck-toothed, bespectacled murderers or as dehumanized snakes in the grass. Mayors continued to declare War Bond holidays. Stores and offices closed, freeing businessmen to canvass every home. In the fifth drive, the *Clayton County Register* compared home front efforts to the recently completed D-day invasion of Normandy. During lengthy rural canvasses, townspeople anxiously fretted about "failing our boys" in an unsuccessful campaign. To kick off the seventh drive in 1945, Marine Lieutenant Jim Lucas described the hard fight for Iwo Jima. "The Japs did not want to surrender and we did not want them to," he said grimly. "The United States must win to have the world it wants." Buying bonds ensured that victory, he concluded.[31]

Starting in summer 1941, town and county patriots took part in many other war-related drives that often transformed school children, Boy and Girl Scouts, and 4-H clubs into active scrap collectors. During the 1942 Salvage for Victory Campaign, Iowans contributed scrap iron and 9.54 pounds of rubber per capita. Even though the nation gathered 450,000 tons as an alternative to conserving tires through gasoline rationing, the president still banned pleasure driving. In the zealous collection of iron, the American Legion even turned in the Clayton County Courthouse cannon used in the last war for freedom. Patrons paid iron for tickets to the Elkader High School "Scrap Dance" and to the Elkader Theatre "Scrap Matinee." The town garnered eighty-five tons; organizers donated sale proceeds to the war effort. Scrap iron drives continued through 1944, but collections lagged statewide and Iowa lost its earlier twelfth-place national ranking.[32]

The Elkader Commercial Club, American Legion, and Boy Scouts often solicited money to send cartons of cigarettes to overseas servicemen. Each one hundred dollars raised bought forty thousand smokes at five cents a pack from a leading cigarette manufacturer. The War Chest drive, carried out by fifty canvassers, annually topped its twelve hundred dollar goal to support nineteen agencies, including the USO (United Service Organizations), War Prisoners' Aid, and United States Committee for the Care of European Children. The Red Cross exceeded its eight hundred dollar quota in 1943 and two years later gathered more than eighteen hundred dollars as Father and others went door-to-door. In 1944, country schoolchildren gathered four thousand bags of milkweed pods in Clayton County toward the national goal of 2.5 million bushels to be used in manufacturing one million life preservers.[33]

In 1942, the USDA Clayton County War Board named local committees and put salvage collection on a permanent basis. Women assumed major responsibilities in these efforts. The War Production Board created a Women's Salvage Army in each state and Iowa established chairs and assistants in each county, totaling more than eight hundred workers. As Clayton County Chair Helen Fitzpatrick said, "Women cannot win the war, but the war cannot be won without women." Housewives saved silk and nylon hose, tin cans, fats, and paper. Stockings became gunpowder bags. Fats contributed to the manufacture of everything from explosives to soap. Wastepaper, collected by Scouts and other boys in coaster wagons, made cartons for shipping military supplies. The small change they received from the salvage yard provided spending money for many and cabin tents for the Scouts. The committee, aided by churches, also saved clothing for war-torn countries and the United Nations Relief and Rehabilitation Administration.[34]

As participants in the "Share the Meat" campaign, women made four-pound pot roasts into main dishes for three meals; served variety meats such as brains, heart, kidney, liver, sweet breads, and tongue; and used the iconic canned Spam or other stretched meats. They drank less coffee or blended it with fillers such as cereal grains, chick-peas, and nuts. They joined the USDA National Victory Garden Program, producing "Vegetables for Vitality and for Victory." Soon after Pearl Harbor, Clayton County USDA Chair Stephen G. Donlon urged planting more gardens to expand shipments of commercially grown vegetables to Great Britain and American cities. The Elkader Commercial Club made "victory gardens" a project, renting land to residents and soliciting expertise from Iowa State College extension specialists. The USDA distributed a five-cent pamphlet titled "Growing Vegetables in Town and City." Among 701,000 Iowa families, approximately 476,690 planted victory gardens.[35]

Meanwhile, Iowa editors exhorted housewives to put up large stocks of homegrown fruits and vegetables. Women from 62 percent of the state's families responded, totaling more than eighty million quarts valued at twenty-three million dollars. To boost fruit canning, the county rationing board eased sugar allotments, raising it to twenty-five pounds in 1943, but cutting it to twenty the next summer. Even so, local stores had no sugar by September due to declining beet production and off-shore supplies. Rationing thus persisted into peacetime.[36]

Allied advances in Europe prompted local preparation for victory day observances in September 1944. Sadly, official news of Germany's surrender did not arrive in Iowa until Tuesday evening, May 8, 1945. When Elkader observed v-e day two days later, a strong wind kept the church bells and fire whistle from being heard in all parts of town. Many stores closed. The populace filled churches, praying and giving thanks. On August 14, the community greeted the news of Japan's surrender more jubilantly. The fire whistle sounded, fire trucks with sirens wailing traversed the streets, automobile drivers blew their horns, and city officials exploded dynamite charges near the reservoir on Kramer Hill overlooking the town. The next day churches opened for prayer and mourned the thirty-eight Clayton County boys who would not return; most businesses remained closed; the Central State Bank, courthouse, and post office took the two-day holiday declared by President Truman; and the government ended rationing on gasoline, fruits, and vegetables.[37]

Wartime sacrifice produced heartfelt hopes for peace and a return to normal lives. Public and congressional pressure on the administration compelled rapid demobilization. The *Clayton County Register* weekly announced the numbers of county men discharged, which totaled 1,442 (excluding those still in the reserves) by the end of 1946. The First Congregational Church backed a cooperative world order when its members signed a document patterned after the historic 1620 Mayflower Compact. In an issue of the *Clayton County Register* that headlined the death of President Roosevelt, an advertisement from Bink's Department Store stated: "For our fallen president a gold star shines throughout the world. To our new president we pledge ourselves for a speedy, permanent and lasting peace." Others similarly endorsed the United Nations and its plan "to live securely and happily in a world of peace."[38]

POSTWAR ECONOMIC uncertainties briefly clouded war-induced prosperity for Iowa farms and towns. Scarcity of goods and the lifting of price controls drove prices 33 percent higher by the end of 1946 than on the day the United States entered the war. Mother complained about the rising cost of bread. Father groused about paying bribes to buy new cars. Both denounced UMW President John L. Lewis, who headed a coal strike that created shortages of electricity and heating fuel. From hearing their talk and listening to newscasts, I pictured Lewis as a man with horns and a forked tail. Cartoons published by the *Clayton County Register* mirrored hostility to unions. When telephone workers walked out for twenty-nine days against Northwestern Bell, residents agreed with company claims that no strike is justified. The firm's wages already exceeded the community standard. Nonetheless, tensions faded by 1947 as store shelves filled, strikes dwindled, and black marketers vanished.[39]

Iowa and Elkader prospered until 1953. The Commercial Club began planning expansion even before the war ended. A survey of residents revealed that many intended to buy new automobiles, appliances, and home furnishings. Several expected to purchase or build new homes with garages attached. Others proposed remodeling and repair. Wives dreamed of efficiently designed kitchens equipped with more convenient ranges financed by war bond savings as a reward for their home front sacrifices.[40]

"Modernizing Main Street" remained a promotional touchstone because retailers knew that attractive stores drew customers. Schmidt's Rexall Drugs added display cases, shelving, a wallpaper department, and soda fountain booths. Oleson's Ben Franklin doubled its floor space and installed new fixtures. Wagner and Matt launched an appliance store in the former Rivola Theatre building. Arno Gossman put a deluxe hamburger trailer next to the Opera House. Veteran Leo Hanson took over Eberhart Jewelry. Kenneth Newburn purchased the Kleinpell Hardware Company while Howard Danaher bought the plumbing and heating departments.

George Schmidt (standing second from left) remodeled his drugstore soon
after the Second World War. I worked here before school my junior year.
Courtesy Clarence and Barbara Stahl.

Navy veteran D. H. Walke started a new hardware store directly across the street. Veterans Everett and Kenneth Carnes took over Hagensick Electric Service and added radio work. Walch Ford erected a much larger showroom and shop. Elmer Miehe acquired Hochhaus Brothers' John Deere and Oliver Implement Company. George Miller began an ice cream plant in the former Len-Ha-Ha Dairy. Thor Fisko established a cement block factory for building prefabricated homes.[41]

Not since autumn 1941, when Dittmer Motor exhibited a few 1942 Studebaker President Eights, Commanders, and Champions respectively priced at $1,205, $1,075, and $785, had dealers offered new vehicles for sale. Annual model changes invented by General Motors in the mid-1920s still drew onlookers when they reappeared in November 1945 at Donlon Chevrolet. The 1950 Studebaker offered the most striking postwar transformation. Its new front with four air vents resembled a three-motored airplane and made it appear in motion even when standing still. County motor vehicle registrations grew steadily; national sales totaled nearly seventy million for the fifties with General Motors accounting for almost one-half of this amount. By decade's end, Dittmer Motor listed the new

Studebaker Lark for $1,925, about the average new car price, but more than twice that of the Champion eighteen years earlier.[42]

The war also stimulated small-town airport development. Congress enacted a national plan supervised by the Civilian Aeronautics Authority, which envisioned more than four hundred thousand private and commercial planes using three thousand fields. Residents Harold Griffith, Harold Hall, and Arthur Meyer established the Elkader Flying Service, an Aeronea Airplane Dealership, and the Elkader Air Park at an old farm southeast of town. They built two runways, three hangers, an office, and a restaurant. They employed a manager, licensed mechanic, and instructor who conducted a flight school. On their first anniversary, an April 1947 air show attracted two thousand spectators. My family attended after watching pilots practice aerial stunts from our farm. We knew them only by the color of their planes. After the red one disappeared, we learned it had crashed in southeastern Iowa. Air shows ended, but flight instruction, charter trips, and aerial crop spraying continued; local pilots took part in the Civil Air Patrol; and the Airport Inn became a popular eating spot.[43]

The Commercial Club transformed itself into the Chamber of Commerce, which continued boosterism. Retailers, attempting to sooth inflation fears, pledged "no unwarranted price advances" and "full value in every dollar's worth of merchandise." They marked the Wednesday night opening in summer with "Dollar Days," reducing prices on groceries, appliances, and other items. They welcomed patrons to the Elkader Fair with a hearty "Hello Neighbor!" They sponsored an on the street "Voice of Iowa" broadcast by Dean Landfear, a WMT radio personality from Cedar Rapids. They held "Roman Holiday" and "Circus Days" sales that coincided with the showing of blockbusters *Quo Vadis* and *The Greatest Show on Earth* at the Elkader Theatre.[44]

National and religious holidays remained occasions for promotion. A celebration of the town and state centennial on July 4, 1946, attracted more than twelve thousand people. The American Legion and the Veterans of Foreign Wars (VFW) sponsored baseball games and fireworks displays on two nights. Six high school bands marched in the long parade. KDTH radio stars Mack and Sandy as well as midway rides entertained at the fairgrounds. Retailers offered a new Kaiser-Frazer car as the grand prize. On July 4th two years later, nine thousand came for the Pioneer Days parade, baseball games, and other events.[45]

Santa Claus drew me and several hundred other kids on the two Saturdays that he distributed free bags of candy, nuts, and fruit. We packed free matinees featuring Popeye or another cartoon, a *Three Stooges* short, and a movie starring Red Ryder, Gene Autry, or Abbot and Costello. Town workers strung colored lights across the business streets between evergreen-wrapped lampposts. Merchants decorated display windows, held drawings for prizes, and placed full- or half-page advertisements for toys and gifts in the newspaper. They opened on Wednesday as well as Saturday evenings in December, stayed open every night during Christmas week, and did not close until 6:00 P.M. on Christmas Eve. At Easter, kids hunted for twelve hundred eggs while their parents shopped for specials listed by the newspaper.[46]

Chamber of Commerce members normally controlled municipal government in Elkader and other towns. Mayor and council upheld quality of life by maintaining the water and sewer systems as well as lighted and paved streets. Discussions that avoided decisions until reaching consensus typified politics and usually resolved issues without disrupting community peace. Yet, in 1948, the Progressive Citizens Ticket headed by Avron Oleson elected three candidates to the five-man council as he narrowly defeated incumbent Mayor W. W. Davidson, who had served thirty-six years. Energized citizens cast more than eight hundred ballots in contrast to fewer than one hundred in previous elections. The contest did not permanently divide the town. Two years later, the council appointed Davidson to fill the unexpired term of Harley Downey who died after serving only thirteen days.[47]

The mayor and council revamped street lighting on the eve of World War II. After the war, they blacktopped the formerly noisy brick-surfaced principal streets and paved twenty-nine additional blocks. They put up street signs and assigned addresses to every residence, making possible telephone directory listings and rural free delivery for those who put up mailboxes. They changed the former Front Street into Main Street and transformed the old Main Street (running from the cement block plant across the river to the jail) into Bridge Street. They kept permanent stop signs in place and installed flashing red and amber traffic signals at the busiest intersections of State Highway 13 that ran directly through town. They enacted a two-hour parking ordinance for the business district, installed meters (despite strong opposition), and put parking lots at each end of Main Street. They approved the Grandview subdivision that overlooked the scenic Turkey River Valley.[48]

Citizens also sought civic improvements through joining lodges, service clubs, and women's groups. The Masons included prominent Protestants; their wives joined the Order of the Eastern Star. The two groups jointly installed their officers at the Masonic Hall, located on the third floor of the bank building. When the female auxiliary instituted a chapter for Rainbow Girls in 1946, it hosted a banquet for more than one hundred at the First Congregational Church. For girls between ages eleven and twenty from Masonic and Eastern Star homes as well as their friends, Rainbow aimed at building character and self-esteem. Rituals focused on faith in a Supreme Being, hope in all you do, and charity toward others. Girls wore white dresses and memorized wordings for monthly meetings as well as for initiation and installation ceremonies. They marched in various formations to enter and took places according to office. They held a formal winter dance that I attended once. Rainbow had deep meaning for some; others objected to its exclusion of Catholics and people of color.[49]

Prominent Catholic men joined the Knights of Columbus that met upstairs at Dittmer Motor before moving above Burlingame's Grocery. Pete Dougherty, who managed the Production Credit Association, led his own band in which three daughters of his large family performed as vocalists. His 1943 initiation as Grand Knight typified the order's activities. It included a ten o'clock Sunday mass at St. Joseph's, an evening banquet at its fellowship hall served by women from Elkader and Monona, and a Tuesday evening smoker. Rotary and Lions clubs, founded in 1945 and 1957 respectively, gave opportunities for fellowship and service without the formalism of older fraternal lodges.[50]

Coterie and Proteus, affiliated with the Iowa Federation of Women's Clubs, did civic housekeeping. They surveyed the town's lack of modern health standards and compelled house-to-house garbage service. For a monthly fee, saloon owner Albert Geno collected twice weekly and fed the refuse to his hogs. He did not pick up glass, cans, razor blades, and other "inedibles," which residents personally deposited at the town dump. The women beautified Riverfront Park, painting the tables, benches, and bandstand and planting shrubs and trees. They spurred the purchase of new playground equipment for Elkader Recreation Park. They started the public library, served on its seven-member board appointed by the council, and supplemented the annual municipal appropriation with tag sale proceeds and interest from a five thousand dollar legacy. The collection of forty-five hundred books occupied the old council chambers on the second floor of the remodeled Opera House. Librarian Helena Niemeyer provided friendly assistance in searching for books on my frequent Wednesday and Saturday afternoon and evening visits.[51]

To fund conservation, the Rod and Gun Club held a fish fry each spring at the fairgrounds shelter house. More than three hundred people consumed a few hundred pounds of catfish, buns, coleslaw, and potatoes as well as a lot of liquor. The next day's talk always told who had drunk too much and who had won the boat or other prizes. The club initiated the drive to build a municipal swimming pool in 1954. It backed the newly created Clayton County Conservation Board in stocking the Turkey River with wall-eyed pike four years later.[52]

The American Legion and the VFW expanded membership and activities after the war. Both met upstairs at Dittmer Motor and created a Vets Club there that admitted members only by key and also sponsored public dances. The veterans organized a semiprofessional baseball team in 1947 that symbolized the town's postwar prosperity, optimism, and confidence.[53]

During the next four seasons, the Vets won 119 games and lost just twenty-two. They captured a Northeast Iowa League title; dedicated a ten thousand dollar lighted baseball park; and played Max Lanier's All-Stars, a team with Sal Maglie and other former big leaguers who had been suspended for signing Mexican League contracts. During their glory years, the Vets drew thousands of fans with local stars like Jack Dittmer, Glenn Drahn, Lee Glesne, and recruits such as hurlers Florian "Lefty" Cassutt and former Iowa Hawkeye "Moose" Faber. Father and Don attended games while Mother and I went to the movies. The team disbanded in early August 1951 after winning just six games. After another abbreviated eight-game season by a team of former high school players, veterans leased the lights and field to the town for public and Catholic school sporting events.[54]

At war's end, civic leaders called for a modern hospital to replace one with a few beds for maternity and emergency cases that had served for more than thirty years. Initially, plans proposed raising thirty-eight thousand dollars, housing a Memorial County Hospital at the insane asylum, and relocating inmates to the county poor farm. Shortage of materials derailed this initiative. The *Clayton County Register* urged renewed effort when Elkader received top priority under a federal program that covered one-third of construction costs in rural and low-income areas. A large voter turnout rejected this proposal by a nearly two-to-one margin in a 1947 bond election. Support from Elkader and a few hamlets could not overcome opposition from the larger towns of Guttenberg, McGregor, and Monona. Not until 1959 did the newly formed Central Community Hospital Association successfully carry out a three hundred thousand dollar campaign. Local businessmen took great pride in this big accomplishment.[55]

Meanwhile, fear of polio intensified as the number of cases initially climbed from nine thousand (1941) to forty thousand (1949), and later peaked at fifty-eight thousand (1952). The media, which headlined outbreaks and tallied victims, presented polio as the nation's number one health threat even though youth, statistically, had a small chance of infection, physical disability, or death. The highly contagious virus tended to strike without warning in late summer endangering adults more than kids. My first cousin, stricken in the evening while milking, died before morning. He left behind a wife and two young children. A rural Elkader mother of five died from polio of the throat at University Hospital in Iowa City. There seemed to be little anyone could do. Doctors warned mothers to attend to respiratory and intestinal illnesses; give their children plenty of rest; have them wash their hands; and keep them from crowds, extreme exercise, and swimming holes.[56]

Because human feces contained the virus that was also found on the legs of flies, Elkader and municipal officials everywhere conducted annual DDT-spraying campaigns. After trash piles had been removed from behind homes and businesses, the council ordered spraying in the downtown and at the dump, fairgrounds, and elsewhere. Extension agents urged farmers to clean up manure piles, spray the walls of all barns housing livestock, and treat outdoor toilets with borax.[57]

The National Foundation for Infantile Paralysis led the fight against polio. Its fund-raising arm, known as the March of Dimes, collected $250 million between 1951 and 1955 by involving students and mothers in door-to-door solicitations. The *Clayton County Register* publicized these annual campaigns by highlighting the number of Iowa cases. Foundation funding for medical research at last reaped success when the Salk dead virus vaccine was shown to have been 60 to 80 percent effective. Elkader doctors then donated their time and vaccinated all first and second graders. The rest of us at school received our shots as soon as serum became available. Even though everyone hailed Jonas Salk as a hero, Albert Sabin's live virus vaccine replaced that of his competitor in the early sixties because it offered lifetime protection with a single dose administered orally.[58]

Next to polio, we most feared Communist subversion and incineration in atomic blasts. The rock-ribbed Republican values instilled by my family and hometown conditioned these cold war anxieties. The party elected every Clayton County official in 1946 and all but three representatives to the 108-seat Iowa House, a feat it duplicated in 1952. Many midwestern Republicans found their political faith affirmed by the *Chicago Tribune* and its publisher, Colonel Robert McCormick. The newspaper distrusted change, foreigners, Eastern party leaders, corporate power, labor unions, federal regulation and spending, and frequent Democratic majorities in Washington that threatened GOP control of small towns. Barber "Stub" Hyde made the *Tribune* available in his shop for patrons. Its bulk and front-page editorial cartoons impressed me even as a child.[59]

The *Clayton County Register* propagated Republican beliefs with a weekly column entitled "In the Squared Circle with MRS." After former

President Harry Truman proposed a Democratic solution to the Republican recession in 1958, the columnist exploded: "How silly can you get? ... Even Uncle Sam can't go on spending money promiscuously without collecting it sometime, somewhere, and somehow." Another column condemned the 85th Congress for "one of the biggest spending sprees in history—$83 billion with a $12 billion deficit." Such reckless spending dangerously extended "federal control over states, communities, private businesses, and the people."[60]

MRS also believed that Communists instigated civil rights agitation. He charged that the NAACP, Roy Wilkins, Martin Luther King, Jr., Thurgood Marshall, and their white supporters were "aiding the Reds more than ... helping our own common people." Little Rock and other demonstrations had harmed United States race relations, which would improve only if the teachings of Booker T. Washington were followed and "the politicians and the press ... shut their mouths." These strident views expressed small-town fears about African American demands for racial equality, Communism, and an emerging consensus on domestic and foreign policy among Democrats and eastern Republicans.[61]

Clayton County Register cartoons revealed postwar anxiety about America's wartime ally. In one, a Russian hand holding a pin pricked a bubble labeled "Hope of World Peace." In another—captioned "Russia Rules"—a United Nations figure watched as Joseph Stalin raked in poker chips representing small East European nations and said "Let's play this my way!" Chamber of Commerce and Rotarian speakers, who appeared at the Elkader Opera House, additionally fueled fears of Communist subversion. H. J. Dollinger warned against socialized medicine coming to the United States as it had to England. Father Lloyd Glass told how Reds had subverted fourteen countries in six years without firing a shot. To safeguard free elections in 1952, the Chamber of Commerce announced in the newspaper: "It's your privilege! It's your responsibility! Don't let your citizenship down!" By not voting, Americans validated Stalin's charge they were too money-crazy, confused, or slothful to do their civic duty.[62]

Cold war issues impressed me as a child. Russians replaced Japanese and Germans as enemies in my games of war. Voices of radio newscasters sounded an urgent note as they announced the Chinese Nationalist government fall, Soviet explosion of an atomic bomb, and trial of State Department official Alger Hiss. These shocking reports in 1949 challenged midwestern illusions of omnipotence. For many family friends and neighbors, Senator Joseph McCarthy's charges of "betrayal" seemed a reasonable explanation for the surprising international setbacks suffered by the powerful United States. His attacks on New Dealers and the Eastern elite tapped deep wells of small-town and rural resentment, suspicion, and anti-intellectualism fed by earlier House Un-American Activities Committee (HUAC) investigations of Communism in Hollywood movies.[63]

Several thought the high school principal and foreign language teacher must be Communists. His slender frame, bald head, and wire-rim spectacles resembled those eggheads and radicals attacked by McCarthy and other anti-Communists. Her unusual habit of walking everywhere and snapping photographs convinced some she might be spying; her lack of an automobile did not matter to those who drew this conclusion. The senator's aggressive interrogation and frequent interruption of witnesses during the televised Army-McCarthy hearings in the summer of 1954 enthralled a school friend and me by appealing to our adolescent masculinity. We thought it a good thing that such a patriot protected us from Communist subversion. We did not understand the paranoia that had made him prominent or the threat to rights his antics posed.[64]

At the peak of McCarthyism, I viewed three troubling Red Scare pictures. *Invasion U.S.A.*, which the Office of Civilian Defense urged everyone to see, showed the conquest of America by an unnamed presumably Communist foe, and an ineffectual response by a stunned president, military, and people. Scenes depicting the A-bombing of major cities, the destruction of Boulder Dam, and the dropping of paratroopers on Washington D.C., scared "our pants off," as columnist Hedda Hopper had promised. *I Was a Communist for the FBI* suggested that Kremlin-instigated efforts strengthening the Bill of Rights weakened HUAC. *Big Jim McLain*, starring John Wayne as a HUAC investigator, justified the arrest and prosecution of Commies, who used the Constitution for self-protection while trying to destroy it. I readily accepted these cinematic arguments that totalitarian threats necessitated extraordinary counter-supervision efforts.[65]

Universal military service resumed during the cold war. Registration of men between ages eighteen and twenty-four started in Clayton County on August 30, 1948. After this group had enrolled, all males registered when they turned eighteen. The first induction call from the county for the Korean War came in early September 1950. North Korea's surprise invasion of South Korea in June had found the United States poorly prepared. Throughout that summer, on maps published in the *Dubuque Telegraph-Herald*, I anxiously followed the steady Communist advance until the United States and its Korean allies held only a small pocket at the tip of the peninsula. I rejoiced when United Nations commander General Douglas MacArthur launched a successful counterattack and grieved when Chinese intervention ended MacArthur's advance near the border of Red China in late November. The contest settled into a stalemate, heightening American anxieties and frustrations as well as boosting United States military spending and forces.[66]

Cold war tensions also touched Elkader through the Ground Observer Corps. The United States Air Force demanded an early warning system after Soviets successfully tested an atomic bomb in 1949. Like the system England organized during the Second World War, corps volunteers supplemented the nation's radar defenses by observing and reporting all aircraft over a special telephone network. Airport Manager Arthur Meyer, who headed the local post, recruited observers to stand watch during periodic alerts. By 1952 he needed eighty-four to staff "Sky-Watch" twenty-four hours each day. He worked for weeks enlisting high school students, wives, couples, and a few farmers. Their sighting of a glowing metallic object excited us, but we never volunteered in sufficient numbers to sustain the system. The corps disbanded after "Exercise Sky Train" in 1955.[67]

The cold war capitalized on the patriotism of veterans and revitalized that of their home front backers. More people took part in Memorial Day observances. In 1952, the high school band led the parade followed by the American Legion, VFW, women's auxiliaries, Service Star Legion, Boy and Cub Scouts, and Campfire Girls. The march halted for ceremonies at St. Joseph's and East Side cemeteries, Keystone Arch Bridge, and courthouse lawn. An airplane dropped a wreath in the Turkey River to honor marine and navy dead, veterans decorated graves, a rifle squad fired a volley and boys scrambled for shell casings, and a bugler played taps. The veterans presented history and citizenship awards to Catholic and public school students. The Reverend Albert Hoffman from Loras College delivered an address entitled "Americanism vs. Communism."[68]

Elkader hosted the first All-Vets Day on October 13, 1953, at the height of the cold war. A Chamber of Commerce full-page advertisement in the *Clayton County Register* proclaimed, "Unity, Freedom, Strength" and "Welcome Veterans." It concluded, "I am an American. What proud words these are. . . . Ours is a proud heritage." Iowa Governor William Beardsley in a Cadillac convertible headed the parade of seven high school bands followed by five hundred veterans. As he passed two friends and me sitting on the curb by the public school, he greeted us, "Hello, boys!" An estimated crowd of five thousand heard Beardsley honor Korean War veterans by saying, "Let's not forget the sacrifices of these men and their buddies who did not return." He also spoke of home front responsibilities. Three flights of jet planes appeared overhead. That night the Vet's Club hosted a street and a ballroom dance. Clayton County observed the second and third All-Vets Days at Guttenberg and Monona respectively.[69]

Despite concern about juvenile delinquency, Elkader's three constables had little to do. Major Jensen—a retired military man—walked the daytime beat with a meanspirited toy poodle in his arms. He loved Bingo, but youngsters did not. A teenager shot the dog while hunting squirrels in nearby woods. The major probably never found his pet. Policemen initially patrolled in their own cars. Ralph Possehl could not apprehend teenagers driving v-8s. He invested one hundred dollars in an overhaul of his 1955 Plymouth Coupe, but did not improve its top speed of seventy-eight miles per hour. Bill Doeppke did better in the first town-owned patrol car—a mid-fifties two-tone-green station wagon with wood paneling on the sides and back door. After he pulled kids over, he addressed them in his German accent that we imitated behind his back. Bill maintained that he only drew his pistol when he shot rats at the town dump. As he described his simple duties: "Vell, I checks da doors on da businesses, sees dat der locked, and sometimes somebody runs out of gas. I opens up da station and gets dem der gas."[70]

Alarmed by a national trend toward more delinquency, the Rotary Club sponsored a countywide fund drive for scouting. Aided by the Chamber of Commerce and veterans' groups, Rotarians backed Cub, Boy, and Explorer Scout Troops in Elkader. Several school friends joined; after-school chores excluded me. They took pride in wearing uniforms, earning merit badges, engaging in outdoor activities, and doing community service.[71]

Rotarians also invited youth to discuss local problems. Football star Bill "Big Train" Colvin based his prizewinning essay on the premise, "Teen-agers grow up just waiting to get out of Elkader because it offers them nothing." The town lacked recreational facilities. A bowling alley and a youth center had closed. The nine-hole golf course had deteriorated. The tennis court needed repair. Several responded to these needs. An athletic club staged boxing matches at the fairgrounds that attracted crowds of several hundred. Despite heavyweight John Ehrhardt winning three consecutive Golden Glove state titles, the sport faded. Dean's Roller Rink offered skating three evenings weekly at the Opera House. Proteus and Coterie created an ice-skating rink on the high school athletic field. They additionally ran the Red Cross "Learn to Swim" program in which as many as eighty youngsters traveled by school buses to classes at Forestville, a man-made lake near Strawberry Point.[72]

Although twenty teenagers submitted a petition signed by 344 voters to the council in 1946, the swimming pool project languished until the Rod and Gun Club took up the cause eight years later. After 552 residents signed another appeal, civic leaders posed the question: "Shall the town council construct a pool at cost not to exceed $70,000?" Boosters said wholesome recreation for children justified the tax increase. The women's clubs joined sportsmen in getting out the vote. Citizens approved the measure by an overwhelming margin of 616 to 184. The August 1955 dedication featured Olympic and national champions as well as synchronized swimmers. The pool attracted more than fifteen thousand in just forty-nine days of operation. The next season, it opened eight hours daily from Memorial Day to Labor Day. More than 750 enrolled for Red Cross lessons, and nearly as many swam every hot afternoon.[73]

During summer 1951, the Chamber of Commerce sponsored youth recreation for which 120 children registered. Proteus and Coterie women supervised lower elementary activities two afternoons weekly as part of the General Federation "Build Freedom for Youth" program. Fourth-through eighth-grade boys met two hours weekday mornings, and girls met two hours on three weekday afternoons. By the next season, the large number of boys sustained Pee Wee and Midget baseball teams. Fewer girls reduced them to just two afternoons weekly. Even though farm work often kept me away, I came when I could. In games with other towns, I caught; played infield and outfield; and pitched disastrously, giving up five runs in one third of an inning. I did not let the reality of mediocre performance intrude on my fantasy of becoming a major leaguer someday. By 1957, baby boomer boys stocked several teams that played a regular league schedule. This worked better because the squads did not need to be transported to out-of-town games.[74]

High school boys tried out for junior legion baseball and the team played a sixteen-game schedule throughout the decade. Interested girls participated in competitive softball on Monday evenings. Their success in the Tri-County League raised the question of why the new Central School District did not offer women's basketball. Twenty-seven girls responded with a letter to the *Clayton County Register* in which they thanked fans for their interest in girls' athletics and said they had enjoyed softball. They claimed a girl's basketball team had been promised when the junior college closed. Several girls resented that this pledge was not kept until mandated by Title IX years later.[75]

Community interest in youth manifested itself in annual athletic banquets sponsored by the Chamber of Commerce. Two hundred or more attended these dinners often served by the women's guild in the basement of the Evangelical and Reformed Church. Coaches from the public and Catholic schools introduced their players. Coaches, players, or athletic directors from the University of Iowa and other state or private colleges provided the program.[76]

The town celebrated the achievements of other athletes as well. The

Clayton County Register reported how native Jack Dittmer won nine letters in three sports at the University of Iowa before he joined the Boston
Braves as the starting second baseman in 1952. After the Braves moved to
Milwaukee the next season, residents waged a campaign to elect him to
the All-Star team. Many of us voted early and often. The American Legion and the Chamber of Commerce sponsored two special excursions
by train to Milwaukee that summer for doubleheaders. The chamber
also honored women's basketball teams from the county that competed
for state championships between 1951 and 1955. Monona took second
twice. The chamber feted them with lunch and a viewing of the *Har-
lem Globetrotters* at the Elkader Theatre. When the Garnavillo "Candy
Kids" became only the fifth team to win consecutive championships the
next two years, the high school band and hundreds of fans hailed their
return.[77]

HISTORIAN Richard O. Davies has identified the mid- to late-1950s as
pivotal for the economic and social decay of Camden, Ohio, and other
small towns. Elkader residents, however, retained an upbeat, can-do at-
titude well expressed by Floyd Tesreau's 1958 letter to the *Clayton County
Register*. He took pride in the town's cleanliness, paved streets and sidewalks, water supply, and fire protection. The beautiful recreational park
had playground equipment, a swimming pool, and a well-lighted baseball diamond. A recently constructed six-lane bowling alley gave additional opportunities for diversion. Tesreau said progress should continue
with building a good hospital and an up-to-date motel and improving
trash and garbage removal.[78]

The bowling alley spawned one women's and three men's leagues that
competed four nights weekly. The Clayton County Concert Association
annually provided high culture by subscription to a three-concert series.
Pianists, harpists, or baritones appeared at the high school auditorium.
The popular Annual Barbershop Parade packed the Opera House auditorium with singing by the Keystone Chorus and visiting quartets.[79]

Twice-daily passenger trains no longer ran, and daily freight service
ended in 1951. Higher costs, lower revenues, and smaller profits dictated
Iowa Railroad Commission approval of the Milwaukee Road's request

for a new tri-weekly schedule. The train arrived at 6:30 P.M. on Monday, Wednesday, and Friday. It departed as soon as trainmen completed switching and make-up work. Milwaukee managers said the new schedule adequately served livestock shippers. Town fathers protested to no avail and feared that all trains would be dropped, as they eventually were. Meanwhile, improved roads decreased the need for rail service and increased commercial competition from larger places. Until the forties, spring thaws often turned gravel roads into impassable seas of mud and compelled county supervisors to impose weight limits. By the late fifties, the state had blacktopped Highway 56 between Elkader and West Union and the supervisors had started paving the Postville to Colesburg route that bisected the county from north to south.[80]

Television came to Elkader on October 13, 1949, when appliance dealer Carl Flack received signals from Chicago and Davenport on his twelve-inch square screen. Soon six stores advertised Admiral, Crosley, Dumont, Motorola, RCA Victor, Sylvania, and Zenith models at prices ranging from $190 to $300. Men and boys gathered at Matt and Frye Electric to watch the grainy black and white telecast of Saturday Night Boxing. Reception improved in 1955 after the town council awarded a cable franchise to the Carnes Brothers, who put a large antenna on Kramer Hill and attached it by co-axial cable to homes in the river valley below.[81]

Television as well as accessibility to cities and urban lifestyles altered small-town shopping and socializing on summertime Wednesday and Saturday nights. Elkader merchants shifted to just Fridays on July 1, 1955. Storekeepers liked reduced evening hours, but their rural patrons did not. Father and other farmers bitterly protested and even shopped in other towns for a time. After seven months of controversy, the Chamber of Commerce relented and resumed Saturday night openings on January 30, 1956. On April 27, with farmers in the field, stores also opened Friday evenings for their convenience.[82]

As television sets occupied more living rooms, movie attendance dropped by nearly 40 percent, and many cinemas closed. The Elkader Theatre expanded its screen, and in 1954 presented *The Robe*—the first feature film made in Cinemascope. I enjoyed seeing the movie, but the

poorly installed extensions limited its panoramic effect. Crowds continued dwindling and prompted the theater to shut down in early 1958. The
town had not been without movies since 1914 when the Majestic opened
in the Molumby Building. By adopting a reduced four-day schedule—
Sunday, Monday, Friday, and Saturday—the theater reopened with *The
Ten Commandments* and resumed advertising in the *Clayton County Register*. It operated in this fashion for several years and at times sold out
such comedies as *Alias Jesse James*.[83]

The annual four-day Elkader Fair also declined. More than ten thousand came in each of three seasons immediately after the Second World
War, drawn by horse shows and races, 4-H exhibits, baseball games,
stage shows, and midway attractions. Then attendance dropped to sev-
enty-four hundred and sometimes as low as five thousand between 1948
and 1954, despite popular automobile thrill shows like Joie Chitwood and
His Daredevils. After the 4-H exhibits relocated to the Clayton County
Fair at National, even awarding free tickets to children, staging Home
Talent Shows, and backing by the Chamber of Commerce and Rotary
Club could not save the fair.[84]

Several long-term businesses perished. In 1951, druggist Charles Oehring passed away in his sleep. The drugstore he had owned for sixty years
closed, and the empty building fell into decay. D. E. Livingood's death
in 1958 shut the shop he had operated on Mulberry Street since 1912. As
the need for harnesses disappeared, the aged leather worker had turned
to repairing shoes and selling saddles. Niemeyer's ceased trade in August 1959. For forty-five years in a building his grandfather erected in
1891, Norb Niemeyer sold groceries, shoes, boots, jeans, overalls, shirts,
socks, and Hanes underwear for men. He had operated on trust and had
not modernized since 1941 because he and his long-term customers liked
keeping things as they were. Now he gave way to the new, leasing his
space for a Laundromat.[85]

The passing of some businesses created opportunities for others.
McTaggart's Furniture expanded across the street by acquiring the
Cheeseman Building, where father William and sons Dale and Byron
had done car repair since 1946, sold the short-lived Kaiser and Frazer
automobiles, and then held a Jeep and Nash dealership. Siblings Al and

South Main Street changed by the late 1950s as Grahams occupied
the former Bink's Department Store and Niemeyer's grocery closed.
Courtesy Clarence and Barbara Stahl.

Marion Bink closed the firm their family had run for more than a half century. Graham's Department Store, a small chain, and the Clayton County Extension Service occupied the former dry goods and grocery spaces. The Farmers Cooperative Creamery sold its plant for ten thousand dollars in 1958 to William Becker of Wisconsin. By manufacturing only cheese, he expected to meet space and refrigeration standards in the old building. The plant again failed inspection when I worked there in 1961, compelling a new facility to be built on Gunder Road.[86]

Other businesses started, remodeled, and expanded. In 1954, Claude Powell purchased the Hochhaus Building and established a shoe store. Ray Schrody bought Economy Grocery, moved his Clover Farm Store to that location, and renamed it Schrody's Superette. Jessen's Supermarket opened the next year on North Highway 13. Jessen's offered the convenience of parking and a well-lighted seventy-five-hundred-square-foot interior designed for self-service. Burlingame's General Store enlarged by taking over the space occupied by the Lauer and Patrick Tavern, which moved across the street. After the Molumby Building sustained tornado damage in 1958, owners Reynold Hedeman and D. H. Walke removed the third floor and replaced the old-style front with a modern design. Their stores and Theis Clothing remained on the ground floor while apartments occupied the second story.[87]

ELKADER CHANGED greatly during my boyhood. The number of stores diminished. The fair died. The theater struggled. Rural travel increased, and shopping centers in nearby cities expanded. The exodus of farmers from the land continued, decreasing Clayton County population by nearly 10 percent. More high school graduates left for urban jobs or higher education never to return. While the town's plight was typical, its response was not. A succession of exceptional business and civic leaders worked cooperatively during the next half century to sustain economic and cultural vitality. They engaged in a common small town strategy of "elephant hunting," hoping to attract a manufacturing plant or distribution center. This worked well, initially. Elkader led the state in per capita retail sales during the sixties. Its population peaked at 1,688 in 1980 before dropping in that decade's rural crisis.[88]

To offset rural decline, sixty-two Iowa communities by 1956 had set aside land and drawn plans for industrial development. Several mayors formed the Clayton County Economic Development Corporation in October 1958. Shortly thereafter the Elkader Rotary Club, Lions Club, and Chamber of Commerce created an industry committee and a development commission. These bodies cataloged the town's assets and liabilities, and then prepared a brochure for attracting manufacturers. Ill-fated efforts to build grain boxes for the Dakotas and wooden parts for a plastic molded "Rollo Pony" ended in bankruptcy. Yet the Elkader Wire and Display Manufacturing Company and the Polaris Plating Works succeeded in creating fifty jobs. The former made display racks and pegboard hooks that it shipped to Canada, France, and South America. The latter electro-plated wire and metal products with chrome, nickel, copper, and brass.[89]

As the Clayton County seat, Elkader remained a commercial and government center. It offered year-round employment for nearly six hundred people. The *Clayton County Register* kept its circulation of twenty-six hundred covering most of the county's trade area. Schmidt's Rexall Drugs, McTaggart's Furniture, Theis Clothing, Fashion Shoppe,

Burlingame's General Store, and other retailers created an advertising shopper program that publicized a common sales theme about twice each month. These promotions sustained retail sales at a brisk pace for a number of years. At the same time, a new Jaycee chapter brought youthful energy to the community. The award-winning group grew to seventy members; it cleaned up the Turkey River, held polio vaccine clinics and teen dances, and started Elkader Sweet Corn Days. Residents now demanded and obtained such urban amenities as better medical facilities, a new sewage disposal plant, enhanced fire protection, modern kitchens and homes, paved tennis courts, a golf course, and a swimming pool. These made Elkader vital and viable economically and culturally for its residents.[90]

As Elkader changed, our family did, too. Don and I married and joined the exodus of young people. After working six years for Farm Service following a hitch in the army, Don and his new wife found better paying jobs in Cedar Rapids. My wife and I moved to Moorhead, Minnesota, where I took a teaching position. Mother and Father lamented the end of small-scale diversified farming and the changes it brought to Main Street. Yet they enjoyed the improvements that civic leaders had made when they retired to town from the farm in December 1974.

4

CHURCH

IN THE LIVING ROOM of our farm home on December 14, 1941, the Reverend Paul Kitterer baptized me as Carroll Lee. Grandparents Adolph and Ruth Olson were sponsors; brother Don, perched on Uncle Kenny's lap, watched. Our parents gave us names that could not be shortened because Father disdained that practice.[1]

I came of age at a time of religious renewal. United States church membership climbed from 43 percent in 1920 until it peaked at 69 percent in 1960. Nearly 67 percent said Satan existed and 90 percent thought Christ divine. Religious readers made best sellers of the Reverend Norman Vincent Peale's *Guide to Confident Living* and *The Power of Positive Thinking*. Dial-a-prayer promised "one minute of inspiration." Jane Russell called God "a living Doll" in a *Modern Screen* series on faith. Billy Graham conducted urban evangelical crusades that drew thousands and networks televised. President Dwight Eisenhower joined the Presbyterian Church after being baptized at the White House. He opened cabinet meetings with prayer, held national prayer breakfasts, and signed the law adding "one nation under God" to the Pledge of Allegiance. He also famously stated, "Our government makes no sense unless it is founded on a deeply felt religious faith—and I don't care what it is."[2]

Religion comprised an essential part of small-town life. Like most places, Elkader had several denominations—Roman Catholic, Congregational, Evangelical and Reformed, Jehovah's Witnesses, and two Lutheran bodies after some families withdrew from the Missouri Synod church and formed an American Lutheran congregation. Few knew how denominations differed even though members frequently socialized with one another and attended weddings and funerals at each other's churches. Whatever their affiliation, most parents brought their offspring to religious instruction and worship. They expected church teachings would uphold community moral standards, which forbade the consumption of alcohol by minors, condemned sex before marriage, and limited most interactions with the opposite sex to church-sponsored meetings, school functions, or dates with specified destinations and times. Yet automobiles parked on country lanes afforded opportunity to escape adult supervision. The closed car may not have been "a house of prostitution on wheels" as a "Middletown" judge alleged in the 1920s, but it enabled sexual exploration.[3]

Although not notably devout in praying at table or reading the Bible, our family attended the Peace Evangelical and Reformed Church. In conversation with friends, Father once questioned the divine inspiration of scripture. Mother changed the subject when she noticed me listening. Whatever Father's doubts, he insisted upon a religious education for Don and me. I played in the nursery sandbox at an early age, and being bitten by a dog on a walk did not drive me from the fold. I went to Sunday School faithfully, joined junior and senior high youth groups, and became a church member in 1955 upon completing the yearlong confirmation course. Church taught me about other and larger worlds than the insular community of my birth.

THE GERMAN immigrant congregation into which I had been baptized originated in the late nineteenth century when a Lutheran pastor from Clayton Center conducted "union" services and a Sunday School in the Methodist Episcopal Church. In 1898, the Methodists moved their building two blocks from 308 First Street Northwest to 111 Cedar Street, placed it over a new basement, and veneered it with brick. After the Methodists dwindled away, ten German families hired the Lutheran pastor from Farmersburg who led worship in the vacant building on every other Sunday.[4]

In 1905, the group requested affiliation with the Evangelical Synod of

German immigrants founded the Peace Evangelical and Reformed Church where my family worshipped. Courtesy Clarence and Barbara Stahl.

North America. "Unionizing" German immigrants had formed this body as an American counterpart of the Prussian Evangelical United Church that fused Lutheran and Reformed believers on the three-hundredth anniversary of the Protestant Reformation. The synodical mission board sent the Reverend J. Frederick Leonhardt, who preached his first sermon in early October. German-born and –educated, Leonhardt expanded the congregation, which established Friedens Evangelical Church on the last day of the year.[5]

The fledgling congregation soon bought the Methodist building and an adjoining home that became a parsonage. In 1908, the Reverend Charles H. Franke—a German-born graduate of the denomination's Elmhurst College and Eden Theological Seminary—replaced Leonhardt, who had resigned due to ill health. By 1915, Friedens had seventy-eight members, one hundred Sunday School pupils, and an excellent choir. That year the church began departing from an exclusive use of German, confirming its first class in English.[6]

Xenophobic zeal aroused by United States entry into the First World War advanced English usage. Native-born Protestants attacked Germans for opposing statewide prohibition in 1916; state officials questioned their

patriotism after the first statewide liberty bond drive did not attain its
goal in 1917; and Iowa Governor William L. Harding banned the public
use of all languages other than English on May 23, 1918. After these attacks, the congregation in January 1919 approved two monthly English
services and two years later recorded the annual meeting minutes in
English. By 1931, German had been limited to a single monthly Sunday afternoon service, which soon vanished. Because older congregants
retained the language of their homeland, the minister spoke *deutsch* on
pastoral calls to them and used German phrases to make sermon points.[7]

Growing numbers compelled purchase of a lot at 301 North Main
for a new church in 1917, but the war delayed dedicating the structure
until December 12, 1923. Once the congregation retired the debt, it built
a handsome brick parsonage on an adjoining lot in 1938. The Frauen
Verein—organized in 1906 by twenty-four female members to "further the purpose of the church"—paid one-half the nearly thirty-three
hundred dollar expenditure for a new pipe organ. The group also spent
nearly forty-six hundred dollars on various church projects during its
first decade.[8]

Frauen Verein became the Women's Guild in 1948 at the request of
the national synod. On the church's golden anniversary, it had 176 members who had sustained youth activities for decades with food, funds,
and teachers. Mother often attended its bimonthly meetings at which
members presented programs. The women visited shut-ins, wrote military personnel, provided meals for various groups, assisted with weddings and other special occasions, and held an annual bazaar in October
to raise funds. Booths offered aprons, baked goods, candy, fancy work,
rugs, and other items. The dinner consisted of such standard midwestern
fare as roast chicken, mashed potatoes and gravy, creamed green beans,
noodles, sauerkraut, light and dark bread, pickles and jelly, assorted pies,
and coffee. Mother helped set up, but never served the meal and our
family never attended. She returned home to prepare supper for us after
we had finished chores. She sometimes gave me a present of an inexpensive item that she had drawn from the fishpond.[9]

The guild grew with an expanding congregation shepherded by two
successful ministers. When Reverend Franke concluded his pastorate in

September 1931, he had baptized 683, confirmed 484, married 382 couples, performed 463 funerals, served as Iowa Synod president, and recommended the Reverend Paul Kitterer as his replacement. Born in Milwaukee and reared in Detroit, Kitterer graduated from Elmhurst in 1918 and Eden Seminary three years later. He came to Elkader from Dysart, Iowa, remained until he retired on April 1, 1960, and continued as pastor emeritus until his death a decade later. He baptized 898, confirmed 654, and performed 562 marriages and 699 funerals. The church became Friedens Evangelical and Reformed after the Evangelical Synod and German Reformed Church merged in 1934. Members adopted Peace, the English equivalent of its German name, at the end of World War II.[10]

Peace Evangelical and Reformed (Peace E and R) grew to nine hundred congregants by mid-century while its activities and schedule changed little. Sunday School started at 9:30 (later advanced to 9:15) followed by worship at 10:30. The Young People's Society gathered at 6:30 on Sunday evenings until 1953 when the congregation called a second pastor who organized junior and senior high groups. As the community had designated Thursdays as "church night," the Women's Guild met at 2:00, the senior and junior high youth convened at 7:00 on alternate weeks, and the choir rehearsed at 8:00. Classes of confirmands assembled on Saturday mornings from 9:00 until noon throughout the school year. When the minister vacationed in July, neither adults nor children met that month. Once the council hired an associate pastor, they began scheduling worship at that time.[11]

THE CRUELTIES OF the Second World War and cold war and fears of Fascism and Communism tested the United States and its churches during the forties and fifties. The Frauen Verein in 1944 collected clothing for Russia and liberated Europe; it shipped fourteen boxes (some with heavy coats), which the United Nations Relief and Rehabilitation Administration distributed as needed. Worries about wartime delinquency prompted creation of a short-lived youth center located in the Opera House, where Friedens women served refreshments for several months. The church tolled its bells and held prayer services to observe the victory in Europe and in Asia. Once peace had returned, the congregation dedicated a plaque to its war dead—Harvey Glawe, Orrin Kuehl, and Robert Dittmer.[12]

Peace E and R took part in the Christian unity movement by joining the recently formed United Church of Christ (UCC) in 1957. Delegates to the Iowa Synod planned the union for several years. The new church united two earlier mergers—the 1929 Congregational-Christian Alliance and the 1934 Evangelical and Reformed Church. English Congregational and German Reformed bodies respectively came to the New World in the seventeenth and eighteenth centuries. Their merger signified the first crossing of the sixteenth-century English Congregational and German Reformed divide, but not without difficulty. Congregationalists objected to joining with the more centralized polity of former German churches. Evangelical and Reformed midwesterners uneasily embraced New Englanders and their urban mentality. Synodical polity eased the way for Peace E and R into the UCC. Our sister First Congregational Church initially joined, but congregational independence impelled its later withdrawal. UCC founders hoped that blending diverse traditions would create a stronger, energetic, and more faithful church.[13]

The UCC soon took part in the Consultation on Church Union with the United Presbyterian, United Methodist Episcopal, Disciples of Christ, Evangelical United Brethren, and African Methodist Episcopal churches. Inclusion of a large black denomination marked a significant step across the racial divide for previously all-white Protestant ecumenism. By taking part in an ecumenical merger, Peace UCC stood apart from the conservative evangelical movement headed by revivalist Billy Graham, which attacked the World Council of Churches and the National Council for being too secular and too soft on Communism in addressing issues of social justice and world peace. Well-known UCC pastor and theologian, Reinhold Niebuhr, was a frequent target of these conservative criticisms.[14]

My home congregation mirrored the national growth of church membership, attendance, monetary giving, and building outlay that pundits regarded as signs of religious renewal. Growing numbers at last compelled calling an associate pastor and expanding physical plant after years of discussion. The congregation installed the Reverend Robert

Jacobs on September 5, 1953. He took charge of the Sunday School, confirmation class, and youth groups, and shared preaching duties. At the time Jacobs arrived, classes had overflowed the basement auditorium into the sanctuary and parsonage. A Christian education planning committee formed in January 1955; it broke ground for an addition two years later. The congregation dedicated the L-shaped, five-thousand-square-foot building on April 20, 1958. The seventy-thousand-dollar structure with its ten new rooms for classes and meetings more adequately housed an expanded education program, which had always been an important part of the church mission.[15]

A prominent, highly regarded churchman, the Reverend Kitterer fully engaged the moderate Christian agenda. He served as president of the Iowa Synod in 1944. He gave the opening address at the state convention that elected him as delegate to the national meeting at York, Pennsylvania. In 1949, he urged the public to support a national rally for religion backed by the Federal Council of Churches, the Jewish Synagogue Council in America, and President Harry Truman in a Sunday evening broadcast over the four major radio networks. Three years later, Kitterer toured war-torn western Europe for two months with a twenty-four-member study group sponsored by the Congregational Christian Church. On the occasion of a dinner at Peace E and R Church upon his return, Kitterer shared a common European saying: "We are not poor because we are Communists; we are Communists because we are poor." This proved to him the need for American foreign aid to save western Europe from Communist take-over.[16]

Reverend Kitterer also embraced popular culture. He frequently showed movies at Sunday evening meetings of the Young People's Society. The youth sometimes shared these with a larger audience. For example, two showings of Maxwell Anderson's 1941 stage play, *Journey to Jerusalem*, drew a large crowd. A few years later, Peace E and R and First Congregational jointly sponsored *For All People*, which dealt with racial understanding between the pastor of a community church and Mexican youth, and collected a free-will offering for overseas relief by Church World Service. I found the films Kitterer presented in Sunday School disappointing compared to the superior and more exciting fare

at the Elkader Theatre. Neither he nor Jacobs specifically banned movies and at times suggested ones of better quality such as *Martin Luther*
and *A Man Called Peter*, based on a best-selling spiritual biography of a
congressional chaplain by his widow Catherine Marshall. Jacobs even
took our youth group to see the latter at the theater.[17]

Sometimes East Indian missionaries spoke at worship, and the congregation donated that day's offering for their work. Their descriptions
of poverty, starvation, leprosy, and other diseases expanded globally the
localized horizons of our small-town congregation. Congregants who
had visited Denmark and England as Farm Bureau delegates as well as
newspaper reports similarly raised awareness of how hunger had followed the Second World War's devastation in Europe and Asia. Natural
disasters such as floods in China or drought in South Africa worsened
these conditions. Yet Americans who responded to calls for aid were
always dismayed if Africans, Asians, and Europeans responded with
anti-Americanism instead of affection.[18]

For our most significant youth event, we traveled by chartered bus to
the Winnebago Indian Mission School at Neillsville, Wisconsin. The
boarding school—established in 1921 by German Reformed missionaries
—offered elementary education, manual arts training, and religious instruction. We toured some of the buildings and a small museum; the
Reverend and Assistant Superintendent Jacob Grether explained the
school programs and challenges faced by the institution.[19] I recall sitting
on the grass of the picturesque campus and lunching on peanut butter sandwiches with several silent Native American students. The trip
afforded us a brief glimpse into an important mission outreach of the
Evangelical and Reformed Church among native peoples we could not
begin to comprehend. As a teenager more interested in girls and a budding social life, I was ill prepared to fully grasp the importance of the trip
Reverend Jacobs had arranged. I remember more about our boisterous
bus trip than I do about meeting the Native Americans and their pastor.

Reverend Kitterer impressed me as a somber, sad man whose face
mirrored his sorrow at the loss of loved ones. His wife died after a linger-
ing illness in 1942, and his teenaged daughter passed away two years later
following an appendectomy.[20] When we applauded a well-sung solo by a

five-year-old girl during a Christmas program rehearsal, he gravely and kindly reprimanded us for inappropriate behavior. I still recall his words every time my congregation mistakes acts of worship for entertainment and applauds choir anthems. Despite Kitterer's accomplishments, having the younger Jacobs as youth pastor pleased me; he shaped my life more than his sad-faced colleague. Even so, his reverend title set him apart as an elevated form of humanity. Not until adulthood did I come to understand that pastors were as ordinary as the parishioners they served.

As a child, church services seemed interminable. I waited impatiently for the offering signaled by the heavy tread of the four ushers (usually beefy farmers stuffed into suits) marching forward in step. Passing those plates meant my liberation would soon be at hand! These childhood experiences led me to avoid worship as an adolescent and an adult. Yet I enjoyed Sunday School and almost attained perfect attendance for several years except for missing a single day due to illness.

More than two hundred children normally enrolled in the classes ordered by grades from kindergarten through sixth in addition to those for junior and senior high youth. The primary pupils met in the lower auditorium, for which the church clerk had built an exact walnut replica of the main altar. Songs, prayer, and a brief homily preceded lessons based on Bible stories taught at folding tables set up around the room's perimeter. Older youth met upstairs in the sanctuary and followed a similar plan. With one exception, I do not recall the homilies or what we discussed in our classes. Once Reverend Jacobs talked about a man who had recorded all the hours he had devoted to various activities in his lifetime. Although the pastor said the man should have paid more attention to quality, I have similarly tracked my time throughout life.[21]

Jacobs started a weeklong Vacation Bible School in 1954. Twenty-one teachers presented lessons from materials produced by the National Council of Churches. At week's end, the children led Sunday worship followed by the annual picnic at Elkader Recreation Park. The church provided coffee, soft drinks, and ice cream while each family brought plates, silverware, and a dish to share for the potluck dinner. I found the picnics great fun, even though Mother frequently fretted that I might make myself sick by consuming too much ice cream and taking too many turns on the merry-go-round. Despite the power of suggestion, her nagging never made me ill. Sadly, Father disliked picnics so we stopped attending.[22]

Our confirmation class of eighteen met weekly on Saturday mornings at 9:00 in the lower auditorium from September 11, 1954, until we were confirmed during the Palm Sunday service on April 3, 1955. We memorized the Apostle's Creed, Lord's Prayer, Ten Commandments, and Twenty-Third Psalm. We completed workbook assignments dealing with the Bible; Christian beliefs, way of life, church, and action; and questions about confirmation and our need for the church. Even though I do not remember content, my written answers demonstrate that I dutifully did assignments. I wrote down dates for the principal English translations of the Bible; diagramed the Trinity, showing that God is Father, Son, and Holy Spirit; and copied this statement: "The Kingdom of God is the rule of God in hearts and minds of men." We were taught to distrust the idolatrous and authoritarian Roman Catholic Church, which reinforced the Protestant rule of my family that I should not date Catholic girls.[23]

On Confirmation Sunday we nervously answered questions before the entire congregation. Some still remember if they "bumbled" their response. After this ordeal, we took our first communion. It seemed strange to attain membership just one year after my paternal grandparents, who had joined by Letter of Transfer and Reaffirmation of Faith.[24]

On the previous day—a beautiful early spring afternoon—we had our class picnic at Pikes Peak State Park. We took in the natural beauty of the Wisconsin River entering the Mississippi. We examined Indian mounds, hiked trails, and gathered colored sand from pits located in woodland ravines. At sunset we cooked hamburgers wrapped in tinfoil in the coals of a wood fire. The warmth of our fellowship and the dying flames suggested God's presence and eased the chill of approaching nightfall.[25]

Later that summer I had a similarly enjoyable week at Blake's Grove near Eldora. The Women's Guild annually funded church camp. The women also held a bake sale and contributed the proceeds for equipping the camp kitchen. Upon our return, we reported our experiences at a guild meeting. We slept in cabins, ate in the dining hall, made woodland

*My confirmation occasioned this Palm Sunday
photograph of Mother and me.*

hikes, did crafts, played softball, swam in the nearby lake, and took part in evening vespers. The last night turned so cold that a roommate and I stayed warm by sleeping back to back in his sleeping bag. We paired up with girls and even exchanged letters before romance faded with time and distance. One of the counselors similarly had written to my brother. I did see my roommate from Clarence again at Band Day in Cedar Rapids and the girl from Ackley at a college track meet in Cedar Falls. After a warm hello, none of us had words or any desire to resume our relationships.[26]

I attended bimonthly youth group meetings in the church basement from seventh through twelfth grade. Membership ranged between twenty-five and forty for the junior and senior high groups. Reverend Jacobs opened with prayer and gave a short talk on some relevant topic. In one he criticized Norman Vincent Peale's positive thinking for its inadequate understanding of Christianity. In another he pointed out the shortcomings of Billy Graham's revival crusades; a one-time conversion experience did not provide an adequate Christian life without involvement in a church fellowship. On another occasion he gave this memorable definition: "Necking is what occurs above the shoulders and petting is what happens below." His statement described where I had been and pointed out where I wanted to go just like all other hormone-crazed males. None of us likely heeded his warnings against sexual experimentation. A business meeting followed devotions, and then we played Ping-Pong, talked with friends, and had refreshments—invariably Kool-Aid and bars or cookies provided by a Women's Guild member.[27]

We went caroling each Christmas season, visiting members who were shut-ins as well as the sometimes-unnerving folks at the Clayton County Insane Asylum and the Poor Farm. In the summer we went to drive-in movies at nearby towns, sitting in the stadium seats provided by slightly elevating the box of a farm truck. We had picnics at family cabins on the Mississippi River where we swam, water skied, and devoured hamburgers, hot dogs, Jell-O salads, and deserts. After the formation of the United Church of Christ, we sometimes met jointly with youth from the Elkader First Congregational Church and the Waukon ucc.[28]

Mine and most other families filled the church at Easter and Christmas. Easter Sunday began with a sunrise service conducted by the youth on Kramer Hill. Afterward, we ravenously consumed an abundant breakfast in the church basement prepared by the Women's Guild. Lilies decorated the brightly lighted sanctuary for the 10:30 worship as the well-dressed audience celebrated the Resurrection and partook of the Lord's Supper.[29]

The annual Christmas Eve program featured each Sunday School class reciting or singing part of the Christmas story. Two large evergreens lighted with white globes framed the chancel where the children performed. Electric candles placed on windowsills festooned with red bows and evergreen boughs decorated the side aisles. Children anxiously hoped to perform their parts without error before pews packed with relatives and neighbors. My class once sang "Silent Night" in German.

Elderly members wept during our performance, and I wondered, "Were we that bad?" On another occasion, during which I recited at length, I was told, "You should be a preacher! I could hear you at the back of the church!" To my mind, one's loud voice did not constitute a call to ministry. No matter how large or small our part, we were all relieved to be done and to reap our reward: a paper sack filled with hard candy, peanut brittle, unshelled peanuts, an apple, and an orange. This replenished the treats that Santa Claus had distributed earlier after the free movies sponsored by the Elkader Chamber of Commerce.[30]

Small-town residents rarely discussed divisive religious issues publicly. An environment in which everyone interacted frequently dictated that hard feelings should be avoided and a spirit of cooperation maintained. Yet within their respective churches, youth often learned to distrust Catholics. At Norway Lutheran—a country church near the hamlet of St. Olaf—one of my classmates received strict religious instruction. She memorized Bible verses and *Luther's Small Catechism.* Her teacher warned pupils not to date Catholics, dance, swear, tell lies, or walk on the sidewalk beside a tavern or they would go to hell. My mother likely received similar teachings at this church a generation earlier. Schoolmates at First Congregational in Elkader also learned that this religious divide should not be crossed. At Peace E and R we heard about Roman Catholic faults as well as the unhappiness interfaith marriages caused. We lamented the loss of progeny to the "false faith" even when the parent from "our side" did not convert.[31]

Schoolmates reared as Catholics in Elkader had Protestant neighbors and playmates. They often transferred to the public high school after attending elementary grades at St. Joseph's Catholic School. Sisters, who "were exceptionally kind and often fairly smart," taught them well. Single women of the parish and relatives hoped they might develop a religious vocation, an idea that they usually did not take seriously. They did not learn much about Protestantism, "a regrettable but mostly harmless mistake not worth more than a passing reference." They did not hear prejudiced talk about Protestants at home or derogatory attacks on them from the pulpit or as part of their religious instruction. They knew that Protestants disagreed with Catholic doctrines about the "one true church," papal authority, and parochial schools. The church discouraged interfaith dating and marriage as most denominations did.[32]

Catholic friends recollect instances of religious prejudice. One told her best friend that she could not go to heaven because she was not a Catholic. On another occasion, public school kids threw gravel at her as she passed the playground on her way to the "lower school," a term the sisters asked pupils never to use and to correct people who did. A Catholic boy invited a classmate to the prom. She initially accepted but later declined when her Lutheran parents objected. The superintendent heard about the incident, expressed his sorrow, and said the school tried to discourage such bigotry. The same boy also recalls his father—a devout Catholic—speaking with uncharacteristic bitterness about religious discrimination in recounting how his sister could not find a teaching position. She had graduated from Northwestern University, yet being Roman Catholic disqualified her from consideration.[33]

Catholic attitudes, ideas, and practices varied within and between parishes. A schoolmate recalls a Friday afternoon excursion on a Mississippi River paddleboat. It ran aground and remained stuck for some time. When she and her siblings became hungry, their parents permitted them to eat hot dogs. "Mom and Dad assured us God would understand and it wouldn't be considered a sin!" Her brother remembers his future wife, an Iowa City girl, being surprised "by our family critiques of the sermon and other matters" after attending mass.[34]

Catholic and Protestant teachings had varied impacts on individuals. A Lutheran classmate ended a serious relationship with a Catholic because she feared alienating her grandmother; "I . . . felt bad when I did it, but because of what I was taught, I thought it was the best thing to do." A Congregationalist recalls that when her younger sister married a Catholic, some family members threatened to boycott the wedding. "In the end, we all did attend, and learned to love our new brother-in-law." A member of Peace UCC married a Catholic and reports, "We have never had any problems regarding religion." A Catholic, whose brother married a Protestant, asks, "Now, fifty years later . . . does it really matter?"[35]

RELIGION AT mid-century appeared in assorted public spaces nationally and locally. Christmas and Easter boosted retail sales everywhere.
Elkader merchants announced the yuletide season in the *Clayton County
Register* with advertisements for toys, gifts, and numerous drawings.
They festively decorated stores and the business district, and awarded
prizes to homeowners who mounted the best-lighted displays. For the
convenience of late shoppers, they opened additional evenings and did
not close until six o'clock on Christmas Eve.[36]

Commerce did not preclude piety. The *Clayton County Register* front
page invariably featured "Come to Church for Christmas Services,"
which listed times for Catholic masses and Protestant Sunday School
programs. The Reverend Robert Jacobs—recently arrived as Peace E
and R associate pastor—twice organized religious parades. Floats depicted the "Herald Angels," "Three Wise Men," "The Nativity," and
other scenes from the Savior's birth. The parade halted at the Interstate
Light and Power Company for a community sing by several choirs conducted by Jacobs. An illuminated nativity scene appeared on the light
company lawn in subsequent years, which added "considerable attraction
to Elkader's Main Street" according to the newspaper.[37]

The *Clayton County Register* always advertised "Easter specials," listed
church services on the front page, and mentioned the numerous families who hosted Sunday dinner guests. The Chamber of Commerce
sponsored egg hunts and at times placed newspaper notices "in a sincere
attempt to bring to our community a spiritual rebirth on this Easter
season." The chamber expressed an ongoing need for religion: "Attend
church . . . and pay tribute to . . . the resurrection of Christ. May the
joyous communion lend you strength to meet the complexities of the
world today."[38]

Religious renewal brought crowds to the biblical epics that Hollywood
produced to reclaim the audience it had lost to television. I loved these
recreations of ancient worlds with scantily clad women, Roman orgies,
battles, triumphal entries into Rome, victories against overwhelming
odds, and miracles revealing the reality of God. Among those playing
in Elkader during the fifties, *Samson and Delilah* appeared first, followed

by *David and Bathsheba*, which the theater opened as an Easter Sunday attraction and advertised as the "Most Forbidden of [the] World's Great Love Stories!" Others included *Salome*, and, in Cinemascope, *The Robe* and *Demetrius and the Gladiators*, and, in Vistavision, *The Ten Commandments. Quo Vadis*—my favorite—became MGM's biggest hit, spurring other studios to profit similarly. Its ending echoed the cold war as Roman Centurion and Christian convert Marcus Vinicius (Robert Taylor) spoke to Americans threatened by Communism: "A more permanent world is not possible without a more permanent faith."[39]

Other media made religion available to millions as well. While working in her kitchen, Mother often listened to *The Lutheran Hour*, a radio program that proclaimed Christ's message on several hundred stations throughout North America. Pioneer Pentecostal televangelist Oral Roberts also attracted a large audience. An adolescent friend regularly watched his program for the spectacle of faith healing, although Roberts denied the label, saying, "God heals, I don't." He brought Pentecostals into the American religious mainstream before he followed "the sectarian cycle" and became a Methodist. His ministry's global impact rivaled that of Billy Graham.[40]

Somewhat surprisingly, our Protestant household more often tuned the television to Roman Catholic Monsignor Fulton J. Sheen than to evangelist Billy Graham. Father enjoyed watching *Life Is Worth Living*, and I sometimes joined him. Sheen's ability to speak for twenty-eight minutes without notes impressed us both. He had a doctorate and earlier had contributed to the spread of Thomistic philosophy by publishing *God and Intelligence in the United States*. His later best-selling *Peace of Soul* declared that conversion cured depression and improved health by enabling the soul to live in the consciousness of God's presence. Sheen won an Emmy as "Outstanding Television Personality," but he had strained relations with the jealous Cardinal Francis Spellman, who eventually ordered him off the air.[41]

American educators long advocated moral and religious training in public schools as requisite for good citizenship, social order, and stability of the American republic. In refuting attacks on godless schools, educational founder Horace Mann stressed the prevailing practice of nonsectarian religious instruction in common moral elements and Bible reading without comment, which nineteen-century Iowa school law incorporated and the State Supreme Court upheld. Reading and history textbooks, American flag ceremonies, special day observances, and the sterling example provided by Christian teachers continued to convey explicit and implicit moral and religious lessons well into the twentieth century. Due to efforts by the Iowa State Teachers Association Committee on Bible Study in Schools, supported by the State Superintendent of Public Instruction, 132 secondary schools gave credit for Bible study to 4,394 students as late as 1927. Although such formal training had disappeared by the time I enrolled, the tradition of nonsectarian religious instruction persisted in Christmas observances.[42]

From before the Second World War until after I graduated, the entire school attended a Christmas chapel program of prayer, scripture and other readings, and sacred music performed by vocal and instrumental ensembles. The Girls' and Boys' Glee Clubs and later the Mixed Chorus also presented a Christmas Cantata for the public. The director organized this program around such themes as "Peace on Earth," "Night of Holy Memories," "The Choir of Bethlehem," and "The Music of Christmas." High school students decorated baskets of candy and fruit that were displayed for all pupils to view and judged for appearance, appropriateness, economy, and originality. Class delegates accompanied by vocal groups delivered them to shut-ins and sang Christmas carols. Every elementary room had its own tree in addition to one placed in the lower hallway. Each grade decorated, sang carols, and drew names for exchanging presents at "cheer parties." The school newspaper headlined "Season's Greetings" and ran articles on Christmas legends and American yuletide customs.[43]

Religious litigation grew significantly after the Supreme Court applied the First Amendment to states in 1940, requiring them to respect religious freedom and to avoid establishment of religion. Expanding religious pluralism and liberals demanding a more secular state prompted the American Civil Liberties Union and other organizations to bring more test cases. Eventually the Supreme Court in *Engel v. Vitale* (1962) and *Abington School District v. Schempp* (1963) qualified or eliminated

Bible reading and prayer from the public schools. Even though some Protestant theologians praised the court for valuing religious conscience, many religious and political leaders condemned the decisions as atheistic and Communist-inspired. The Hearst and several big city newspapers also disapproved. Some schools continued these practices while others stopped. Conservative Christians began an ongoing campaign for a constitutional amendment authorizing prayer in the public schools.[44]

I encountered local displeasure with the court rulings at the time of Father's funeral in 1979. William Witt—a World War II veteran, a former school board member, and the funeral director who had buried all my family members—brought up the issue in conversation with me. He did not think Bible reading, prayer, and other religious observances should be removed. "It has always been that way," he complained, "why should it be changed?" I could not explain why freedom of conscience and the separation of church and state now justified ending long-practiced and commonly accepted customs.

FOR MOST RURAL and Elkader residents throughout my youth, Sundays normally included religion and usually passed quietly. My family rarely worked on the Sabbath apart from our daily chores or harvesting hay in summer. We put on our best clothes for church school and worship. Father stopped for the *Des Moines Sunday Register* at Schmidt's Rexall Drugs before it closed at noon. No other businesses opened except for the gas stations, Bridge and Checkerboard cafés, and movie theater. We hurried home so Mother could place an elaborate meal on the table as close as possible to the noontime dinner hour. She managed by preparing several courses in advance, keeping them warm in the stove during her absence, and then quickly reheating everything when she returned.

In the afternoon, we might call on relatives or be visited by them. If we did not go anywhere, my parents examined the newspaper and often napped. I read the comics and sports section before turning to toys or books. No one listened to the radio because classical music did not appeal. Once I turned ten, I frequently took in Sunday matinees and checked out the televised Chicago Bears football game at the Bayless Hotel lobby before the film started. In the evenings, my and other families often socialized with friends at neighborhood card parties, or listened to radio and in later years watched television at home. Obviously, piety did not preclude enjoyment of popular culture on the Sabbath.

Religious education had varied effects on schoolmates and me. Several report that religion—an essential part of their youth—has remained important in helping them "though some very tough times" throughout their lives. Due to personal experience, one now understands how people are "born again." For others, their religious faith gradually slipped away into indifference.[45]

In my case, religion did not save me from sinful acts, spare me from doubt, or equip me for theological reflection. It did not give me an experience of the presence and transcendence of God or provide me with the spiritual discipline required to seek such encounters. Made aware from attending neighborhood wakes as a child that all humans eventually died, I early pondered the subject of immortality. I considered whether anything lived forever and decided that the rock outcroppings on the hillsides of our farm survived longer than everything I could conceive. As their existence did not seem nearly as interesting as mine, I soon abandoned reflection on the subject.

Once I began taking communion after confirmation, I felt uncomfortable with the spiritual perfection the ritual seemed to require. Father often grumbled about this as well. Dark-lit Maundy Thursday and Good Friday evening services depressed me. A Catholic friend returning home from a Lenten service at St. Joseph's witnessed me taking Mother to Peace E and R Church shortly after seeing my brother—who no longer lived at home—entering a tavern on lower Main Street. She gave me credit for religious piety that I did not deserve.

In a required humanities course at college, I encountered deism through reading Voltaire's *Candide* and readily embraced its rationalistic critique of Christian theology. Thus began my twelve-year repudiation of formal religious observance. Even though I studied the history of American Christianity in graduate school and prepared a master's thesis on prominent theologian Reinhold Niebuhr, I did not enter a church except for weddings or funerals.

I have long since resumed active membership in the United Church

5

SCHOOL

ON TUESDAY, September 3, 1946, Mother and I entered the northeast door of the Elkader Public School to be greeted by the pungent odor of cleaning chemicals and the sight of freshly waxed floors that I subsequently noticed on the first day of every new year. We climbed one flight of stairs, crossed the hallway, and stepped up into the kindergarten room located behind the auditorium stage. Mrs. Florence Hamilton warmly welcomed me and the seventeen other children who enrolled that day. The lower and upper elementary grade classrooms were on the other side of the hallway of the first and second stories. For the next seven years I came through the same door and ascended the same stairway. These familiar surroundings eased my annual transitions to new rooms, grades, and teachers.[1]

The school sat on the 400-block of North Main Street and overlooked Molumby Athletic Field, situated beside the Turkey River below. A newly equipped playground on the northeast corner adjoined the junior college housed in an old three-story structure built in 1912. Yellow buses parked on the less elevated southeast corner near the "new" gymnasium, which survived the fire that destroyed the old school in 1936. To replace it, the board erected Iowa's first glass-block schoolhouse at a cost of $148,000 paid by fire insurance, a bond issue, and the Public Works Administration. Des Moines architect Oren R. Thomas designed the 173 × 148 feet, two-story, fireproof, air-conditioned edifice.[2]

The corrugated, translucent glass blocks in theory admitted the maximum amount of properly transfused light without glare, shut out noise,

The Elkader glass-block school that Don and I attended.

and provided insulation against extreme heat and cold. In reality, rooms facing west required Venetian blinds and curtains to reduce glare and heat. Hot days overwhelmed the ventilating system, stifling pupils inside the building. Asphalt tiles covered the floors and chemically treated hard rubber topped the tables in classrooms and laboratories. A landscaped lawn, shrubs, and trees decorated the front entrance on First Street Northwest. A magazine editor called it "the most beautiful and efficient schoolhouse it has ever been my privilege to visit."[3]

Unlike most farm children, I never attended country school. I graduated thirteen years after entering kindergarten in a class more than doubled by the statewide consolidation movement of the early 1950s. The newly formed Central Community School District absorbed rural pupils as well as secondary students from the nearby hamlets of Elkport, Garber, Littleport, and St. Olaf. Several Roman Catholics transferred after taking eight grades at St. Joseph's parochial school. The Elkader district bused children from the countryside even before consolidation. As these did not stop at our farm, Don and I walked the mile and one-quarter to school. In the middle grades, he rode his bicycle in good weather as I did after he passed it on to me. By his junior year, he owned a car and in winter I rode with him. When I became a senior, a classmate, Eric Meisgeier, picked me up mornings during the football season and dropped me off after practice. Otherwise I walked home daily.

School started at nine and ended at four o'clock before consolidation brought an earlier dismissal. Recess relieved tedium and pent-up energy twice daily. An hour at lunchtime permitted town children to eat at home and allowed additional playtime for those bringing their lunches or purchasing the hot meals available after December 1947. Recess disappeared in junior high and academic work increased. Yet it remained minimal throughout high school, usually finished in study hall if completed at all. As years passed, the opposite sex appeared more interesting and desirable, and extracurricular activities afforded additional instruction and diversion.

GREGARIOUS, CAPABLE Superintendent George Manus—a ruddy-faced individual whose bushy eyebrows bracketed a small scar—always seemed a frightening figure to me. One day he unexpectedly entered the noisy boys' bathroom, ostensibly to wash his hands. Unnerved in my haste to finish and depart, I zipped part of me into my fly. Timid elementary pupils fortunately had few opportunities to encounter such an imposing man. He came as a teacher, soon became dean of the junior college, and in June 1940, replaced Superintendent D. L. Wood, who had embezzled nearly twenty-three hundred dollars from the school activity fund. Manus left for military service during the Second World War but afterward resumed his position until he resigned in 1952, during onset of the baby boom and consolidation. His successor, M. F. Whitney, coped with expanding enrollments, overcrowding, and skeptical voters who blocked new construction.[4]

The superintendent and Chamber of Commerce advertised public education each autumn in the *Clayton County Register.* "The World-renowned Glass Block School" and its senior and junior high, elementary grades, and kindergarten promised "Education for Citizenship." The fully accredited junior college offered a well-trained faculty, free textbooks, and an approved two-year teacher training and secretarial course at only forty-five dollars each semester. Rural students comprised 60 percent of high school enrollment. Buses gathered them from the

Gunder Road through St. Olaf to Highway 13; the Pony Hollow Road to the Garber-Garnavillo Road junction and along Highways 128 and 13; and south Highway 13 through Mederville to the Downey and Dohrer Schools. Soon new routes ran on Highway 13 to Communia and the Elkport Bridge and on Highway 56 to the Frietag Farm and the Highland Church.[5]

The progressive, life-adjustment ideals of United States education at midcentury dominated my schooling. Teachers avoided dismissal during the Red Scare by self-censoring what they taught and by identifying American society with the highest possible attainment of democracy. Manus articulated his vision in a series of *Clayton County Register* articles. "Your school," he wrote, "embodies the organized effort of society to train children to live efficiently and effectively." Its program of curricular and extracurricular activities "successfully orients students to intelligent living" and "continually throws its weight on the side of community improvement and civic betterment." It fosters feelings of unity and thereby educates for democracy and safeguards against Fascism.[6]

The school attained these political objectives by imparting knowledge of history as well as national political and economic institutions. It gave fundamental training in science and physical education. Its well-cataloged library made magazines and books more readily available. The high school and junior college annually produced two plays and competed in the state one-act play contest. The junior high offered dramatic play reading and each spring put on one or two children's plays. Seventy-five instrumentalists who participated in three bands received "invaluable" training and opportunity for "the future enjoyment, understanding, and appreciation of music." In light of Wood's recent crime, Manus assured the public that the school conducted its business "with the most modern and efficient methods" and carefully audited student activity funds.[7]

Founded in 1929 as one of several municipal institutions in the state, the junior college graduated its largest class of twenty-eight in 1941. About one-half its alumni were teachers, commercial workers, and students. Seventeen housewives, fourteen professionals, and thirteen military personnel comprised the remainder. Enrollment dropped sharply from eighty-four (1940) to sixteen (1944). Just four graduated in 1945. At that time, the Iowa Taxpayers Association reported that Elkader had a high-cost school, expending $161 per pupil compared to $105 averaged by all others. When postwar enrollment did not reach the number recommended by state officials—despite ambitious recruiting efforts—the board of education in 1948 closed the institution.[8]

The Iowa consolidation movement dated from an 1897 law that created 439 merged districts by 1921 when depression stalled activity. It resumed at the end of World War II with the general assembly appropriating two million dollars for transportation, shifting the school-funding burden from local property taxes to the state treasury, and enacting the community school district as the new unit of public education. Reform cut 12,611 rural schools, decreased districts from 4,558 (1953) to 452 (1972), and gave farm and town kids similar schooling.[9]

The Clayton County superintendent of education urged consolidating districts to provide the schooling modern society required. A Clayton County board elected in 1948 to devise a better system filed its plan with the State Board of Education four years later. It called for eight secondary schools and kept grade schools in each village as a concession to residents who insisted on retaining institutions that sustained their communities. Voters approved the proposed consolidated Central Community School District based in Elkader by a 271-vote margin among the 916 polled. Country folk only narrowly backed the measure, however, while six of seven ballots cast by Elkader residents supported it. Five months later, a large majority of St. Olaf, Elkport, Garber, and Elkader inhabitants approved joining together with Littleport in the new district.[10]

Consolidation ended an era. In August 1946, 112 rural teachers attended the annual meeting conducted by Clayton County Superintendent H. F. Oelberg at the Elkader Courthouse. Their monthly salaries averaged $129, ranging from three who received only $70 to the royal personage paid $188. They learned that 121 country schools would open for the fall term even though five still did not have instructors. Because eight hundred schools in the state lacked teachers, thirty-seven closed in the county—ten more than the previous year. Speakers talked about public education, history and English textbooks, and state plans for rural schools. The distribution of supplies concluded the meeting. The following June, eighth graders and their parents gathered for graduation ceremonies at the Elkader High School Auditorium where Superintendent Oelberg presented diplomas.[11]

Within a decade, twenty-six country schoolhouses in the Central Community School District had disappeared. The Glesne and Hughes schools were moved to St. Olaf and Littleport, supplementing educational facilities there. The Cox Creek Township Trustees bought the Robbins School near Osborne for use as a town hall. Central netted over fourteen thousand dollars from twenty-two buildings sold at auction. Prices ranged from ninety-five dollars paid for the abandoned Motor School to eight hundred dollars for the Cain School on Highway 56.[12]

Friends fondly recall their rural educations. Buildings functioned as neighborhood centers. Some had a stage or a curtain for performing plays, which often accompanied box socials. Yet many lacked indoor plumbing and electricity. Pupils relieved themselves in a nearby privy or two. They fetched drinking water from the nearest farm. They huddled around wood-burning stoves on the frigid days and created their own hot lunch program by heating soup, potatoes, or other dishes. They usually walked to school and received rides only in the wettest or coldest weather. They went sledding or played fox and geese, hide-and-seek, tag, and ball according to the season at recess or the noon hour. Teachers changed frequently or returned for several terms according to the whim of district board members. While some "were not very good," others were more professional, imposed discipline, and "made us work."[13]

Numbers in the eight grades ranged from as few as four to more than twenty. When a school became too small or a teacher could not be hired, the board closed it and had the pupils bused to Elkader. Country kids found this an adjustment socially but not scholastically. One friend, LeRoy Larson, felt overwhelmed by a room filled with thirty children his own age. Yet the many books available for him to read eased his anxiety. Most believed the individual attention they received from their rural teachers and older classmates prepared them well academically.[14]

Initially, the Elkader building had space available for the influx of students brought by consolidation. Yet a school census projected an annual enrollment increase until 1959. To combat overcrowding, the board proposed erecting a farm shop, twelve elementary classrooms, and a garage for twelve buses with an enclosed maintenance and washing area. In August and October 1955, voters twice narrowly rejected the $340,000 bond issue. Strong Elkader support did not offset the more than 80 percent in Littleport who voted no. The *Clayton County Register* grieved, "What price education? [It is] necessary to preserve a democratic way of life in a world threatened by Communism." Yet democracy dictated congested conditions during my high school years. Not until June 11, 1958, did the electorate approve a $395,000 Elkader addition as well as all-purpose rooms at Elkport, Littleport, and St. Olaf. The satellite school structures at last gave the victory margin.[15]

A CLASSMATE remembers kindergarten as "a very good way to start out." Mrs. Hamilton "treated us all the same." Another says he can still hum tunes from "Peter and the Wolf" because she played the record for us so many times. During that critical nine-month gestation period, we became acquainted with one another, played with colorful, enameled wood blocks, practiced lacing tennis shoes so we could play in the gymnasium, and performed noisily in a rhythm band. We learned to read from a folio of the Dick and Jane Reader mounted on a stand that we all could see. We filled jelly jars with water, placed them outside on a cold November night, and observed that water froze, expanded, and cracked the jar. We memorized nursery rhymes about Jack Sprat, Dick Horner, and other colorful characters. We painted with brushes and fingers on paper. We pressed our right hands in a circle of damp clay that Mrs. Hamilton signed and dated for us. Mother kept mine on the living room wall for many years.[16]

A total of twenty-one students eventually made up our class. Nearly one-half graduated thirteen years later. Four returned after attending parochial or country school for a time. Three others continued into high school, when they dropped out to marry. Our elementary classes numbered about twenty through the fifth grade. In sixth, thirteen rural pupils joined us, pushing the total to thirty. After Mrs. Hamilton, Pelagia

Shimek, Annella Gleim and Mary Feeney, Arlene Schoien, Melba Ruigh, Wanda Winter, and Vivian Whitney nurtured us in turn as we ascended the educational ladder. Most held two-year degrees from Iowa State Teachers, Upper Iowa, or some other college. Four soon left teaching to wed. One never married and taught until she retired. Mrs. Hamilton, Mrs. Feeney, and Mrs. Whitney stepped aside between 1949 and 1958.[17]

School reinforced moral lessons taught at home, and parents generally upheld the sanctions educators imposed on miscreants. Teachers recorded attendance and tardiness daily. They expected pupils to apply themselves diligently and disciplined through humiliation. They reprimanded the unruly, made them write repetitiously on the board, kept them after school, placed them outside in the hall, sent notes home to their parents, or—all else failing—ordered them to the principal's office. Despite rumors of a paddle in his desk, he administered stern lectures rather than spankings. I do not recall anyone being inflicted with corporal punishment or even expulsion. A classmate had his mouth washed out with soap by Miss Winter for using one of the vulgar words that most of us eagerly learned from big kids. *Fart, poop, pee,* and more adult obscenities often elicited laughs unless overheard by a teacher, and then the comedian risked discovering whether or not Ivory soap really was 99 $^{44}/_{100}$ percent pure as advertised.[18]

At the end of each six-week term, the superintendent underscored the importance of application and achievement by listing those who had attained perfect attendance and the honor roll in the *Clayton County Register.* Among the total enrolled, the percentage of those who qualified as honor students by earning a B average ranged between the high of 35 percent (1946–1947) to the low of 27 percent (1949–1950). I made the honor roll more frequently in the upper elementary grades (94 percent) than I did in the lower elementary grades (67 percent). My perfect attendance rate improved as well from 53 to 65 percent. Even though my failure to achieve these distinctions never troubled me, I did enjoy the recognition when given and especially liked seeing my name in the newspaper once I learned to read. About one-half of us made the honor roll in the first and second grades. Those numbers dropped to about one-third for the third and fourth grades and one-quarter or less for the fifth and sixth grades.[19]

Elementary teachers daily drilled us in the three Rs. In first grade we learned how to print and spell our first and last names. Mine ranked as the longest, narrowly edging out Linda Lou Livingston. After visiting the school library, we all printed thank you notes. The teacher selected the neatest and best-written one to send. In second grade we studied phonics and wrote poetry. A brown-eyed girl, who spoke with a southern drawl, joined us from Texas. She told us about segregation, saying white people were mean to Negroes. To calm us after noontime play, instructors read aloud. We especially enjoyed *The Bobbsey Twins at the Seashore* and *The Story of Babar the Elephant*. We marveled at going on vacation, a phenomenon unknown to most of us, and the adventures of a Parisian-educated elephant that favored bright green suits. After Babar returned to the jungle and as the king spread civilization, we did not mind his "gentle authoritarianism" in upholding French colonialism.[20]

As we gained proficiency through the years, we took turns reading aloud; many believed they always received the longest or most difficult paragraphs. Our readers instilled moral values, condemning greed and dishonesty and upholding kindness and industry. To foster study and to reward those who finished their work early, teachers checked out library books to our classroom. I preferred exciting tales about English heroes King Arthur and Robin Hood as well as American pioneers Davy Crockett and Kit Carson. Weekly spelling tests and daily arithmetic work sheets challenged us in every grade. The subjects of science, social science, and history appeared as we acquired basic skills and knowledge. We conquered the complexity of cursive writing by practicing penmanship frequently. Starting in fifth grade, standardized achievement tests measured our educational progress. Such instruments appeared after the Second World War, aiming to create a democratic meritocracy.[21]

Teachers assigned art projects for Halloween, Thanksgiving, Christmas, and the birthdays of Lincoln and Washington. Dutch windmills indicated that March had arrived. We learned how to darn and occasionally made gifts for our mothers such as potholders in honor of her day. We carved animals or other objects from bars of soap, which ranged from excellent to unrecognizable. I rarely cared for these tasks. I preferred free periods in which I recreated scenes of modern combat or Robin Hood's band battling the Sheriff of Nottingham's armored knights. My genius went unrecognized.

Two or three times weekly, we marched to the music room or the gymnasium for instruction. We welcomed the chance to escape confinement even though it tested our ability to remain quiet in the halls. In music, we sang an assortment of songs, but most enjoyed American folk and patriotic tunes. My pleasure ceased when classmates snickered at my off-key solo delivered at the teacher's request; the humiliation kept me from ever trying out for vocal music in secondary school.

In the gym, we learned never to walk across the floor in street shoes. Fred Wistrick, janitor for more than four decades, always kept it spotless. We heard stories about seniors selling tickets to freshmen for admission to the swimming pool under the hardwood surface. Because its facility had the largest seating capacity, Elkader hosted the county basketball tournament until 1952 when the finals moved to the new Garnavillo gymnasium.[22] During the primary grades, the women's PE instructor taught us kickball and other games. In upper elementary, girls stayed with her while boys moved to the men's coach. We now wore gym clothes and took showers. Hot water never completely relieved the soreness caused by tumbling.

Music and physical education obligated everyone through twelfth grade to display their skills publicly. At a May Fete devoted to the theme "Battle between Spring and Winter," we debuted in kindergarten under the glare of spotlights as snowflakes and raindrops costumed in crepe paper. In second grade we jumped rope as the high school band played "Country Gardens" and "Festival March." During fourth grade the girls did Indian dances and the boys tumbled for "Rip Van Winkle," written and narrated by a high school student. For "Rhythm Rodeo" two years later, the girls performed "Whoa Back" while the boys portrayed "Cowboy Championship Steer Wrestling Contest" with backbends, chest balance, pyramids, and elephant races. For a vocal music concert as fifth graders, we sang "Whale Song," "Dreams," and "Dear Elvina."[23]

The vocal music instructor additionally staged operettas such as "Kentucky Sue" or "Polly Make Believe," casting seventh and eighth graders in speaking roles and using elementary pupils in the chorus or as dancers. For adolescent boys, Miss Sinning—the shapely and well-dressed director —proved aptly named for the fantasies she inspired. Instrumental and vocal instructors also directed the annual Christmas Chapel program for assemblies and the Christmas Cantata for the public.[24]

Throughout elementary school we welcomed the liberation afforded by the noon hour as well as morning and afternoon recess. We had an opportunity as first graders to eat hot lunches. Georgia Senator Richard Russell had sponsored the National School Lunch Act the previous year to benefit American agriculture, relieve southern poverty, and create healthier children. Female nutritionists and food reformers also shaped the law. Assuming that poor children were malnourished, they called for "a high-calorie diet based on whole milk, cream-based sauces, rich puddings, and butter on every slice of bread." The women invested the program with an idealism it did not deliver.[25]

Instead, male agricultural economists in the USDA used school lunches for distributing surplus commodities. They did not ensure participation of black schools or provide free meals for poor children. Only about 50 percent of schools took part nationally; many did not serve Type A meals and all based their menus on surplus foods. While appropriations increased throughout the fifties from sixty-five to ninety-four million dollars, the inconsistent choice of available foods limited nutrition. Schools regularly received milk, lard, flour, rice, and corn meal; deliveries of beef and eggs fluctuated wildly from one year to the next.[26]

At the start in Elkader, the home economics teacher and her student assistants prepared the food. A federal subsidy of six cents and a student fee of twenty cents per meal covered costs. By September 1950, the program operated throughout the academic year and daily fed one hundred students—about one-third of those enrolled. Primary pupils paid twenty, others expended twenty-five, and the government spent five cents on each meal served in the basement of the junior college building. The lower grades ate at 11:45 in the same room as the kitchen and cafeteria line. Older students ate at noon in a separate and larger lunchroom.[27]

Mothers and housewives, who wanted part-time jobs, were now hired as cooks at minimum wage. They were trained on-the-job or at workshops and in-service programs. They cooked according to standards set by dieticians employed by the Hot Lunch Division of the Iowa Department of Education. Besides half-pints of milk, meals consisted of what the federal government supplied: canned peas, peaches, tomato paste, and tomatoes; peanut butter, dry beans, dried apricots, grapefruit sections, and orange juice; processed cheese, butter, and cotton seed oil shortening; frozen ground beef or canned beef and gravy. School lunches today are different from those I experienced. Now nearly thirty million kids in ninety-eight thousand schools eat them daily; almost 60 percent of these get their food free. States started free meals with funds from the 1965 Elementary and Secondary Education Act, and within a decade school lunches had evolved into America's favorite welfare program.[28]

Disliking long lines and unappealing meals, I rarely bought hot lunch except on days when sloppy joes were served and everyone endured onion breath throughout the afternoon. I preferred the more tasty items Mother packed—sandwich, fruit, bars or cookies supplemented with hot cocoa or soup during frigid weather. In the wintertime, I carried my thermos bottle and food in a black workman's lunch bucket. Mother never dreamed of buying a Roy Rogers or another celebrity-endorsed pail! In the warmer months, she placed my wax-paper-wrapped sandwiches and desserts in brown paper sacks. She instructed me to fold and save both paper and sack, which she frugally reused. I commonly traded food with others. Mother's baked goods always attracted offers, but her sandwiches prepared with homemade bread could not compete with tasteless store-bought varieties.

After lunch we headed to the playground, which had a crushed-rock surface, making it usable in wet weather, and a large slide, a set of six swings with wooden seats, and high bars with a trapeze for swinging, a low bar for chin-ups or hanging, and a ladder for climbing to the top. Only the most adventurous, athletic boys used the bars. A classmate, John Lenhart, recalls, "I was never able to slide down that infernal contraption as I was sure I would . . . plunge to my death." Older boys talked about "going over the top" on the swing set but no one ever did. Girls played hopscotch or jumped rope on the sidewalk; their skill usually kept boys from joining them. On winter days with newly fallen snow, we slid down a small hill between the playground and the bus park, or took part in fox and geese on Molumby Athletic Field. As we grew, we competed there in softball and touch or even tackle football. We also staged games of tag or hide-and-seek around the buses or in the trees and shrubs that decorated the front of the building.[29]

During frigid weather the girls put on snow pants or wore blue jeans under their dresses. The coldest days kept us indoors for recess and in the gymnasium during the noon hour. At those times, accidents occurred frequently as supervisors could not adequately monitor the frenzied activity of so many children. We commonly scraped knees and experienced cuts or bruises through falls and collisions. While sliding one morning on a piece of tin, I fell forward when the makeshift sled stopped abruptly on striking dirt. A nasty cut above my eye ended that activity for everyone. Another boy knocked himself out from his drop when the trapeze chain broke.

Teachers banned chewing gum, eating candy, noisy outbursts, talking back, whispering, fighting, or leaving the room without permission. They rewarded good behavior with Christmas and Valentine's Day parties. For deportment, the brightest and best-behaved girls got As. Other girls attained Bs. The Bs and Cs boys usually received reflected our immaturity and proclivity for rowdiness. When a sixth-grade classmate came with a Mohawk haircut, exceeding the limits for acceptable deportment, the principal did not suspend him. The boy did not continue the style, and no one else adopted it. Two fights I witnessed went undetected and unpunished. Two girls engaged in a ferocious hairpulling brawl until, exhausted, they stopped and everyone went home. Another in which a boy defended himself in classic pugilistic style ended quickly without blows.

Our sitting at fixed desks ordered in rows reflected the traditional pedagogical methods we experienced. We occasionally had a filmstrip shown in the room or a film in the auditorium. We also attended assemblies at which high school dramatic or musical groups often performed. At times visiting speakers presented edifying yet entertaining programs. In fourth grade we sold fifty dollars worth of tickets for the high school play. In sixth grade we held a mock presidential election in which we reflected our parents' Republican affiliations by liking Ike, too. We took field trips to the Municipal Water Plant and the newspaper office. Class picnics at Elkader Recreation Park marked each year's end.

On our most memorable and favorite elementary school field trip, we attended *Cinderella* at the Elkader Theatre. We loved Jacque and Gus-Gus, two adorable mice, and hated Lucifer, the stepmother's villainous cat, that Walt Disney added to the tale. His productions modeled the virtues of industry, honesty, and thrift that adults wanted to instill in children. Most of us had seen *Snow White and the Seven Dwarfs*, *Bambi*, and *Pinocchio* at the theater and knew about good winning over evil through work, self-denial, and bravery. We were less enthralled with Disney's *True-Life Adventure* nature documentaries. These domesticated "nature's never-ending drama" by calling animals mom, dad, and the kids while showing their desert or prairie habitats.[30]

Teachers acknowledged birthdays, giving classmates an opportunity to sing. Some families hosted parties, inviting friends from the neighborhood and class. These defined peer groups, inculcated manners, and taught us that females planned and reported them in the *Clayton County Register*. I attended several birthday parties for my two closest friends. For Larry Dohrer's eighth birthday, Pete Meder and I rode home with him on the school bus, had dinner with his family, played, and stayed overnight. For his eleventh birthday, three other friends joined us and we went to a movie at the Elkader Theatre in the evening. For Pete's eleventh birthday, he asked fourteen boys to an afternoon party at the family cottage on the Mississippi River near McGregor. We hiked to Pikes Peak State Park, played games, and ate a supper his mother served.[31]

In keeping with the philosophy of life adjustment education, schools assisted with preventive health care. Each class marched out of the building to a mobile X-ray unit that screened for tuberculosis. We received sight and hearing tests as well as smallpox and other immunizations such as the Salk polio vaccine when it became available. Hygiene classes encouraged annual dental examinations and taught everyone how to keep their hands, hair, bodies, and teeth clean.[32]

Accidents, deaths, and national crises sometimes disturbed our idyllic lives. During first grade, classmate Karen Crane coasted on her sled directly in front of a car. She received severe bruises, remained unconscious for more than twenty-four hours, and spent three weeks in the hospital. In third grade, high school senior and only son Milo Murphy died one month short of graduation when he lost control of his 1933 Oldsmobile while driving from Clayton Center toward Elkader. His parents kept the death vehicle near their rural home. Visible from the highway, it reminded us all what could happen in a careless moment. In sixth grade, Pete Meder's mother died in an accident just north of Iowa City. She had taught several of us at Peace E and R Sunday School, and we awkwardly expressed our sympathy to him when he returned to class. My brother's close friend Richard Nelson died of leukemia shortly before their graduation. A coal strike caused a national crisis, angered adults, and closed school for one week during third grade. It troubled us only when we made up the classes on Saturdays and a vacation day.[33]

RISING ENROLLMENT and crowding marked my junior and senior high years. Numbers in the building jumped 23 percent to 480 in 1953, and grew another 8 percent to 524 the next fall. Administrators separated the seventh and eighth grades, putting them in rooms carved from the former high school study hall. An Elkader Chamber of Commerce full-page advertisement in the *Clayton County Register* proudly declaimed: "Meet Your Schools! The factories which turn out the Central District's most important product—Your children with a sound basic education. Your schools offer a complete course of study, plus broadening extra-curricular activity for the best all-around education."[34] The chamber's analogy of school and industry pointed to the need to expand the plant for processing baby boomers.

Junior high marked a bewildering transition for my classmates and me. Past practices continued, but new prospects beckoned. We retained fixed desks, and one teacher instructed us in most subjects. We still left our room for music and physical education as well as for eighth-grade civics and science. Males now played on athletic teams, but females did not. Girls could be cheerleaders for boys' basketball. They might also learn to twirl batons or play instruments and join the senior band. Girls and boys now took an interest in one another. They sometimes danced together at seventh- and eighth-grade parties while others looked on with disbelief, disdain, or desire. Some trooped downtown for lunch at the soda fountains of the Walgreens or Rexall drugstores. They preferred spending quarters on hot fudge sundaes instead of nutritious meals made from agricultural surpluses. A few went to the Bridge Café for the "the best chili and hamburgers ever!"[35]

Mrs. Gertrude Scully, newly employed at Elkader after extensive experience in country schools, taught us in seventh grade when we numbered thirty-three. Our rowdiness tested the patience and discipline of this good teacher. We whispered, passed notes, and fired projectiles from peashooters that rattled noisily down the Venetian blinds. As Harold Biedermann heard our eruptions in the adjoining eighth-grade classroom, he would pause and tell his students, "I can't wait to get my hands on them next year!" After two decades instructing rural pupils, he had joined the faculty in 1946 as junior high principal, teacher, and coach. He anticipated every misdeed and his scolding effectively shamed even the most disobedient. We knew his reputation as a stern disciplinarian; no one in our group of thirty-one challenged him, and our year together passed quietly.[36]

Adolescent hormonal urges surprised us and impelled interest in the opposite sex. We had little guidance for dealing with turbulent emotions further stimulated by movies, music, and magazines marketing goods through sex appeal. Most parents did not talk about "it." Older peers imparted only half-truths. We shared information gleaned from fumbling encounters and gossiped about girls who had gotten pregnant. By the 1940s, Parent Teacher Associations (PTA) backed formal sex education that focused on health, family living, and human relations. Courses taught youth to avoid sexual activity viewed as immoral and dangerous outside marriage. An Elkader PTA did not form until late 1955, and the district did not formally teach about sex in our time. Yet freshmen and sophomore girls learned domestic science skills in home economics. Sophomores studied sexual growth and reproduction in biology. And women's magazines and other media shared facts from college marriage courses.[37]

Pedagogues, parents, and popular culture fostered heterosexual growth by encouraging youth to care for their appearance, seek popularity, and date. To develop appropriate masculine and feminine behaviors and prepare students for marriage and procreation, schools carried out informal sex education through sponsored social activities. These consisted of class parties each semester starting in junior high, Friday night senior high sock hops after home football and basketball games, and the more formal annual homecoming dances and junior-senior proms. Teachers chaperoned, maintained decorum, enforced the ban on alcohol and cigarettes, and concluded these events at a suitable hour.[38]

At seventh- and eighth-grade parties we played games, danced, and ate. Girls more quickly mastered ballroom dancing perhaps because they did folk dances in physical education and practiced with one another at slumber parties. Boys lacked lessons and could not imagine rehearsing steps with another male. The socially adventurous Sandra Lemka and Julie Stebor even invited boys as well as girls to their thirteenth birthday celebrations. At one we had a chaperoned hayride; at the other we danced; and at both we took part in games, gave gifts, and had lunch. Larry Dohrer and Pete Meder still observed their natal day with boys only.[39]

Class parties continued with a similar format throughout high school. As second-semester freshmen, we had a picnic at the Elkader Recreation Park on Friday evening and afterward entertained the sophomores at a dance in the gymnasium. At the first-semester senior party, Pete Meder won a drum contest and Clarence Stahl played his guitar and sang in addition to the normal routine of games, dancing, and food. Alcohol-free sock hops featured a high-fidelity record player, a stack of Glenn Miller LPs, and couples dancing (a few more skillfully than most) in the semi-darkened gymnasium. We evolved to the bunny hop and rock and roll music, which did not entirely displace classic swing for dance-ability and listening pleasure. Once sock hops concluded, many boys and girls left together in cars and carried on informal sexuality studies unsupervised by adults.[40]

Our senior class trip in May to the Wisconsin Dells formed a party on wheels. We left by chartered bus accompanied by two chaperones at 6:15 A.M.; took a midday boat tour of the scenic geological formations at the Dells; and then rode horses, boated, hiked, or played volleyball and softball in the afternoon at Devil's Lake State Park. After a picnic supper, we headed home, arriving at 11:30 P.M. We had resisted this customary senior class trip, but the sensual pleasure of a perfect spring day eased our disappointment. A few celebrated the occasion with alcohol. Three boarded the bus with hangovers from drinking the night before; three others got tipsy while boating and capsized their craft. Even though their misbehavior scandalized some, no one informed the chaperones, who could not discipline rule violators they failed to detect.[41]

Homecoming our senior year resembled those of previous autumns that had copied college and university practices. A Thursday night parade started at the school and proceeded through the business district. The band led the class floats and the king and queen candidates who rode as couples in four convertibles. The procession stopped twice for cheers before continuing to Molumby Athletic Field for the pep rally and bonfire. At halftime of the Friday night football game the band performed, and the Chamber of Commerce announced the prizewinning floats. Our class finished second with a hypodermic needle and the slogan "Get 'Em in the End" (an idea we had stolen from the University of Iowa School of Pharmacy). We had won as juniors with "Sail Past the Pirates" and as freshmen with a motto lost to memory. The 1957 queen crowned Pete Meder and Janice Carolan. They and their court dressed in suits and formals were again presented to students and alumni at the postgame dance in the gymnasium.[42]

As juniors we sold magazine subscriptions and worked the concession stand at football games to raise money for hosting the seniors at the spring banquet and prom. Parents sanctioned these activities, fostering adult behaviors in their offspring. We donned suits and formal dresses, minded our manners, and danced to an orchestra rather than records. We adopted the oriental theme of "Shangra La," which we willfully misspelled, and decorated the gymnasium with assorted structures and colorful streamers of crepe paper.[43]

Juniors entertained us in turn the following year. The Women's Guild again served the banquet at Peace UCC. Myrna Voss, our class president, gave the welcome, and her junior counterpart responded. Vocal groups entertained us with "Bali Hai" and "Some Enchanted Evening" from *South Pacific*. Readers related our class history and prophecy, comically recounting our past as well as predicting the future of each senior. A

"Treasure Chest" theme transformed the gymnasium for the dance. The "Melody Maestros" played from a stockade, and sophomore girls served punch from a hut. As proms had been all-night affairs since 1955, we viewed an early morning showing of *Torpedo Run* and *The Mating Game* at the Elkader Theatre. To our disappointment, parents no longer served a sunrise breakfast. By first light, I drove my date back to Garnavillo and headed home to sleep. Father interrupted my all-too-brief slumber by putting me to work, but even spending all day on a tractor did not erase my pleasant feelings about an evening that we all expected to remember forever.[44]

Almost everyone wanted a date for important events like the prom and homecoming dance because it validated acceptance by our peers. Yet we learned early and painfully that all were not equal in the competitive dating system. For males to rate, we needed proper clothes, access to a car, and cash for tickets, gas, and food. For females to rate, they must have beauty and personality for attracting boys who could provide for them on dates. A popular and pretty girl who caught the attention of an upperclassman might be invited to four proms. The rest of us were limited to two or none if we could not fund or attract dates as dictated by convention. To some degree, the system transformed both sexes into commodities. Boys became "wallets" who were valued for what they could afford. Girls were "show horses" prized for their head-turning appearance. They emulated models and actresses who typified ideal beauty and revealed the breast fetish of American men. Boys early learned to admire large breasts, but did not realize how these could be faked with "falsies" or padded brassieres by the less endowed.[45]

The routine representation of couples instilled in us the notion of heterosexual pairing as natural, normal, and expected. Each senior high class selected nominees for spring carnival king and queen. Seniors named homecoming king and queen candidates who were presented as couples at the parade, pep rally, football game, and dance. When the yearbook featured senior superlatives for success, dress, looks, dance, humor, personality, and studiousness, the editor photographed the winning pairs as couples. In the *Central Community School Tatler* (*CCS Tatler*) "Who's Whose" recounted the activities of steadies, a few of whom eventually married. "Klassroom Kapers" sometimes made jokes about those who had trouble finding a partner or perhaps found one too frequently. For example, someone asked, "Can You Imagine?" and answered "Cookie without a suitor." As the prom approached, Eric Meisgeier exclaimed, "I'll buy a corsage on only one condition—that a girl comes with it."[46]

Yearbook pictures of senior superlatives document our shared middle-class masculine and feminine concern for appearance. We had learned that stylish clothes and careful grooming facilitated personal relations. Boys have flat-tops or neatly trimmed longer hairstyles. They wear tan or black slacks, short-sleeved polo or long-sleeved sport shirts at times with button-down collars and V-neck sweaters, and often white bucks or penny loafers. The girls are attired in flats, skirts and blouses (sometimes with sweaters), or dresses. Some wear lipstick and all have their hair neatly arranged. Yet urban class distinctions blurred in our rural and small-town high school. As farm kids, we often wore working-class blue jeans or Levis, flannel shirts, and even the rebellious ducktail as well as flattops and chinos.[47]

Females differed from males as Wini Breines, Caryl Rivers, and Susan Allen Toth have recounted in their memoirs about coming of age in the fifties. They say girls knew more and had more experience in presenting themselves. Girlfriends typically provided a sense of security and information about fashion, hairstyles, beauty products, and diets gleaned from the *Ladies Home Journal*, *McCall's*, and *Seventeen*. Girls taught one another about living together in equality, which may have been the best marriage preparation any of them received. Girls wanted to be popular, which meant being valued for beauty, dress, ability, or personality. Even though girls wanted to capture a man, Breines contends they rebelled at times against this expectation and sublimated sexual yearnings for an Elvis Presley or James Dean, hoping for lives different from their mothers.[48]

Many of us did not date until high school, and a few delayed until college. Parents made sexual experimentation logistically difficult. They limited our access to the family car, insisted on verifiable destinations, restricted us to supervised events, and imposed curfews. Yet some of us paired up in junior high at movies or school parties, which did not involve couples being alone in automobiles or require parental permission. On three Saturday evenings one winter as our parents shopped or worked downtown, three pairs gathered at a friend's house in the absence of his widower father. The housekeeper stayed in the kitchen, popped corn, and served soft drinks. We sat in the darkened living room, watched television, and necked despite being just twelve-year-old seventh graders. Without being aware, our acts mirrored cultural trends. War- and depression-spawned insecurities raised the marriage rate and reduced the average wedded age. The media celebrated youthful matrimony and emphasized dating as essential for mate selection, and kids like us entered the courtship system at earlier ages.[49]

Despite societal norms, boys expected necking and even petting on dates and in romantic relationships. Dating promoted sexual exploration in the privacy afforded by automobiles as well as by a sense of obligation in girls fostered by having boys pay. The dating system made women the controllers of sex. By her more virtuous nature and the logic of sexual economy, she must enforce limits, and he must accept them despite his more libidinous nature. Girls kept their value with boys by making sex a scarce commodity. Males wanted intercourse, but did not value promiscuous females. Experts claimed these conventions sustained couples who eventually married and preserved a woman's social status by limiting premarital sex. Girls varied in what they permitted. Most kissed, but a few did not or limited their date to a good-night kiss at the door. Most did not pet, but some did if they were sure a boy would not tell. These rules changed for some going steady who engaged in sexual intercourse while others did not progress beyond necking.[50]

The system especially burdened females by pressuring them to be sexually interesting without being permissive. They endured the male gaze on the street and in school as well as harassment by overly aggressive males on dates. They set sexual exploration limits in regard to touching body parts above or below the waist and inside or outside of clothes. They might engage in petting that stopped short of penetration and still remain virgins technically, or they might pleasurably experience sex with a steady partner.[51]

According to Wini Breines, behavior deviated from social norms and expectations exceeded reality in the fifties. The Kinsey report revealed that 50 percent of females had engaged in premarital sexual intercourse. Fiction and memoirs suggested frustration with initial sexual experiences. Couples going steady imitated peers seeking security in early marriage. They pledged fidelity and exchanged class rings, assuring themselves dates and greater sexual intimacy. At times these relationships blossomed into matrimony, enabling males and females to escape competitive dating and the premarital sex taboo. For these reasons, women's magazines endorsed early marriage, and experts argued that the practice benefited couples as well as society.[52]

Among twenty-nine girls in our class at the start of high school, six dropped out and married. Seven others wed within twelve months of graduation. Some enjoyed happy, long-lasting marriages, but others did not. These women likely paid a price for not taking advantage of their educational opportunities. Popular culture assured them that academic achievement did not count in competing for boys and dates. School prepared them for marriage by requiring two years of home economics. Parents who considered higher education unnecessary for daughters advised them to take commercial subjects like typing, shorthand, and bookkeeping. They did not anticipate a future in which women worked at low-wage jobs throughout their lives.[53]

In addition to the informal sex education that provided our most important lifelong learning, every graduate needed sixteen units from the academic curriculum. All freshmen enrolled in English, general mathematics, and general science. Sophomores took algebra, biology, and English. They might elect drivers education as a fifth subject. Boys chose either agriculture or shop and girls home economics for their two-year vocational education requirement. Every junior had American history, American literature, and two selected from world history, geometry, physics, physiology-anatomy, bookkeeping, typing, and agriculture. All seniors took American government and elected three from advanced algebra, chemistry, English literature or speech, shorthand, and agriculture. In theory, the curriculum prepared well-adjusted graduates to live effectively as family members, workers, and citizens. In practice, it lacked academic rigor and failed to challenge those who went on to college. It did not offer trigonometry, calculus, foreign language, or any guidance counseling.[54]

By my senior year, the high school faculty numbered nine men and four women. Only one woman was married even though the postwar prohibition on hiring them had been dropped. Most transmitted knowledge by teaching the text; they lectured and we recited from the assigned reading. They rarely employed films, filmstrips, or any other audiovisual aids. Assemblies supplemented our academic work. As first-semester seniors, for example, we heard talks on Yosemite National Park, the United States Merchant Marine, and Ethiopia. Frequent turnover of staff subjected us to a succession of inexperienced and at times inept teachers. Only five remained throughout our four years. The most capable such as skilled math instructor Gerald Robinson—a tall man with slicked-back black hair and a mustache who resembled movie mogul Howard Hughes, according to one of the girls—departed for a superior job in an urban district. Yet two with family in the area stayed until retirement. They became favorite teachers and had yearbooks dedicated to them.[55]

Lorene Lenth—an outstanding director of forensics and plays— taught American and English literature as well as speech. She required us to compose essays on "America's Future Is Up to Youth" for a contest sponsored by the Clayton County VFW. We won seven of the top eight places probably because few from other schools entered the competition. When MRS—the staunch Republican *Clayton County Register* columnist —condemned the civil rights movement and called its leaders Communist stooges, we discussed his allegations in speech. Even though most shared his Republican values, we did not think that protest made someone Communist in a country that valued equality of opportunity and individual rights. Miss Lenth not only urged many to attend college, she prepared them well by assigning research papers and drilling in vocabulary.[56]

Reid Dillon taught biology, world history, American history, and government; advised the newspaper; and coached baseball. A genial quick-tempered man, he kept order without being oppressive. Unwilling to incur his red-faced wrath or being whacked with his grade book, we responded at once to his command: "Settle down!" He praised the objectivity of our American history text which said the "civil war" should be called the "war between the states." We did not think to ask how using the South's preferred term could be more objective than the northern one. Upon completing the government and economics requirement, he ended the year by teaching world geography for the first time. He believed we should learn about other nations in a world shrunk by modern communication and transportation. Our text showed the lives of various peoples by describing their resources, industries, agriculture, and commerce.[57]

In biology we dissected frogs, which Mr. Dillon's best pupils had acquired from the banks of the nearby Turkey River. We also collected leaves and insects. My well-prepared leaf scrapbook earned an A, but my cigar box of ten insects—hastily gathered after I belatedly recalled the due date—justly received a D-. He did not inquire about my inconsistency; I would have been too embarrassed to explain.

In addition to poor teachers, overcrowding compromised the quality of our education. Ever-expanding need for elementary classrooms compressed high school space each year. The board authorized dividing the study hall into two classrooms; using the lunchroom as a study hall; and putting classes in the library and auditorium. For example, we had eighth-grade civics in the upper library; tenth-grade English in the lower library; eleventh-grade typing on the stage; twelfth-grade speech in auditorium seating; and farm shop in the city park shelter house. Congestion dictated new construction. Cost compelled the board to reject building a new high school outside the town. Even so, voters twice rejected a less-costly addition to the existing plant. Not until 1958—too late to help us—did the public finally authorize new construction.[58]

When more seventeen-year-olds began attending high school in the twenties and thirties, vocational education gave them the curricular variety many newcomers craved. The Commission on National Aid to Vocational Education (1914) and the Smith-Hughes Act (1917) had furthered the cause by authorizing federal money for part of the salaries of agricultural, home economics, and industrial arts teachers. While many likely benefited from these courses, schoolmate Pat Keleher who became a farmer maintained he learned nothing from his agriculture classes, which had been poorly organized and taught. For my part, I intensely disliked shop and its instructor. In two years I completed only a walnut lamp and end table that Mother refinished to make presentable. She could not understand my aversion for practical learning, and Father often insisted: "You can't make a living from books!" I did not listen or care, and remained mired in mediocrity.[59]

The Future Farmers of America (FFA) and the Future Homemakers of America (FHA) gave opportunities to many who did not take part in other activities. Members wore national blue corduroy jackets emblazoned with the FFA corn gold emblem. Its motto succinctly stated chapter goals: "Learning to do; Doing to learn; Earning to live; Living to Serve." The chapter enrolled thirty or more and elected six officers annually. Its Green Hand initiates wore bib overalls, twine belts, straw hats with a feather, and work shoes, socks, and shirts. Five delegates attended the National Convention at Kansas City, Missouri. Others took part on judging teams at the National Barrow Show at Austin, Minnesota, the All-Iowa Fair at Cedar Rapids, and the National Dairy Cattle Congress at Waterloo. Members competed at the FFA state speech contest in such events as parliamentary procedure as well as creed, public, and extemporaneous speaking. During FFA Week, which honored first farmer George Washington, the chapter placed displays in store windows and articles in the *Clayton County Register.*[60]

The FHA strengthened the family as the basic unit of society and promoted consumer sciences education. It enrolled twenty members and elected seven officers annually. It prepared boxes of Christmas gifts for the state children's home. Two delegates attended district and state conventions. In addition, the tenth-grade homemaking class modeled the pajamas, dusters, and dresses they had made at a style show held for parents in the auditorium. The ninth-grade class served the punch and cookies they had earlier baked.[61]

When the Soviets launched Sputnik 1 and 2 in autumn 1957, it challenged American technological supremacy and intensified attacks on public education. Critics Arthur Bestor, Jr., and Admiral Hyman Rickover blamed life adjustment pedagogy for not properly preparing smart children. They called for greater academic rigor to match the superior

Soviet education system and to keep pace with its Communist rivals in the global struggle.[62]

Sputnik also confirmed my decision to take as many science and mathematics courses as I could. In retrospect, world history and English literature would have given me greater pleasure. Even though I scored high in quantitative ability on the Iowa State Educational Development Test and excelled in geometry, I generally received average grades in math. I completed a six-week term of advanced algebra, which I had taken as an overload. Then the regular teacher went on medical leave, and his substitute reduced me to such confusion that I dropped the course. I earned better grades in physiology, physics, and chemistry, but neither the football coach nor the principal who taught them fired my passion for these disciplines. Still, I did learn that my interests lay elsewhere and at college tested out of math and physical science general education requirements.

The superintendent continued posting the honor roll at the end of each six-week term throughout junior and senior high. I remained an honor student in seventh grade, but did not qualify during the next three years. This displeased Father, who went ballistic when I brought home Ds in both drivers education and shop. As someone who scored in the 96th percentile on the Iowa State Educational Development Test as a junior, I clearly should have done better. Yet no teacher spoke to me about the disparity between my ability and mediocre grades. Perhaps I stopped "attending" in the eighth, ninth, and tenth grades because adolescent angst and hormonal imbalance afflicted my male classmates and me. Nearly twice as many females made the honor roll, and more of them joined the National Honor Society. Class valedictorian Eric Meisgeier and salutatorian LeRoy Larson were exceptions to this rule of male indifference.[63]

My academic work improved greatly as a junior and senior. I earned a 3.75 grade point average and qualified belatedly for National Honor Society membership. What turned me around? As a sophomore, I became friends with John Niemeyer and Jack Glesne, two college-bound seniors. Their talk of future plans moved me to think about mine. Becoming a high school senior no longer seemed an adequate life goal, and I focused more on academic and extracurricular achievement.

American high schools at midcentury solidified an age-segregated youth culture that shaped my generation, who were the first to be called teenagers. Targeted by corporate marketing, we carefully attended to our appearance, clothes, and tastes; we did not mind when our choices alarmed adults. Cold war fears about juvenile crimes and crumbling families caused Hollywood to make more than sixty delinquency pictures in the 1950s. The genre expressed alarm about the problem while it romanticized sexy, misguided, youthful antiheroes. Marlon Brando thrillingly portrayed the leader of a leather-jacketed motorcycle gang in *The Wild One.* Billed as "the most startling picture in years," *Blackboard Jungle* dramatized urban high school problems and featured the first rock and roll score played by Bill Haley and the Comets. James Dean, Natalie Wood, and Sal Mineo appeared as troubled teens in the popular *Rebel Without a Cause.*[64]

These cinematic celebrations of adolescent anxiety and uncertainty appealed to me, my classmates, and other teenagers throughout the country. We began wearing black engineer boots, tight Levis rolled up at the cuff, and shirts with turned-up collars. I let my hair grow, combed it straight back into the ducktail sported by all rebels, and plastered it in place with gobs of butch wax. Yet the anger and physical violence of such films unnerved me. I felt immense relief after a standoff in an implement dealer's lot with a group of teenagers from Strawberry Point ended without coming to blows. When my father ordered me to cut my "grease-ball hairdo," I meekly complied.

Our musical tastes set us apart and spurred the growth of Top Forty broadcasting. Friends and I rode around Elkader at night or on Sunday afternoons desperately looking for excitement while listening to rock and roll on the car radio. A few peers acquired record players and bought inexpensive 45s at a newly established record shop on Main Street. National sales nearly tripled during the second part of the 1950s, and numerous small stations became outlets for the four hundred new recording companies that appeared. Many of us listened to Dale Wood, a DJ who broadcast Top Forty music on KOEL from nearby Oelwein. Like other DJs, "Mrs. Wood's little boy Dale" used jive talk to sell advertising and himself. He identified with rebellious teens by combing his well-lubricated black hair so that it resembled a duck's posterior and hosted RC Cola dances all over northeast Iowa. His broadcasts gave us access to our favorite black and white musicians like Chuck Berry, Fats Domino, Elvis Presley, Jerry Lee Lewis, Little Richard, and others.[65]

Turning sixteen and having older friends with wheels like Pat Keleher, Glen Huebner, and Daryl Dahling enabled me to follow my parents' example by attending dances usually at Lakeside Ballroom in Guttenberg. There we cruised for girls without much success because both they and the two-step befuddled us. In time I had romances with two women who danced well and taught me to polka, schottische, square dance, waltz, and jitterbug. Popular local bands like Leo Greco and His Pioneers and Andy Doll and His Orchestra played country swing and arrangements of current rock and roll hits. Once each summer, we dressed up and danced more sedately to the Jan Garber Orchestra, one of the finest big bands. We delighted in live performances by the iconic Everly Brothers at Lakeside, Buddy Holly and the Crickets at Decorah's Matters Ballroom, and Johnny Cash and the Tennessee Two at the Fayette County Fair.[66]

Frightened by the specter of juvenile misbehavior, Elkader adults organized a PTA; a speaker from the state office warned that deviance often resulted "from parental delinquency." Town fathers and educators curbed Halloween pranks by arranging entertainment, and eventually created an Elkader T-Inn in the Opera House basement. They invited everyone between ages fourteen and twenty and served refreshments, offered dance instruction, and asked school board members and wives to serve as chaperones. After a successful Halloween party, *Clayton County Register* editor Harold Griffith thanked youth for their "becoming behavior." Yet the ambitious T-Inn initiative collapsed, as had an earlier wartime effort.[67]

J. D. Salinger's 1951 novel *The Catcher in the Rye* expressed the decade's fixation on alienated youth and cultural uncertainty. Our rebellious behavior paled in comparison to that of Holden Caulfield. During our freshmen year, a rumor that someone intended to build a zip gun in shop brought an immediate response from the principal. After interviewing us all individually, he decided it had been just talk. A few girls emulated the Beats by wearing black tights and berets. Boys sometimes copied the hairstyle and dress of James Dean and Marlon Brando. As juniors we took part in Bermuda Shorts Day that administrators subsequently banished. The next year we declared Sunglasses Day with the same result. To prevent these disruptions from evolving into delinquency, pedagogues and parents put their faith in an extracurricular program of wholesome activities at Central Community High School. Music, dramatics, journalism, and athletics focused youthful energies on the team or institution, generated loyalty, created a shared sense of values, and promoted maturity.[68]

ADULT-SUPERVISED adolescent pursuits that fostered equality of opportunity, cooperation, discipline, and leadership accompanied the rapid growth of public secondary education after 1900. No wonder superintendents and the Chamber of Commerce often stated that good education included extracurriculars. The Elkader board boosted involvement by shifting to eight forty-five minute periods in 1941.[69]

Award assemblies ended each academic year, signifying the importance educators placed on achievement in many areas. At these events students performed two or three musical selections. Community groups like the Women's Clubs, PEO, Music Boosters, and Bar Association recognized seniors who ranked highest in scholarship, speech, vocal and instrumental music, and citizenship. The principal or coaches and advisors awarded letters, gold pins, and certificates to class officers and to those taking part in athletics, Girls Recreation Association (GRA), and cheerleading; FHA, FFA, and commercial; drama, speech, and music; and yearbook, *Tatler*, Quill & Scroll, and National Honor Society. The tedious program lasted forever, but recipients valued the tokens acknowledging their work.

As students in a small high school, we had opportunities for participation that would not have been possible in a larger institution. Those who took advantage recall their multiple endeavors as "a great experience," providing "a well-rounded outlook." Another shrewdly observed: "Being in a small pond let me develop some capabilities that might not have emerged in a large pond." Wide involvement taught valuable lessons. We gained knowledge about journalism and other fields. We developed appreciation for the musical and dramatic arts. We acquired skills of self-application, cooperative labor, and time management. Most important, we learned it takes effort and talent to succeed as well as courage and grace to cope with the failures we experienced despite our best efforts. The community also benefited by parents and others attending concerts, plays, and athletic events, which augmented communal bonds and lessened the isolation of their lives.[70]

Writing about his South Dakota boyhood in the forties and fifties, newsman Tom Brokaw declared, "In high school . . . boys were favored. They had the only athletic teams, which were the pride of the town and received the most resources." Females led cheers and dominated other activities, yet received less recognition than males. Elkader similarly discriminated. The Central Community School District added track and wrestling in the fifties but did nothing for girls. Only boys were elected team captains, initiated into the Warriors Club, and named on all-conference or all-state teams.[71]

A half century later, some women still resent their exclusion from interscholastic athletics and restriction to the GRA. The club had a faculty advisor, student officers, and weekly play nights when boys' teams did not use the gym. More than 70 percent of senior girls had taken part before their graduation. They played basketball, volleyball, soccer, and other games. They sometimes held field days at which winners of events received blue ribbons. As the GRA locked the facility on its night, curious boys sometimes stood in the shrubbery under the cover of darkness and watched through the windows. The association's wholesome pursuits did not satisfy our voyeurism, and we soon departed.[72]

Frosty Westering, an influential coach, began his career at Elkader in 1952. He later won an NCAA Division III Championship for Pacific Lutheran University and election to the College Football Hall of Fame. During four years at our school, his squads took two conference football titles and won seventy-one basketball games. He started a Quarterback

Club for boosting sports. He held clinics for fans. He moved football games from Molumby Athletic Field to the Vets' baseball diamond, which had superior lights, seating, and parking. He arranged a "picking bee" to dig out prolific sandburs. After he took a better job at Fairfield High School, a former player spoke for many in praising the coach's sportsmanship and dedication.[73]

With an eye toward building future squads, Westering started midget football. Thirty-three boys from the upper elementary grades at the public and parochial schools took part. Equipped with helmets, pads, and uniforms purchased by the Quarterback Club, we played two Sunday afternoon games and during the homecoming halftime.[74] Westering also taught us basketball and baseball fundamentals in season. Although few attained the athletic success he may have hoped for us, we had great fun and he positively influenced our lives.

Interscholastic athletics began for boys in junior high. In theory anyone could try out, but family circumstances determined who did. Farm chores kept some from ever taking part. Others quit sports to work, if their parents could not give them the goods teenagers desired. Westering initiated a three-game football season for seventh and eighth graders from all Central District schools. I started two years as an undersized end and played without distinction except for a TD pass reception. Several later starred for the varsity squad, which I did not join until twelfth grade. Mr. Biedermann coached those who tried out for basketball and baseball. His sharp tongue at times reduced players to tears. His basketball teams frequently won the county tournament before it ended in 1954. He disliked new Iowa State Athletic Association rules that limited junior high teams to ten afternoon games. The basketball and baseball squads on which I played won few games and marred his record.[75]

Among high school sports, football carried the most prestige, drawing crowds of one thousand or more. Players monopolized nominations for homecoming king, and usually team captains wore the crown. In contrast, female candidates required beauty, personality, and skill in many activities to win. Coach Westering inherited a program that had endured three consecutive losing seasons after the Warriors had won forty straight games over a five-year span. Westering revived team fortunes by installing a fast-hitting split-T offense and taking an Upper Iowa Conference title. Two years later, his squad achieved Elkader's first undefeated season since 1947, and again shared the championship. The coaches who followed Frosty lacked his charisma, but managed three winning seasons without any first-place trophies. Squads numbered between twenty-three and thirty-two; 50 percent of boys who graduated played at least one season. Three individuals made all-state: Gary Embretson—Fourth Team (1954); Daryl Dahling—Seventh Team (1956); and Gary Woods—Sixth Team (1957).[76]

The school had four great basketball teams and Westering coached two of them. The 1946 quintet—led by all-conference stars Jack Dittmer and Glenn Drahn—won twenty-two games, reached the sub-state tournament for the first time in school history, and lost to Marshalltown in the opening round. Five years later, all-conference players Vic Schneider and Roger Huggins carried the Warriors to the sub-state finals where Waverly defeated them. Powered by a fast break installed by Westering and led by brothers Milt and Clyde Kramer and Frank Gilson, the Warriors won twenty-seven games before losing to Dubuque Senior High in the sub-state finals in 1955. The next year, Gilson made third team all-state as the team finished first in the conference. The teams on which I played did not win as often, but garnered another conference title and three Clayton County tournament championships. Usually 40 percent of male seniors took part in at least one season of basketball; about twenty boys annually tried out for the squad.[77]

Westering initially handled all sports aided only by two student managers. When he started track and field, Reid Dillon helped him with baseball and soon took charge of it. After Westering departed, the district added someone to head the new wrestling program for which twenty-five reported in 1956. By my senior year, four men served in five head and three assistant coaching positions. Baseball, track, and wrestling squads each numbered about eighteen and drew fewer fans than football and basketball. Yet a seventy-car caravan greeted the 1945 baseball team after it lost to Cedar Rapids Roosevelt in the state finals. Subsequent squads played an eight- or nine-game schedule and at times claimed the county championship. The track team competed in six meets and finished first

As a senior basketball player,
I launched many jump shots.

in the county three times. The two-mile relay team (Glen Huebner, Frank Gilson, Clyde Kramer, and Wayne Schulte) took fifth in the 1956 state meet; miler Frank Reavis finished second in 1959.[78]

Adding a band room in 1941 freed the auditorium for speech and dramatic work. More students and a higher percentage of girls took part in vocal and instrumental music than any other activity. Females comprised 67 percent of the ninety-two who made up the senior and junior bands. The Girls' Glee Club included between forty and fifty-four singers. The Mixed Chorus had between forty and sixty-eight voices of which 55 percent were women. More girls than boys performed as soloists and as members of vocal and instrumental ensembles. Howard John Steinbeck—a first-rate instrumental instructor and conductor—received a superior rating in band at the 1954 state contest. His brusque personality led to his dismissal the next year. The Senior Band Council questioned this decision in the *Clayton County Register* without changing the outcome. The constant turnover of instructors after that hurt program quality.[79]

I spent four years as a poor percussionist in the band, which gave Wednesday evening summer concerts on the Interstate Power Company lawn and performed fall and spring concerts in the high school auditorium. The *Clayton County Register* publicized these events and a good-sized crowd usually attended. In January, instrumentalists and vocalists joined in a massed band and choral program at the Clayton County Music Festival. Every autumn the marching band executed dance steps and military maneuvers at home football games, homecoming parades at Luther, Wartburg, or some other college, and Veterans Day observances. In the spring it nominated a queen candidate and attended the Eastern Iowa Band Festival at Cedar Rapids or Waterloo. Sheila Mulrony even won Miss Eastern Iowa in 1953.[80]

Participants recalled band trips fondly because good times with friends compensated for the lengthy, jolting ride in an uncomfortable yellow bus and the bad food sometimes prepared by volunteers at festival sites. Even though I did not take part, spring trips to sectional, district, and state contests by vocal and instrumental ensembles likely afforded similar unforgettable bonding experiences. Vocalists usually did better at these events than instrumentalists, bringing home a few superior ratings each year. In 1954, Lyle Kuehl's rendition of "The Happy Wanderer" subsequently brought him an audition on television in New York City. Two years later, tuba player John Niemeyer earned an opportunity to attend the all-state music festival.[81]

The community gave strong support to music programs. During "Band Uniform Week" in 1947, members solicited nearly eighteen hundred dollars at businesses, a public concert, and a motion picture benefit. The uniforms, which we wore with white buck shoes in the fifties, had dark red trousers and double-breasted coats trimmed in white. Almost one decade later, a minstrel show raised money for choir robes. It featured a twenty-four member black-faced chorus, a male quartet, and a soloist. An interlocutor, Tambo, and Bones provided humor. The next year bandleader George Gundacker and vocal instructor Vernon Feuer-

helm directed eighty musicians in a swing show resurrected from vaude-
ville days before overflow crowds at matinee and evening performances.
The Music Boosters Club also raised money with annual carnivals. At
one of these, thirteen boys dressed in drag staged a style show. An ever-
vigilant Superintendent Whitney, however, ordered us to deflate our bal-
loons and thereby curbed our sex appeal.[82]

Drama and speech may have been the best programs at Central High.
Fall productions of well-known Broadway plays that had been made into
movies such as *The Robe, I Remember Mama,* and *Arsenic and Old Lace*
cast between fourteen and thirty-one students. Twenty-seven percent of
graduates took part in at least one play. Forensics annually attracted between thirty and forty participants who were 64 percent female. Among
seniors, 22 percent did some speech work. We began competing in late
January at the Clayton County Speech Festival followed by the Iowa
High School Speech Association sectional (early February), district
(mid-March), and state events (early April). In late February we entered
the District Tournament of the High School Forensic League followed
by the state finals held at the University of Iowa in mid-April.[83]

Many have fond memories of these trips, especially the Hotel Monroe
where we stayed during the state contest hosted by Grinnell College.
This ramshackle firetrap had an observant staff that quickly knocked on
doors whenever a member of either sex frequented a room of the other. A
mid-March snowstorm even trapped Miss Lenth and eleven contestants
at West Union for three days, which upset me because I had returned
home earlier and missed all the fun![84]

Elkader annually excelled at the speech association state meets, and
John Niemeyer additionally won a statewide contest with his original
oration on the Constitution in 1957. Central had perhaps its best season in
1959. At the tough Iowa State Forensic League finals, Lynn Cawthorne
(Serious Play Reading), Martha Liddy (Television Speaking), and Judith
Hughes (Humorous Prose Speaking) received Forensic Keys, the highest
award presented. The one-act play won superior ratings at state and the
University of Iowa play festival. Judges at both sites presented Martha
Liddy and Janice Carolan best actress awards; Lynn Cawthorne also
got one from the university. One Iowa director called the drama "the

finest thing I have ever seen high school students do." Due to Lorene Lenth's consistent success "as a maker of champions," the Chamber of Commerce—represented by Mayor F. E. Sharp—acknowledged her achievements that spring at the Central High Awards Assembly.[85]

Publication of a yearbook, which had been discontinued for some time, resumed in 1953 with consolidation and formation of the Central Community School District. Thirty or more students, nearly 60 percent of them female, comprised the *Shadows* staff. Twenty-three percent of graduates claimed to have taken part in producing at least one book. Over time eleven editors and managers were reduced to five. The *ccs Tatler* had nine editors and a staff of more than forty; women constituted 64 percent of this group. Thirty percent of those who graduated said they had served on the newspaper at least once. Advisor Reid Dillon determined who would be elected co-editors. They made assignments, edited stories, prepared layouts, proofread, and distributed the final copies of the seven issues we prepared as seniors. Ninety column inches qualified one for membership in Quill & Scroll, which numbered between six and nine, 74 percent of them female.[86]

Between our freshmen and senior years, the National Honor Society, which recognized scholastic achievement, increased from eleven to twenty-one. Women made up 60 percent of the members. About twenty lettermen belonged to the Warriors Club. They are pictured in each annual, wearing red cardigan or pullover sweaters emblazoned with a large white E on which gold pins symbolizing each sport are attached. Those with cardigans wore white initials of their name and numerals of their graduation date on their right and left pockets respectively. A white star and chevrons on the left sleeve indicated a captain and the number of years lettered. Willy Warrior (the Cleveland Indians emblem) was proudly displayed on the right sleeve in days before political correctness had been invented. The club initiated new members each autumn with a day of wearing odd dress and an evening of hazing. It did nothing else, showing that some societies exist merely to honor members. About 40 percent of male seniors earned athletic letters.[87]

Each class had a faculty advisor and annually elected a president, vice president, secretary-treasurer, and two representatives to the student

council. Officers and council had limited duties, which included planning class parties, school dances, and other events; deciding class mot-
tos and colors; nominating king and queen candidates; and preparing
Christmas baskets for shut-ins.[88]

A talented few joined every extracurricular activity while others did
nothing or just FFA and FHA. Don did baseball and band as a fresh-
man and class officer and vocal music as a senior. I listed band, baseball,
basketball, track, and class officer my first year; I retained only basketball four years later, but had added the annual, ccs *Tatler*, forensics,
plays, football, and two honor societies. My uneven participation appears
typical of many schoolmates. As we dropped out of one thing, we tried
another. Classes varied in their interests. Those who graduated in 1955
had outstanding football and basketball teams as well as more taking
part in vocal music and the FFA. The 1957 seniors had several talented
individuals, but fewer participated in activities. The 1958 graduates had
the most taking part in band, vocal music, plays, and sports. The class
of 1959 belied its rowdy reputation with the highest percentage joining
the National Honor Society and the ccs *Tatler*.[89]

AN AFTERNOON commencement chapel replaced the traditional Sunday evening baccalaureate services for our commencement. In our class
of forty-four, just forty-one received diplomas in the gymnasium on
Friday evening, May 29, 1959. Edmund Groomes, a farmer and past
president of the Iowa Association of School Boards, gave the address.
Even though he had been billed as having "sufficient humor to make his
message interesting and sufficient philosophy to make it meaningful,"
none of the graduates heard a word he had to say. The following Monday, we attended the alumni banquet at Peace ucc Church. Perry Price,
a Los Angeles attorney who had graduated in 1917, served as master of
ceremonies and attracted a record crowd of nearly two hundred. After
Sarah Riordan had been honored for attending forty-four consecutive
banquets, Price commented that her attendance and his had been quite
good on the average.[90] My father, a 1929 graduate, welcomed our class.
In responding, I expressed the hope that our attendance would be as
good on the average as that of Mr. Price. It was; most never came again.

Graduation marked a new stage in our maturation. For some it represented an opening outward to higher education and a better-paid future in some profession; for others it closed off formal schooling forever and limited them to lower-wage jobs. Thirteen from our class attended college; six went to nursing, medical technology, business, or airline schools; five started farming; three entered the military; ten found jobs in Cedar Rapids, Waterloo, or Elkader; and five married. The previous year, seventeen started college, three entered nursing programs, thirteen found jobs, three farmed, three enlisted, and four married. Twenty from the class of 1956 became collegians, an unusually high 44 percent compared to the 33 and 29 percent respectively of the 1958 and 1959 classes.[91]

Young adults departed small towns for varied reasons: jobs paid better in cities; apart from teaching, few professional opportunities attracted the return of those with university degrees; small farms and family businesses that demanded long hours did not assure future financial security. Harsh financial realities eventually forced out some who undertook farming. Therefore for most of us, as schoolmate John Niemeyer has said, leaving "was the right, indeed the only sensible choice." Many parents simply assumed their offspring would seek higher education. They subsequently related proudly how their children succeeded in gaining bachelor's degrees and good jobs.[92]

For some, college was not an option. They did not have the grades or the desire. Their parents lacked the means or did not see the point. Mothers often reared daughters for domestic roles and therefore did not impart academic ambitions. Others scrimped, worked overtime, and borrowed so their child could attend. In my case, I hated seeing school end. I had received more praise, success, and joy from it than I had on the farm. My conscientious parents reprimanded me often for my many flaws, hoping their constant correction would help me succeed. These circumstances made higher education appealing in its postwar period of remarkable growth. In fact, colleges and universities expanded from two million students and 165,000 faculty in 1946 to eight million students and more than five hundred thousand faculty in 1970.[93]

I watched neighborhood young people depart. I overheard their parents explain the necessity of college and listened as Father urged my

brother to attend. When Luther and Iowa State Teachers College re-
cruiters visited our high school, I learned the former cost one-third
more—about four hundred dollars in 1958–1959. As a lover of history
and school, I had decided to become a social studies teacher; the cheaper
option therefore seemed best. A $620 scholarship, my summer and col-
lege jobs, and Father's $1,300 loan at 4 percent interest paid my bills. He
took great pleasure in this outcome, saying, "It cost me a lot less than
I thought it would." In fact, it cost him nothing because my wife and I
repaid him. College and the successes it enabled for several schoolmates
mirrored the point made by Iowa author Curtis Harnack who wrote,
"In the great democracy of intellect, clodhopper backgrounds made no
difference; with brains and perseverance any height was attainable."[94]

In 2009, twenty-three 1959 graduates attended the fiftieth anniversary celebration of our high school graduation. Twenty-five submitted
memories to a booklet prepared for the occasion including five who did
not attend. Two, who had been part of the class from kindergarten until
tenth grade when they dropped out and married, shared accounts of
their lives. Both earned diplomas subsequently, and the one who came
to the reunion had her name retroactively added to the official class list.[95]

Most of my classmates stayed in the Midwest while others scattered
throughout the United States. Four Iowans had died. Twenty-four still
lived in the state (seven in Elkader). Nine resided in Illinois, Wisconsin,
and Minnesota. Nine others dwelt in California, Oregon, Washington, Idaho, Pennsylvania, Maryland, Virginia, and Florida. Nearly all
had retired from highly varied occupations. A female health care CEO
in an Iowa town had attained the greatest success. Other professionals
included an architect and an operations research analyst; a food service
manager, librarian, lawyer/real estate broker, salesman, pharmacist, and
professor; and three teachers. Four owned and operated small businesses.
Another farmed. Four worked in offices. The jobs of others cannot be so
easily categorized.[96]

Those who returned for the reunion amiably reminisced about school
days but spoke most about their children, grandchildren, activities, and
plans. No one boasted about success or wealth perhaps because these had
been relatively modest for everyone. Returnees apparently felt linked to

⇒ CONCLUSION ⇐

LITERARY GIANTS John Steinbeck and Thomas Wolfe concur in saying, "You can't go home again because home has ceased to exist except in the moth balls of memory." Yet reminiscence can be a "pilgrimage of renewal" or "a journey of discovery," as Tom Brokaw suggests in his memoir about growing up in South Dakota.[1] I visited Elkader two or three times annually until my widowed mother died in 1997. Her passing ended the Christmas and Easter dinners, where my brother and I had an opportunity to visit. Since then, Don and I telephoned each other on our birthdays, but saw one another only four more times before he died on May 3, 2011. My rare trips home for high school class reunions at five-year intervals revealed ongoing alterations in the town and rural landscape. The Old Volga Road now ends at our former farmstead. The house looks ill-used by an owner who suffers from drug and alcohol abuse. The outbuildings are gone or falling into decay. The land is posted for hunting and the fields planted in trees. I can no longer walk the hills or visit Holstein Dip where I played as a boy.

Since 1920, 75 percent fewer midwestern farm residents have increased their corn crop thirteenfold on larger holdings of several hundred acres. Suburban-style houses as well as metal machine sheds and grain bins are displacing traditional barns and granaries. In Clayton County a few hog- and cattle-feeding operations now produce several thousand animals, and dairy herds may number four hundred cows. The presence of fewer families in the countryside has diminished Elkader's Main Street. The largest retailers of my childhood—druggist George Schmidt, clothier Emmet Whalen, and McTaggart's Furniture—did not transmit their economic clout to successors. Only gravestones mark the four generations of my family who lived here for about 150 years. Awareness that a world has vanished in my lifetime saddens me.[2]

Expanding cities have steadily eclipsed the countryside for more than two centuries in the United States, and small-town decline as a percentage of total population in the Midwest persists into the twenty-first century. Elkader seemingly bucked these trends, growing by 4.3 percent in the sixties and 6 percent in the seventies to reach 1,688 people. The town at that time boasted about its economic prowess. It occupied the hub of a 470,000-acre trade area that yielded an annual income in excess of twenty million dollars. Its sales tax reports placed it first in the state for per capita business volume. Annual payrolls for county and state offices, contractors, utilities, and small manufacturers totaled over one million dollars.[3]

The 1980s farm crisis halted Elkader's growth and dropped its population by 13 percent to just 1,465 inhabitants by century's end. The state rerouted Highway 13 and the more than four thousand cars that once daily passed through town. Heavy rains caused successive historic floods that ravaged businesses and homes. Residents combated these disasters by undertaking new initiatives that required a high degree of community unity and participation. They held a "Rally for the Positive" in which the high school jazz band—playing a Dixieland dirge—led a New Orleans style funeral procession down Main Street to bury the Despair Brothers—Gloom and Doom. They created the Elkader Development Corporation (EDC) to grow business, industry, and jobs, and Main Street Elkader to revitalize the downtown. The Chamber of Commerce guided these efforts and marketed the community with a new motto—"We've got it here in Elkader."[4]

The EDC raised money for constructing the scenic River Walk from the Keystone Arch Bridge to a new campground at the City Park. It recruited new businesses by offering incentives with funding provided by local, state, and federal programs. Land's End created thirty-five new jobs when it put a cut and sew operation in the former SuperValu store. Local contractor Keith Knospe purchased two deteriorating buildings on South Main Street, and transformed them into a higher-end restaurant that fulfilled a typical small-town need. New radio stations at

The 1980s farm crisis brought unwelcome change to Elkader,
but the Keystone Arch Bridge and courthouse landmarks remained.
Courtesy Clarence and Barbara Stahl.

nearby Clayton Center broadcast country and adult contemporary music sponsored by local businesses and community groups.[5]

Meanwhile, Main Street Elkader promoted redevelopment and historic preservation by attracting numerous investors who put two million dollars into seventy-seven buildings. Contractors stripped steel siding from several structures and put new lights on the bridge. Volunteers paved the downtown crosswalks with brick. Modernization efforts of the nineties in many ways resembled those of the thirties as local boosters battled economic decay through community organization, commercial growth, and architectural design. Yet the two programs differed in one crucial respect. During the Great Depression, promoters pushed renewal through visually striking contemporary designs. The National Trust for Historic Preservation, however, favored restoring "traditional commercial architecture." As a result of its renewal efforts, Elkader in 2001 received a National Main Street Center Award from the National Trust at Indianapolis, Indiana, as well as a State of Iowa Spirit of Main Street Award.[6]

Elkader today continues its promotion efforts. Leaders seek expertise for making more sustainable streetscapes, buildings, and businesses.

They promote community health and prosperity through walkability. They set advocacy and education agendas, and seek the technical and financial resources needed for success. They employ branding and marketing tools to foster commercial growth. They mount effective cooperative advertising campaigns by utilizing Web sites and well-illustrated brochures, which underscore historic, scenic, recreational, cultural, and commercial themes, assuring visitors "Life Can Be This Good."[7]

The Elkader Historical Society formed in the early seventies to preserve and publicize the town's heritage. It gathered information for nine structures put on the National Historic Register. It published a self-guided walking tour to twenty-seven places of historical interest. It bought and restored the Carter House, one of Iowa's best examples of Greek revival architecture. The museum exhibits Victorian clothing, furniture, and photographs; military and pharmacy objects; and antique tools. Its Web site announces additional events and provides links to the other National Historic sites as well as nearby Lover's Leap and Motor Mill. The George Maier Rural Heritage Center, located by the City Park in the rebuilt 1919 Sale Barn, displays an extensive personal collection of rural Iowa artifacts. The town also formed a sister city relationship with the Algerian city of Mascara, home of Emir Abd el Kader.[8]

The Chamber of Commerce markets Elkader's location at the heart of Iowa's "Little Switzerland." Hunters come in autumn and cross-country skiers in winter. In summer, anglers seek bass, catfish, or pike in the Turkey River, and trout in other streams. Families go canoeing and tubing on the river. Bikers and hikers use the picturesque Pony Hollow Trail as well as those available at the Osborne Conservation Park. The City Park has picnic areas, tennis and sand volleyball courts, horseshoe pits, a swimming pool, a campground, and RV camping at the adjacent Deer Run Resort. The Elkader Country Club, housed appropriately in a remodeled barn, has a nine-hole golf course.[9]

Renovating old theaters and starting new restaurants are steps often taken by small communities seeking growth. The Elkader Theatre, closed since the early 1990s, has reopened and shows first-run movies nightly. At the restored Opera House the Keystone Chorus still puts on the Annual Barbershop Parade every autumn, and the Opera House

Players present two, three, or four shows annually. Orchestra Iowa, the Smothers Brothers, and other popular acts are booked, ensuring that the theater is well used. Inhabitants and tourists may dine at Fennellys' Irish Pub or enjoy Algerian, North African, Mediterranean, and midwestern cuisines at Schera's Restaurant & Bar.[10]

A walk in downtown Elkader today reveals that much has changed in a half century. Four onetime car dealerships have been absorbed by Brown's Sales & Leasing at 109 Gunder Road. The Elkader Floral Shop sells fresh cut flowers, plants, and home accessories in the former Ben Franklin. NAPA Auto Parts operates in the original McTaggart's store, and the Elkader Carpet & Design Center is in the old creamery plant next door. On NAPA's other side, Wilke's offers the goods once supplied by five groceries. Theis Clothing is the Backstitch and Folk Art & Primitives. Apartments fill the Bell Telephone and Miller Ice Cream buildings on First Street NW.

Some businesses remain the same. As his father before him, Alan Johnson is president of the Central State Bank much expanded by opening a drive-up facility and by acquiring the St. Olaf, Volga, and Marquette–McGregor depositories. A third-generation Glesne runs True Value Hardware (once Coast to Coast) and a descendent operates Lutz Locker. Schmidt's Rexall Drugs, where I worked my junior year, is now Moser Healthmart Family Pharmacy. Ishman's Jewelry, Elkader Dry Cleaners, Pedretti's Bakery, and *Clayton County Register* are what they were in my youth under new ownership. The Pronto Market and The Store occupy the former D-X and Sinclair station sites. They still sell gasoline, but have added snacks, sandwiches, soft serve, ice, pop, and beer. The eateries of my day are gone except for the Two Mit Hamburger Stand, which is Arno Gossman's trailer relocated to 201 West Bridge Street and renamed to commemorate constable Bill Doeppke's German accent.

Antiques on Main has primitives and fine quality Victorian goods. The Buttery offers antiques, gifts, and decorative accessories. The Turkey River Mall overflows the lobby, restaurant, barbershop, drug store, and guest rooms of the former Bayless Hotel and markets antiques, gifts, crafts, collectibles, and more. The Willow Creek Wine & Garden sells garden and home décor, gifts, pottery, wine, and more. One might ask, "Do customers buy enough 'more' for these shops to survive?" The Elkader Bed and Breakfast occupies a stately Victorian mansion built in 1892. The Riverside Cooperage Mill 'N' Retreat overlooks the dam. The Cedar Street Suites are in the old Methodist church. At the former Clayton County Jail, the proprietor of the Jailhouse Inn promises, "This stay in jail will be one to talk about . . . not fret about."

The Central State Bank president is developing the Johnson Industrial and Business Park, an eighty-one acre site located on the north side of Gunder Road and High Street NE. Tenants include Caterpillar Elkader, which employs seventy-five workers in making scrapers, forty-ton dump trailers, and other machines; Mobile Track Solutions, a new local company, is preparing to manufacture construction equipment including the MT-450 tractor; Alpine Communications, an essential lure for attracting new businesses; the Clayton County office for the USDA conservation, natural resources, and other services; an Emergency Services Building, housing fire and medical personnel; and Clayton County offices in the former DeLong Sportswear facility.[11]

Despite talk of small towns dying, Elkader has a bakery, grocery, pharmacy, and an appliance and hardware stores for daily needs. It has a modern landfill, a sewage treatment plant, and adequate health care through the Central Community Hospital, several physicians, a dentist, an optometrist, two chiropractors, and the Elkader Care Center, a forty-four-bed facility for the elderly. Three attorneys are at hand. The Elkader Public Library, relocated to the former Interstate Power Company building, offers expanded services. In addition to the churches of my day, the newer Grace Evangelical Free and Grace Reformed Baptist congregations show the growth of conservative evangelical Christianity in America.[12]

Although quality of life has improved in the past half century, the town still faces problems. In Iowa, one out of six falls below the poverty line and the rate approaches 30 percent in some counties. In Elkader, 8.5 percent of those above sixty-five and 4.3 percent of those under eighteen are poor. In addition, the record-setting Turkey River flood in 2008 damaged thirty businesses and forced removal of twenty-eight houses. This shrinks the number of available homes and further depopulates the town. According to the 2010 United States Census, numbers in Elkader dropped 13 percent to 1,273 people and those in Clayton County dipped 2.9 percent to 18,129. Whether or not Elkader can win the numbers game will depend upon the quality of local leadership, new jobs, and an attractive lifestyle appealing to young people. Residents hope that grants and charitable gifts will grow and that new telecommunications and manufacturing technologies will reverse population trends.[13]

To halt decline, Iowa launched a program aimed at bringing back former residents. Some communities even offered low-interest home loans to returning natives. Elkader's natural beauty has drawn retirees and other newcomers, who have built homes and started new businesses. These and other present-day inhabitants are less provincial and better educated than my parents' generation. They more readily enjoy life by dining out frequently and traveling extensively.[14]

Many schoolmates still live in the town and area. Some have remained since high school if they married or found jobs. Others left for education or work and returned if economic opportunity beckoned or elderly parents needed them. Some retired there after spending their working lives elsewhere. They have enjoyed holding responsible positions in church, school, and community and rearing children in a safe environment close to family and old friends. In retirement they have what they need and most are enjoying the many amenities of small-town life.[15]

WHEN I STARTED reading history as a youngster, I thought it happened only to important people in earlier times and other places. I did not perceive my life, my parents' farm, or our hometown as in any sense historical. I first began reflecting upon my upbringing when I encountered graduate students whose superior preparation for historical study prompted me to seek an explanation for my shortcomings. I also saw some of my parents' ideas in Richard Hofstadter's explanation of the agrarian myth and our postwar experiences in Eric Goldman's account of that decade. Through years of study and teaching, I at last perceived that history happens to us all and embarked on this book.

You can take the boy off the farm and away from the small town yet never remove the lessons and memories he retains from coming of age in these locales. I married college classmate Joan Hartman in part because her family background mirrored my own. We practiced our parents' work ethic and frugal ways in our jobs, household, and child rearing. In some respects, we did not move far from our small-town upbringing. I taught history for nearly four decades and she worked as a secretary almost as long at Concordia College, an institution that Norwegian American Lutherans founded in 1891. The Scandinavian heritage of the college and Red River Valley where three great-great-uncles pioneered made my arrival a homecoming of sorts. The Fargo-Moorhead metropolitan area of more than two hundred thousand people exhibits the neighborliness of its rural hinterland. The First Congregational United Church of Christ where we worship and our daughters Kristen and Rachel were confirmed similarly exudes friendliness as an open and affirming congregation.

Our lives also differed from those of our parents. We had greater physical comforts and did less hard physical labor. We made more money and spent more. We traveled to Europe, Mexico, and Africa. My parents would be proud of these markers of a successful life as well as the books I have written. Yet they would be uncomfortable about having their privacy violated in this one. In spite of that, I hope they would see that I have treated their lives with respect and gratitude. They helped me attain my portion of the American Dream articulated in a passage from Thomas Wolfe that I memorized for high school American literature: "So, then, to every man his chance—to every man, regardless of his birth, his shining, golden opportunity—to every man the right to live, to work, to be himself, and to become whatever thing his manhood and his vision can combine to make him—this, seeker, is the promise of America."[16]

FAMILY TREES

MATERNAL LINEAGE

My great-great-grandparents Ole Pederson Lerkerud (1807–1890) and Anne Marie Iversdatter (1807–?) married on June 7, 1837, at Rakkestad, Norway. Their son, my great-grandfather Johan (John) Christian Olson (1840–1890), emigrated from Norway. On January 16, 1874, he married my great-grandmother Rachel Halstenson (1856–1932), the daughter of great-great-grandparents Torkel Halstenson Groth (1826–1872; emigrated 1849) and Anne Blakkestad (birth and death dates unknown; married in 1856). Johan and Rachel's son, Adolph Olson (1884–1970), was my grandfather.

My great-great-grandparents Endre Olson Vold (1816–1892) and Brynhild Thorsdatter (birth, marriage, and death dates unknown) emigrated from Hallingdahl, Norway, in 1853. Their son, great-grandfather Ole A. Wold (1846–1937), married Carrie Johnson Rodegarde (1846–1907) on January 1, 1865. Ole and Carrie's daughter, my grandmother Ruth Wold (1885–1950), married Adolph Olson on October 28, 1909. Adolph and Ruth's daughter, my mother Ruby Olson (1913–1997), had one sibling, my uncle Kenneth Olson (1911–1984).

PATERNAL LINEAGE

My great-great-grandparents John Engelhardt (1818–1901) and Mary Smith (1819–1887) married in 1840, and emigrated from Anklam, Pomerania (Germany), in 1862. Their son, my great-grandfather Rudolph Engelhardt (1841–1893) on January 9, 1867, married Marie Schmidt (1850–1930), daughter of my great-great-grandparents John Schmidt (dates unknown; emigrated from Anklam in 1860) and Lena Gumtow (dates unknown). Rudolph and Marie's son, Robert Henry Engelhardt (1886–1958) was my grandfather.

My great-great-grandparents Frederick Faber (dates unknown; emigrated 1865) and Kathrena (last name and dates unknown) were the parents of my great-grandfather John G. Faber (1855–1940; born in Mecklenburg, Germany; emigrated 1865). On January 15, 1878, John married my great-grandmother Isabelle Hulverson (1854–1922; born in Norway), daughter of Lars C. Hulverson (1819–1901) and Mary (last name unknown; dates unknown; married January

24, 1844), who both emigrated from Norway in 1859. John and Isabelle's daughter, my grandmother Ella Marie Faber (1889–1962), married Robert Engelhardt on October 11, 1906. They had three children: Isabelle Fredericka (1907-1934), my father Curtis Rudolph (1912-1979), and Allan Robert (1924-2003).

IMMEDIATE FAMILY

Ruby Olson (1913-1997) and Curtis Engelhardt (1912-1979) married on June 21, 1934. They are the parents of Don Engelhardt (1935-2011) and Carroll Engelhardt (1941-).

NOTES

PREFACE AND ACKNOWLEDGMENTS

1. Janice Hamilton to author, November 9, 2009; Susan Allen Toth, *Blooming*, 3, 8, 10, 14, 18–19, 21.
2. George McJimsey, "Naturalized Iowan"; H. Roger Grant, "An Albia Childhood"; John D. Buenker, "Growing Up Iowan"; Dorothy Schwieder, *Growing Up with the Town* (hereinafter *Growing*), 103, 118–119, 125–126; Tom Brokaw, *A Long Way from Home* (hereinafter *Long Way*), 179; Mildred Armstrong Kalish, *Little Heathens*, 6–7, 82; Kenneth Hassebrock, *Rural Reminiscences*, xi.
3. McJimsey, "Naturalized Iowan," 181, 194–195; Kriste Lindenmeyer, *The Greatest Generation Grows Up* (hereinafter *Greatest Generation*), 204–205; Joseph A. Amato, *Rethinking Home*, 1–3, 7, 9–11, 29, 47; Richard O. Davies, *Main Street Blues*, x–xii, 1–2, 4–5, 7.
4. Michael Wood, *America in the Movies*, 16–17, 23, 192–193; also see Toth, *Blooming*, 203, 205–206 and Caryl Rivers, *Aphrodite at Mid-Century*, 102–103, 108–111.
5. Amato, *Rethinking Home*, 3.
6. Schwieder, *Growing*, xiii–xii.

INTRODUCTION

1. Will quoted in James R. Shortridge, *The Middle West*, 143; also see 59–62, 68, 72, 97, 99, 100.
2. Joseph Frazier Wall, *Iowa*, xvii–xviii; William Cronon, *Nature's Metropolis*, 309.
3. Herman L. Nelson, "The Beautiful Land," 7, 10; Federal Writers' Project, *Iowa*, 362–363; *Clayton County Register* (herinafter *CCR*), June 20, 1946.
4. Edward W. Olson, *Look What You Started Mr. Davis* (hereinafter *Look*), 37, 39; Wall, *Iowa*, 74–75.
5. Lyell D. Henry, Jr., *Was This Heaven?*, 79–80; *CCR*, June 27, 1946; Larry and Anne Lerch, "Building a Railroad," *The Milwaukee Railroader*, 6, 8, 11–12.
6. *CCR*, February 9, 1941, June 27, 1946; Realto E. Price, ed., *History of Clayton County, Iowa* (hereinafter *History*), Vol. 1: 331–332.

7. Federal Writers, *Iowa*, 363; CCR, February 19 and March 12, 1941, June 27, 1946, July 6, 1977; Nick Lamberto, "How Iowans Live," *Des Moines Sunday Register*, 12; Henry, *Was This Heaven?*, 80–81, 149.

8. CCR, July 6, 1977.

9. Price, *History*, Vol. 1: 330.

10. Wall, *Iowa*, xvi; Cronon, *Nature's Metropolis*, 267–269.

11. Cronon, *Nature's Metropolis*, 308–309; Leland L. Sage, *A History of Iowa*, 310–311, 314, 318; James L. Sunquist, *Dynamics of the Party System*, 257–258; Lisa L. Ossian, *The Home Fronts of Iowa* (hereinafter *Home Fronts*), 10–11, 16–17.

12. Carlton C. Qualey and Jon A. Gjerde, "The Norwegians," 220–222; Jon A. Gjerde, *From Peasants to Farmers* (hereinafter *Peasants*), 4; Leonard Dinnerstein and David M. Reimers, *Ethnic Americans*, 29, 36–39; Odd S. Lovoll, *The Promise of America*, 107.

13. Ron Gunderson to author, July 28, 1997; Lloyd A. Svendsbye, *"I Paid All My Debts,"* 23.

14. "Ole A. Wold Obituary," CCR, March 10, 1937.

15. *Olson Family History*; "Rachel Olson Obituary," CCR, December 1, 1932.

16. Clayton County Genealogical Society, *1984 History*, 209; Price, *History*, Vol. 2: 110–111; "Rudolph Engelhardt Obituary," *Elkader Register*, September 14, 1893.

17. "Marie Engelhardt Obituary," CCR, April 10, 1930.

18. Price, *History*, Vol. 2: 187; Betty Engelhardt to author, September 25, 2009; "Isabelle Faber Obituary" and "John G. Faber Obituary," CCR, March 2, 1922 and March 13, 1940.

19. Betty Engelhardt to author, September 25, 2009.

20. "Ruth Olson Obituary," "Adolph Olson Obituary," and "Kenneth Olson Obituary," CCR, November 30, 1950, August 5, 1970, and July 18, 1984.

21. "Curtis Engelhardt Obituary," CCR, May 2, 1979; Curtis Harnack, *We Have All Gone Away* (hereinafter *Gone Away*), 173; Deborah Fink, *Open Country Iowa*, 32–33.

22. Elaine Felker Smith to author, September 27, 2009; "Curtis Engelhardt."

23. Fink, *Open Country Iowa*, 24, 40, 63–64, 240; Gjerde, *Peasants*, 200; Dinnerstein and Reimers, *Ethnic Americans*, 32, 40.

24. Gjerde, *Peasants*, 11, 200–201, 222; Dinnerstein and Reimers, *Ethnic Americans*, 32, 40; Catherine McNicol Stock, *Main Street in Crisis*, 148, 150, 152, 155, 164.

25. Carroll Engelhardt, "Religion, Morality, and Citizenship," 45–50.

26. Stock, *Main Street in Crisis*, 48–49, 51, 53, 55–56, 58–60, 74–76, 87, 107, 112; John C. Hudson, *Making the Corn Belt*, 189, 192.

27. Dorothy Schwieder, *Iowa*, 276, 279, 282–283; Doris Kearns Goodwin, *No Ordinary Time*, 556, 624–627; William Graebner, *The Age of Doubt*, 13–14.

28. Goodwin, *No Ordinary Time*, 625; David Halberstam, *The Fifties*, 591; United States Bureau of Census, *Census of Population: 1960*, 228; Graebner, *The Age of Doubt*, 78.

I. HOME

1. *CCR*, September 17, 1941.

2. Amato, *Rethinking Home*, 17–18.

3. Lindenmeyer, *Greatest Generation*, 4–6, 16, 240, 246; Wini Breines, *Young, White, and Miserable*, 60; Lisa Jacobson, *Raising Consumers*, 14–15, 81–82, 91–92; Joseph A. Amato, *Jacob's Well*, 224. On character, see Harnack, *Gone Away*; Hassebrock, *Rural Reminiscences*; Schwieder, *Growing*; Kalish, *Little Heathens*.

4. Brokaw, *Long Way*, 82–84; Amato, *Jacob's Well*, 227–228.

5. Fink, *Open Country Iowa*, 47; Lindenmeyer, *Greatest Generation*, 15.

6. Kalish, *Little Heathens*, 162–164.

7. Ronald P. Kline, *Consumers in the Country* (hereinafter *Consumers*), 87, 198–202, 255.

8. Kline, *Consumers*, 206, 255–256, 277.

9. Amato, *Rethinking Home*, 62–63, 65; Barbara J. Scot, *Prairie Reunion*, 123.

10. Nelson, "The Beautiful Land," 7–9; Drake Hokanson, *Reflecting a Prairie Town* (hereinafter *Reflecting*), 35–36.

11. *CCR*, May 14, 1953, November 20, 1958, January 1, 1959.

12. *CCR*, June 19 and July 2, 1947, April 19, 1951.

13. *CCR*, August 6, 1941, August 26, 1948, August 4, 1955.

14. *CCR*, April 15, 1948, January 20 and February 3, 1949, February 1, 1951, January 26, 1956.

15. *CCR*, January 30 and February 6, 1947, March 15, 1951, March 12 and 19, April 2, 1959.

16. Pamela Riney-Kehrberg, *Childhood on the Farm*, 218–219; Hassebrock, *Rural Reminiscences*, 71–72.

17. Bob Artley, *Memories of a Former Kid*, 40.

18. Fink, *Open Country Iowa*, 48; Hassebrock, *Rural Reminiscences*, 144; Scot, *Prairie Reunion*, 133; Dwight Hoover, *A Good Day's Work*, 102; David Edwards to author, March 2, 2010.

19. Fink, *Open Country Iowa*, 48; Ossian, *Home Fronts*, 139; Scot, *Prairie Reunion*, 134–135.

20. Hassebrock, *Rural Reminiscences* 71; Kalish, *Little Heathens*, 156–157, 159.

21. Hassebrock, *Rural Reminiscences*, 174; Kalish, *Little Heathens*, 95, 98–100; Artley, *Memories*, 50.

22. Kalish, *Little Heathens*, 94.

23. *CCR*, December 16, 1943, June 8, 1944, March 16, 1950, March 19, 1953.

24. Kalish, *Little Heathens*, 56.

25. Riney-Kehrberg, *Childhood on the Farm*, 30–32.

26. *CCR*, March 1, 1945; Engelhardt to author, September 25, 2009.

27. Kalish, *Little Heathens*, 40, 46; *CCR*, December 3 and 31, 1953, December 5, 1957.

28. Kalish, *Little Heathens*, 243–245; Riney-Kehrberg, *Childhood on the Farm*, 146; *CCR*, October 29, 1953.

29. Schwieder, *Growing*, 128.

30. *CCR*, March 21 and June 27, 1946, January 16, 1947, June 24, 1948, February 10, 1949, January 10 and March 6, 1952, January 1, 1953, August 21, 1953, March 3, 1955; Clarence Stahl to author, May 8, 2010.

31. Robert D. Putnam, *Bowling Alone*, 216–217, 222–224, 235–236, 242, 246.

32. Stahl to author, May 8, 2010; *CCR*, October 25, 1945, September 12, 1946, July 2, 1947, September 9, 1948, November 17, 1949, January 12, 1950.

33. *CCR*, July 2, 1947, September 9, 1948, November 17, 1949, January 12, 1950.

34. Kline, *Consumers*, 123–125, 261–262; Lindenmeyer, *Greatest Generation*, 164, 168–169; Susan J. Douglas, *Listening In*, 24, 28, 31–32; Michele Hilmes, *Radio Voices*, 1, 5–6.

35. Hilmes, *Radio Voices*, 195, 205–207; Milt Josefsberg, *The Jack Benny Show*, 98–100, 116; Gerald Nachman, *Raised on Radio*, 134–136.

36. Nachman, *Raised on Radio*, 272, 274–278, 282, 285–287.

37. Nachman, *Raised on Radio*, 91, 218–220.

38. Nachman, *Raised on Radio*, 315, 317, 379; "Mr. and Mrs. North," July 16, 2009; "Mr. Keen, Tracer of Lost Persons," May 15, 2009.

39. Lindenmeyer, *Greatest Generation*, 168; Douglas, *Listening In*, 213, 217–218.

40. "Arthur Godfrey," June 6, 2009; Nachman, *Raised on Radio*, 156–158, 170–171.

41. Lindenmeyer, *Greatest Generation*, 156–158, 165–167; "Let's Pretend," November 29, 2008.

42. Jacobson, *Raising Consumers*, 185, 190, 198–199.

43. Russel Nye, *The Unembarrassed Muse*, 395; Nachman, *Raised on Radio*, 400–403, 407.

44. Nachman, *Raised on Radio*, 354–358; Halberstam, *The Fifties*, 195–196.

45. Nye, *The Unembarrassed Muse*, 395–397, 401; Hilmes, *Radio Voices*, 171–172, 174.

46. Kline, *Consumers*, 262–263; Nye, *The Unembarrassed Muse*, 406, 408–409;

Michele Hilmes, *Hollywood and Broadcasting*, 145–146; Stephen J. Whitfield, *The Culture of the Cold War* (hereinafter *Culture*), 153.

47. Eric Barnouw, *Tube of Plenty*, 213–214; Nye, *The Unembarrassed Muse*, 410–411; Nachman, *Raised on Radio*, 203–205.

48. Barnouw, *Tube of Plenty*, 117–118, 187; Halberstam, *The Fifties*, 474–475, 479; "Steve Allen," July 20, 2009.

49. Barnouw, *Tube of Plenty*, 187, 248; Jay S. Harris, ed., *TV Guide*, 281–282; "What's My Line?" August 2, 2009.

50. Hilmes, *Hollywood and Broadcasting*, 148; Josefsberg, *The Jack Benny Show*, 388; Halberstam, *The Fifties*, 509–510; "Bachelor Father," June 1, 2009; "Father Knows Best," July 28, 2009.

51. Riney-Kehrberg, *Childhood on the Farm*, 126–127, 142–143, 157; Jacobson, *Raising Consumers*, 161; Lindenmeyer, *Greatest Generation*, 188.

52. Lindenmeyer, *Greatest Generation*, 186–190; Kalish, *Little Heathens*, 215.

53. Riney-Kehrberg, *Childhood on the Farm*, 124–125, 127; Jacobson, *Raising Consumers*, 179; Kalish, *Little Heathens*, 215.

54. *CCR*, July 2, 1947.

55. Garry Wills, *John Wayne's America*, 149–150, 156; *TV Guide Film and Video Companion*, 67–68, 810, 1002–1003.

56. Herbert Quick, *One Man's Life*, 153–154.

57. "The Open Road for Boys," May 23, 2009; McJimsey, "Naturalized Iowan," 184.

58. "The Mercer Boys," November 16, 2011; "The Hardy Boys," July 8, 2009; "Robert Sidney Bowen," May 22, 2009.

59. Lindenmeyer, *Greatest Generation*, 182–183; Gail Schmunk Murray, *American Children's Literature*, 161–165.

60. Kalish, *Little Heathens*, 63, 68; Carroll Lee Engelhardt, "The Common School and the Ideal Citizen," 150–151, 154–155, 161–163.

61. Murray, *American Children's Literature*, 168; Annie Dillard, *An American Childhood*, 178, 183, 214.

62. Lindenmeyer, *Greatest Generation*, 184.

63. Maria Reidelbach, *Completely Mad*, 22; Rivers, *Aphrodite at Mid-Century*, 25.

64. Jeet Heer and Kent Worcester, "Introduction," 1; Amy Kiste Nyberg, *Seal of Approval*, 3–4, 11, 18–19, 50–52, 86.

65. Nyberg, *Seal of Approval*, 6–8; Delmore Schwartz, "Masterpieces as Cartoons," 52–53, 57, 61.

66. Reidelbach, *Completely Mad*, 30–32; Nyberg, *Seal of Approval*, 83–85; Halberstam, *The Fifties*, 576–580; Ardis Cameron, "Open Secrets," vii–xi, xviii.

67. Reidelbach, *Completely Mad*, 183, 186, 188–190, 197.

2. FARM

1. Sue Meyer, Clayton County Recorder/Registrar, to author, May 21 and 27, 2009. Patent #6057, March 1, 1848; Patent #52587, February 1, 1855; Witt and Rice, August 14, 1897; #96, March 2, 1927; #102, March 2, 1935; #728, March 1, 1937; Land Deed Records, Book 71, 112, 416; Book 69, 15; Book 96, 325; Book 102, 84–85 in Clayton County Recorder's Office. For estimated costs, see *Encyclopedia of American History*, 461–462, and John L. Shover, *First Majority—Last Minority* (hereinafter *First Majority*), 123.

2. Shover, *First Majority*, 4–7; David B. Danbom, *Born in the Country*, 231, 240–248.

3. Hudson, *Making the Corn Belt*, 101–103, 129–130, 140, 151–152; Nelson, "The Beautiful Land," 15; CCR, September 9, 1948.

4. Richard Hofstadter, *The Age of Reform*, 24–25, 46–47, 121–129; CCR, October 28, 1943 and January 23, 1958.

5. Fink, *Open Country Iowa*, 39.

6. Kline, *Consumers*, 26–27, 50, 53, 64–65, 77, 86.

7. Hassebrock, *Rural Reminiscences*, 118–119.

8. Kline, *Consumers*, 162–163, 219–220; CCR, January 1, July 30, and September 3, 1941.

9. Danbom, *Born in the Country*, 189, 202, 211, 230–231.

10. CCR, March 5 and December 17, 1941, December 17 and 24, 1942, June 24, 1943, June 8, 1944, and November 14, 1946; Danbom, *Born in the Country*, 212.

11. Ossian, *Home Fronts*, 40–42; Danbom, *Born in the Country*, 212–213.

12. CCR, July 23, 1953, April 15, 1954.

13. Fink, *Open Country Iowa*, 40; Shover, *First Majority*, 128–129; Kent Meyers, *The Witness of Combines*, 127–133.

14. Hassebrock, *Rural Reminiscences*, 65–66.

15. Kalish, *Little Heathens*, 152–153, 155.

16. Schwieder, *Iowa*, 287–288.

17. Fink, *Open Country Iowa*, 49, 142.

18. CCR, April 17, 1947, April 8, 1948, January 12, 1950; Hoover, *A Good Day's Work*, 22.

19. Fink, *Open Country Iowa*, 50, 125, 150.

20. Hudson, *Making the Corn Belt*, 74, 158.

21. Harnack, *Gone Away*, 36–37.

22. Nelson, "The Beautiful Land," 9; Hoover, *A Good Day's Work*, 16.

23. Hoover, *A Good Day's Work*, 14–15, 33–34.

24. Shover, *First Majority*, 130–131.

25. *CCR*, July 20, 1950, November 8, 1951, June 17, 1954.

26. *CCR*, December 24, 1953.

27. Hudson, *Making the Corn Belt*, 169, 171; Wall, *Iowa*, 131, 133; *CCR*, June 25, 1941, December 6, 1951.

28. Danbom, *Born in the Country*, 236; Hudson, *Making the Corn Belt*, 198–199.

29. Danbom, *Born in the Country*, 236–237.

30. *CCR*, August 14, 1946, May 8 and August 28, 1947, June 9, 1949.

31. J. Sanford Rikoon, *Threshing in the Midwest*, 58, 60–61, 83–84.

32. Steven R. Hoffbeck, *The Haymakers*, 8–9, 14.

33. Shover, *First Majority*, 134–135; Hoffbeck, *The Haymakers*, 10, 60–61, 64, 84.

34. Hoffbeck, *The Haymakers*, 86–90.

35. Hoffbeck, *The Haymakers*, 12, 90–92.

36. Shover, *First Majority*, 158.

37. Shover, *First Majority*, 135.

38. Hoffbeck, *The Haymakers*, 13, 123–125.

39. Harnack, *Gone Away*, 103–104.

40. Harnack, *Gone Away*, 103–105; Rikoon, *Threshing in the Midwest*, 115.

41. Rikoon, *Threshing in the Midwest*, 143–144.

42. Harnack, *Gone Away*, 106–107; Rikoon, *Threshing in the Midwest*, 78.

43. Harnack, *Gone Away*, 112, 114.

44. Harnack, *Gone Away*, 121.

45. Harnack, *Gone Away*, 112–113.

46. Harnack, *Gone Away*, 111–112, 122.

47. Rikoon, *Threshing in the Midwest*, 116–121.

48. Harnack, *Gone Away*, 116, 118–120.

49. Rikoon, *Threshing in the Midwest*, 150, 153, 158, 160, 163.

50. Artley, *Memories*, 44–45; *CCR*, October 21, 1942.

51. Hassebrock, *Rural Reminiscences*, 107; Artley, *Memories*, 45–46.

52. Kalish, *Little Heathens*, 151–152.

53. Kalish, *Little Heathens*, 154–155.

54. Kalish, *Little Heathens*, 250; *CCR*, May 30, 1946.

55. Artley, *Memories*, 19.

56. James Hearst, "Young Poet on the Land," 52–53.

57. Artley, *Memories*, 86; Hoover, *A Good Day's Work*, 46–47.

58. Hoffbeck, *Haymakers*, 85; Hoover, *A Good Day's Work*, 67.

59. Artley, *Memories*, 26; Hoover, *A Good Day's Work*, 167.

60. Hoover, *A Good Day's Work*, 134–139; *CCR*, October 25, 1945.

61. *CCR*, March 18 and April 15, 1948.

62. Hearst, "Young Poet," 55; Riney-Kehrberg, *Childhood on the Farm*, 34, 225, 227.

63. *CCR*, November 4, 1954.

64. Danbom, *Born in the Country*, 255–259; Hudson, *Making the Corn Belt*, 204.

3. TOWN

1. Schwieder, *Growing*, 134; Hokanson, *Reflecting*, 162–163.

2. *CCR*, May 23 and 30, September 19, 1946, November 22, 1951, October 16, 1952.

3. *CCR*, November 4, 1948, September 8, 1949, May 17, 1951; *Leonard Maltin's 2003 Movie and Video Guide*, 164–165, 846–847.

4. Lewis Atherton, *Main Street on the Middle Border* (hereinafter *Main Street*), 181, 183, 355; Kathleen Norris, *Dakota*, 72, 74, 76; Arthur J. Vidich and Joseph Bensman, *Small Town in Mass Society* (hereinafter *Small Town*), 40–42, 45–46.

5. Schwieder, *Growing*, 139; Vidich and Bensman, *Small Town*, 42; Brokaw, *Long Way*, 148.

6. Quoted in Vidich and Bensman, *Small Town*, 32; Schwieder, *Growing*, 144.

7. *CCR*, April 8 and 15, August 26, 1942, June 24, 1943.

8. *CCR*, December 17, 1941, April 8 and December 10, 1942, December 6, 1945.

9. Olson, *Look,* 47.

10. *CCR*, September 24, 1941.

11. Atherton, *Main Street*, 237–238, 348, 350.

12. *CCR*, June 11, August 13, October 29, and November 12, 1941; Gabrielle Esperdy, *Modernizing Main Street*, 7–8.

13. *CCR*, September 17 and 24, 1941.

14. Wall, *Iowa*, 151; Schwieder, *Growing*, 104; Fink, *Open Country Iowa*, 33–34, 65, 196.

15. Schwieder, *Growing*, 104–105; John Niemeyer, July 3, 2009, Ann Boultinghouse, August 15, 2009, to author.

16. Davies, *Main Street Blues*, 121; David Edwards, March 2, 2010, Karen Bossard, December 10, 2009, Hamilton, November 9, 2009, Mary Harstad, September 26, 2009, John Lenhart, April 9, 2010, to author; Kalish, *Little Heathens*, 277–278; Toth, *Blooming*, 123–125, 151.

17. Wall, *Iowa*, 149–151, 154; *CCR*, May 6, 13 and 27, 1942.

18. Ossian, *Home Fronts*, 3, 50–51; Geoffrey Perrett, *Days of Sadness,* 39–40; *CCR*, January 1, 1941.

19. *CCR*, March 26 and October 1, 1941; Ossian, *Home Fronts*, 18.

20. Robert Wm. Kirk, *Earning Their Stripes*, 4, 36, 40–41, 56–57, 77–78; *CCR*, November 12, 1941, April 8, 1942, September 30, 1943.

21. *CCR*, December 31, 1941, February 25 and November 11, 1942, August 2, 1945; Ossian, *Home Fronts*, 88.

22. *CCR*, December 10, 1941, June 29, August 3 and 10, 1944, August 2, 1945; Olson, *Look*, 48.

23. Richard Polenberg, *War and Society*, 29, 36, 67, 132–133; Perrett, *Days of Sadness*, 67, 300.

24. *CCR*, October 7, November 26, and December 17, 1942, August 5 and September 2, 1943.

25. *CCR*, April 8, May 13, and October 21, 1942, February 11, September 2, and October 14, 1943.

26. Danbom, *Born in the Country*, 230; *CCR*, May 20 and July 8, 1942, September 16 and December 9, 1943.

27. *Encyclopedia of American History*, 381; Olson, *Look*, 48; *CCR*, August 10, 1944, April 12, 1945; Perrett, *Days of Sadness*, 303.

28. Ossian, *Home Fronts*, 92–100; *CCR*, August 2, 1945, January 17, 1946.

29. *CCR*, December 17 and 31, 1941, February 25, June 24, and October 21, 1942; Kirk, *Earning Their Stripes*, 86.

30. James J. Kimble, *Mobilizing the Home Front*, 35–39, 50; *CCR*, September 2 and 16, 1943.

31. Kimble, *Mobilizing the Home Front*, 63, 67, 84–85, 93–96; *CCR*, January 27, June 8 and 29, 1944, April 26, 1945.

32. Polenberg, *War and Society*, 16–18; Kirk, *Earning Their Stripes*, 56–57, 68, 74; Ossian, *Home Fronts*, 104–106, *CCR*, January 1, 1941, July 1, September 9, and October 14, 1942, June 15, 1944.

33. *CCR*, July 8, 1943, October 5 and 12, 1944, March 29, 1945; Ossian, *Home Fronts*, 106.

34. Ossian, *Home Fronts*, 101, 105–107, 122, 147–148; *CCR*, March 25, July 22, and December 24, 1942, February 11 and November 25, 1943; Olson, *Look*, 48–49.

35. Ossian, *Home Fronts*, 130–137; *CCR*, December 31, 1941, February 25, 1943.

36. Ossian, *Home Fronts*, 139; *CCR*, May 27 and July 29, 1942, May 27, 1943, May 25 and September 7, 1944.

37. *CCR*, September 7, 1944, May 3 and 10, August 16, 1945.

38. *CCR*, May 18, 1944, January 1, 1947, April 19 and August 16, 1945.

39. Eric Goldman, *The Crucial Decade*, 25, 27, 46; *CCR*, December 5 and 12, 1946, April 10, 1947.

40. *CCR*, April 13 and May 25, 1944; Ossian, *Home Fronts*, 150.

41. Esperdy, *Modernizing Main Street*, 137; *CCR*, August 24 and September 28, 1944, January 15, March 8, July 19, and October 11, 1945, February 7 and March 7, 1946, March 20, April 10, and July 17, 1947, March 4, 1948.

42. *CCR*, September 17, 1941, November 8, 1945, May 12 and September 1, 1949, November 20, 1958; Halberstam, *The Fifties*, 120, 487, 490.

43. *CCR*, October 18 and November 11, 1945, April 10 and 17, 1947, May 6, 1948, October 6, 1949, June 1, 1950.

44. *CCR*, July 11, 1946, February 5, 1948, April 27 and August 10, 1950, March 20 and September 4, 1952, March 18, 1954.

45. *CCR*, June 20 and 27, July 11, 1946, July 8, 1948.

46. *CCR*, April 25 and December 5, 12, and 19, 1946, December 4, 1952, November 10, 1955.

47. Vidich and Bensman, *Small Town*, 135; *CCR*, March 25 and April 1, 1948, September 5, 1950.

48. *CCR*, June 11, 1941, April 17, 1947, March 16 and April 27, 1950, May 8, 1952, May 14 and July 2, 1953, March 28, 1957.

49. Atherton, *Main Street*, 186, 291, 300; *CCR*, November 12, 1941, February 14, 1946, January 16, 1947; Sandra Kramer, October 1, 2009, and Boultinghouse, August 17, 2009, to author.

50. Olson, *Look*, 63; *CCR*, October 28, 1943, March 1, 1945, July 18, 1946, October 17, 1957; Atherton, *Main Street,* 190, 247.

51. *CCR*, August 12, 1942, July 1 and 8, 1943, February 7 and April 25, 1946, November 9, 1950.

52. *CCR*, May 28, 1958, January 1 and June 11, 1959.

53. *CCR*, July 18 and September 26, 1946, March 20, 1947; Davies, *Main Street Blues*, 146.

54. *CCR*, August 28 and October 23, 1947, May 27, June 24 and September 2, 1948, March 30 and September 5, 1950, August 9, 1951, August 28, 1952, May 5, 1955.

55. *CCR*, October 11, 1945, February 14 and August 1, 1946, October 2, 1947, November 6 and 20, December 24, 1947, January 1 and June 11, 1959.

56. David M. Oshinsky, *Polio*, 4–5, 69, 81–85; *CCR*, October 11, 1945, November 30, 1950.

57. Davies, *Main Street Blues*, 152–153; *CCR*, May 22 and June 5, 1947.

58. Oshinsky, *Polio*, 53–55, 81, 86–89, 188, 200–201, 204, 244–246, 255–256, 266–268; *CCR*, October 11, 1945, September 8, 1949.

59. *CCR*, November 7, 1946; Sage, *A History of Iowa*, 320–321; Halberstam, *The Fifties*, 4–5, 214–215, 217.

60. *CCR*, April 24 and September 11, 1958, January 1 and 29, 1959.

61. *CCR*, January 1 and 29, 1959; Goldman, *The Crucial Decade*, 293, 296–297, 326, 341–342.

62. *CCR*, March 28 and April 4, 1946, September 5, 1950, January 31 and October 30, 1952.

63. Goldman, *The Crucial Decade*, 36, 112–113, 127, 144.

64. Goldman, *The Crucial Decade*, 278–279.

65. *CCR*, June 21, 1951, April 2, 1953; Whitfield, *Culture*, 133–135.

66. *CCR*, August 26, 1948, September 5, 1950; Halberstam, *The Fifties*, 67–68.

67. Davies, *Main Street Blues*, 158; *CCR*, July 27 and November 9, 1950, May 1, October 23, 1952, March 31, 1955.

68. *CCR*, June 5, 1952.

69. *CCR*, October 8 and 15, 1953, October 7, 1954, October 20, 1955.

70. Goldman, *The Crucial Decade*, 190–191; Clarence Stahl to author, March 22 and April 18, 2010.

71. *CCR*, June 5 and September 25, 1947; Brokaw, *Long Way*, 130–131.

72. *CCR*, February 24, 1944, May 22, 1947, March 11, 1948, July 21, 1949, June 1, 1950.

73. *CCR*, August 8, 1946, July 22, September 9 and 16, 1954, August 4, 1955, March 1, May 31, and June 14, 1956.

74. *CCR*, May 31, 1951, June 12, 1952, June 18 and August 6, 1953, May 20, 1954, January 1, 1958.

75. *CCR*, July 3, 1952, August 13, 1953, May 20, 1954, April 21, 1955; Boultinghouse to author, August 15, 2009.

76. *CCR*, May 1, 1952.

77. *CCR*, February 15, 1951, March 6, 1952, May 7, June 18, and July 23, 1953, March 11, 1954.

78. Davies, *Main Street Blues*, 164–165; *CCR*, May 22, 1958.

79. *CCR*, September 11, 1952, November 10, 1955, August 29, 1957.

80. *CCR*, March 20, 1947, December 6, 1951, September 1, 1955, January 9, 1958.

81. Davies, *Main Street Blues*, 149–151; *CCR*, October 13, 1949, November 5, 12 and 26, 1953, May 5, 1955.

82. Davies, *Main Street Blues*, 156; *CCR,* June 16, 1955, February 2 and April 19, 1956.

83. Davies, *Main Street Blues*, 151; *CCR*, August 20, 1953, September 9, 1954, February 6 and 27, 1958.

84. *CCR*, August 23, 1945, August 22, 1946, August 21, 1947, August 26, 1948, August 30, 1951, August 5, 1954, April 18, 1957, August 14, 1958.

85. *CCR*, March 29, 1951, December 22, 1955, April 9 and August 6, 1959; Niemeyer to author, August 3, 2009.

86. *CCR*, July 15, 1948, August 20, 1953, April 26 and July 8, 1954, May 23 and October 10, 1957, January 2, 1958.

87. *CCR*, July 15, 1954, October 20, 1955, January 16, 1958, April 2, 1959.

88. Richard E. Wood, *Survival of Rural America* (hereinafter *Survival*), 18, 42, 48; Olson, *Look,* 42.

89. Schwieder, *Iowa*, 289; CCR, January 1, March 5 and 12, 1959; Olson, *Look*, 83–84; Elkader Chamber of Commerce, *Elkader, Iowa*, 12.

90. Olson, *Look*, 84–87; Elkader Chamber of Commerce, *Elkader, Iowa*, 2; Richard O. Davies, Joseph A. Amato, and David R. Pichaske, "Introduction," 3–6.

4. CHURCH

1. Church Records, Peace United Church of Christ, Elkader; CCR, December 17, 1941.

2. Whitfield, *Culture*, 83–84, 86–89; Graebner, *The Age of Doubt*, 62; Goldman, *The Crucial Decade*, 305–306.

3. Schwieder, *Growing*, 137; CCR, June 27, 1946, July 5, 1956, January 1, 1959; Eric Meisgeier to author, January 8, 2010; Davies, *Main Street Blues*, 121–122. Quoted in Frederick Lewis Allen, *Only Yesterday*, 100.

4. *History of Peace*, 1.

5. *History of Peace*, 2; Winthrop S. Hudson, *Religion in America*, 261.

6. *History of Peace*, 3; Price, *History*, 332.

7. *History of Peace*, 4; Carroll Engelhardt, "Citizenship Training," 60–61.

8. *History of Peace*, 3; Price, *History*, 332.

9. CCR, October 25 and December 6, 1945, October 16, 1952, June 16, 1955, February 2, 1956.

10. *History of Peace*, 3–4.

11. Atherton, *Main Street*, 300; CCR, July 9, 1953, January 13 and July 7, 1955.

12. Edwin Gaustad and Leigh Schmidt, *Religious History of America*, 329–332; CCR, October 5, 1944, January 18, May 3 and 10, and August 16, 1945, January 8, 1948.

13. CCR, January 19, 1956; Martin E. Marty, *Righteous Empire*, 251; Hudson, *Religion in America*, 416–417.

14. Marty, *Righteous Empire*, 251; Martin E. Marty, *Pilgrims*, 411–417.

15. Gaustad and Schmidt, *Religious History of America*, 341; *History of Peace*, 4–5; CCR, June 11, 1953, May 9, 1957, April 24, 1958.

16. CCR, May 4 and June 22, 1944, October 27, 1949, September 18, 1952.

17. CCR, April 16, 1941, June 26, 1947, December 31, 1953; Whitfield, *Culture*, 84.

18. CCR, August 17, 1950, March 20, 1952; Goldman, *The Crucial Decade*, 33.

19. "Church [and] Neillsville UCC Winnebago Indian Mission," July 27, 2002.

20. CCR, August 19, 1942, October 26, 1944.

21. CCR, August 10, 1950, June 16, 1955.

22. CCR, May 27, 1954, June 9, 1955.

23. CCR, September 2, 1954, April 7, 1955; *My Confirmation*.

24. Edwards to author, March 21, 2010; Church Records.

25. *CCR*, April 7, 1955.

26. *CCR*, June 16 and August 4, 1955, February 2, 1956.

27. *CCR*, January 13, June 9 and 16, 1955, May 14, 1959.

28. *CCR*, February 2, 1956, August 29, 1957.

29. *CCR*, March 22, 1951, April 4, 1957.

30. *CCR*, December 21, 1950, December 17, 1953, December 23, 1954, April 4, 1957.

31. Schwieder, *Growing*, 127; Bossard, December 10, 2009, Kramer, October 1, 2009, Boultinghouse, August 15, 2009, Larry Dohrer, September 2, 2009, Edwards, March 2, 2010, to author; Toth, *Blooming*, 15–16.

32. Hamilton, November 9, 2009, Niemeyer, August 3 and September 29, 2009, Harstad, September 28, 2009, to author.

33. Harstad, September 26, 2009, Niemeyer, August 3 and 17, 2009, to author.

34. Harstad, September 28, 2009, Niemeyer, August 3, 2009, to author.

35. Bossard, December 10, 2009, Kramer, October 1, 2009, Dohrer, September 2, 2009, Hamilton, November 9, 2009, to author.

36. Gaustad and Schmidt, *Religious History of America*, 349; *CCR*, December 25, 1952.

37. *CCR*, December 28, 1950, December 10, 1953, December 18, 1958.

38. *CCR*, March 22, 1951, April 2, 1953, April 25, 1957.

39. *CCR*, April 3, 1952, March 18, 1954, February 27, 1958; Wood, *America in the Movies*, 170–178.

40. "The Lutheran Hour," March 27, 2010; "Oral Roberts," July 27, 2010; Sydney E. Ahlstrom, *A Religious History*, 822.

41. Ahlstrom, *A Religious History*, 956, 1011, 1088; Whitfield, *Culture*, 170–172.

42. Engelhardt, "Religion, Morality, and Citizenship."

43. *CCR*, December 17, 1941, December 16, 1943, December 9, 1948, December 8, 1949; *CCS Tatler*, December 22, 1958.

44. Gaustad and Schmidt, *Religious History of America*, 349–350, 356–359; Marty, *Righteous Empire*, 249.

45. Bossard, December 10, 2009, Kramer, October 1, 2009, Dohrer, September 2, 2009, Hamilton, November 9, 2009, Niemeyer, September 29, 2009, to author.

46. John H. Hayes, *Introduction to the Bible*, 258–261.

5. SCHOOL

1. *CCR*, September 5, 1946.

2. *CCR*, August 3, 1944, June 27, 1946; Federal Writers, *Iowa*, 362–363.

3. Federal Writers, *Iowa*, 362–363; *CCR*, October 29, 1941.

4. *CCR*, January 1 and 8, 1941, April 10 and May 22, 1952.

5. *CCR*, August 23, 1945, August 29, 1946, September 4, 1947, August 30, 1951.

6. Andrew Hartman, *Education*, 4, 6; Diane Ravitch, *The Troubled Crusade*, 10–11, 43–44, 68, 79–80; *CCR*, April 30 and December 17, 1941.

7. *CCR*, January 8 and 22, April 23, and December 17, 1941, April 15, 1942.

8. Sage, *A History of Iowa*, 330; *CCR*, May 14 and September 3, 1941, July 15, 1943, May 4 and September 7, 1944, May 24, 1945, May 27, 1948.

9. Wall, *Iowa*, 188; Sage, *A History of Iowa*, 330–331.

10. *CCR*, February 24 and March 10, 1949, February 21 and December 18, 1952, May 14, 1953.

11. *CCR*, August 29 and October 3, 1946, June 3, 1948; Ravitch, *The Troubled Crusade*, 5.

12. *CCR*, February 18, 1954.

13. Kramer, October 1, 2009, LeRoy Larson, October 6, 2009, Patrick Keleher, June 23, 2009, Glen Huebner, June 23, 2009, to author; Hoover, *A Good Day's Work*, 125–130.

14. Kramer, October 1, 2009, Larson, October 6, 2009, Dohrer, September 2, 2009, to author.

15. *CCR*, August 28, 1952, February 25 and August 5, 1954, August 25 and October 13, 1955, January 1, 1959.

16. Linda French in *Memories, 1959–2009*; Lenhart to author, October 21, 2009; Carroll Engelhardt, "Looking Back."

17. *CCR*, September 4, 1947, September 2, 1948, September 1, 1949, May 11 and August 31, 1950, August 30, 1951; Engelhardt, "Looking Back."

18. Lindenmeyer, *Greatest Generation*, 114; Kalish, *Little Heathens*, 171–172.

19. *CCR*, January 29, 1948, March 3, 1949, June 8 and November 23, 1950, November 29, 1951, November 20, 1952, May 28, 1953.

20. French; Lenhart to author, October 21, 2009; "Bobbsey Twins," September 13, 2009; "Babar the Elephant," October 19, 2009.

21. Diane Finley to author, October 19, 2009; Atherton, *Main Street*, 267–268; Hartman, *Education*, 64.

22. Olson, *Look*, 69; *CCR*, January 24, 1952, January 5, 1956.

23. *CCR*, May 15, 1947, March 17, 1949, May 3 and October 25, 1951, May 1, 1952.

24. *CCR*, November 24, 1948, March 5, 1953.

25. *CCR*, November 27, 1947; Susan Levine, *School Lunch Politics*, 3–5, 10–11.

26. Levine, *School Lunch Politics*, 39–40, 71–72, 89–91, 93–94.

27. *CCR*, November 27, 1947, September 14, 1950.

28. *CCR*, September 2, 1954; Levine, *School Lunch Politics*, 2, 97–98, 113, 150–151.

29. Lenhart to author, October 21, 2009; Finley to author, October 18, 2009.

30. *TV Guide Film and Video Companion*, 156; Nicholas Sammond, *Babes in Tomorrowland*, 2, 30, 34–35, 202.

31. *CCR*, October 6, 1949, October 4, 1951, June 5 and October 2, 1952.

32. Lindenmeyer, *Greatest Generation*, 119–120; *CCR*, August 17, 1950, January 5, 1956.

33. *CCR*, February 12, 1948, March 2 and 16, April 27, 1950, November 27, 1952, April 15, 1954.

34. *CCR*, September 10, 1953, February 25, August 5, and September 2, 1954.

35. French.

36. *CCR*, August 22, 1946, September 10, 1953, September 16, 1954.

37. Beth L. Bailey, *From Front Porch to Back Seat* (hereinafter *Front Porch*), 126–127, 136; Susan K. Freeman, *Sex Goes to School*, ix–x, 6, 14, 17–19; Toth, *Blooming*, 12–13, 35, 44–46.

38. Freeman, *Sex Goes to School*, 20, 139–140; Bailey, *Front Porch*, 98, 102.

39. Engelhardt, "Looking Back"; *CCR*, October 1, 1953, June 3, September 9, and October 7, 1954.

40. *CCR*, May 10, 1956; *CCS Tatler*, December 22, 1958.

41. *CCS Tatler*, May 28, 1959.

42. Atherton, *Main Street*, 303; *CCR*, October 24, 1957, and October 9, 1958; *Shadows 1958*; *CCS Tatler*, November 1, 1958.

43. William Graebner, *Coming of Age*, 112; *CCS Tatler*, May 28, 1959; *CCR*, October 15, 1953.

44. *CCS Tatler*, May 28, 1959; *CCR*, April 28, 1955.

45. Bailey, *Front Porch*, 55–56, 58–59, 61–62, 67–70.

46. Freeman, *Sex Goes to School*, 130; *Shadows '59*, 22–23; *CCS Tatler*, November 24, 1958, May 8 and 28, 1959.

47. *Shadows '59*, 22–23; Graebner, *Coming of Age*, 43, 46.

48. Rivers, *Aphrodite at Mid-Century*, 211, 236: Breines, *Young, White, and Miserable*, 157, 165–166; Toth, *Blooming*, 60, 66, 72.

49. Bailey, *Front Porch*, 41–43, 47–48, 83–84, 87.

50. Bailey, *Front Porch*, 78–81, 87–88, 94–96; Breines, *Young, White, and Miserable*, 119, 122.

51. Freeman, *Sex Goes to School*, 139–140; Breines, *Young, White, and Miserable*, 118, 123–124.

52. Breines, *Young, White, and Miserable*, 66, 89–90, 122; Bailey, *Front Porch*, 46–47, 49–54.

53. *Shadows 1956*; *CCS Tatler*, October, 1959; Breines, *Young, White, and Miserable*, 162; Davies, *Main Street Blues*, 121.

54. *CCR*, August 16, 1951, November 10, 1955; Boultinghouse to author, August 15, 2009.

55. *Shadows '59*, 5, 7–9; *Shadows 1958*; Ravitch, *The Troubled Crusade*, 263; *CCS Tatler*, November 1 and 24, December 22, 1958; French.

56. *CCR*, April 3, 1958, January 29, 1959.

57. *CCS Tatler*, February 13, 1959.

58. *CCR*, September 10, 1953, August 30, 1956, March 21, 1957, June 19, 1958.

59. Lawrence A. Cremin, *The Transformation of the School*, 55–56; Hoover, *A Good Day's Work*, 136; Keleher to author, June 23, 2009.

60. Hoover, *A Good Day's Work*, 137; *CCS Tatler*, November 1 and 24, 1958, February 13, March 31, and May 28, 1959; *Shadows '59*, 14–21, 69.

61. *CCS Tatler*, February 13 and March 31, 1959; *Shadows '59*, 14–21, 69.

62. Goldman, *The Crucial Decade*, 309–310; Hartman, *Education*, 125, 175–176, 179.

63. *CCS Tatler*, November 21, 1957, May 8, 1959; Gender-based honor statistics compiled from three 1958–1959 posted lists and *Shadows 1956–1959*.

64. Freeman, *Sex Goes to School*, 125; Breines, *Young, White, and Miserable*, 93–94; James Gilbert, *A Cycle of Outrage*, 64, 70–71, 162–163, 188; *CCR*, September 15, 1955, April 12, 1956.

65. Douglas, *Listening In*, 226–230, 246–247; Dohrer, September 2, 2009, Edwards, March 2, 2010, Hamilton, November 9, 2009, to author.

66. *CCR*, August 14, 1958, June 11, 1959; Dohrer to author, September 2, 2009.

67. *CCR*, November 5, 1953, December 15, 1955, October 4, 1956.

68. Breines, *Young, White, and Miserable*, 148; Graebner, *Coming of Age*, 8, 113.

69. *CCR*, April 30 and September 3, 1941, August 5, 1954; Lindenmeyer, *Greatest Generation*, 117.

70. Hamilton, November 9, 2009, Boultinghouse, August 8, 2009, Kramer, October 1, 2009, Niemeyer, August 3, 2009, to author; Kalish, *Little Heathens*, 209–210.

71. Brokaw, *Long Way*, 176–177; *CCS Tatler*, December 22, 1958, May 28, 1959.

72. Boultinghouse to author, August 15, 2009; *CCS Tatler*, November 24, 1958. Participation calculated from *Shadows 1955, 1957–1959*.

73. *CCR*, October 2, 1952, August 20 and September 10, 1953, April 12 and 26, 1956.

74. *CCR*, October 2, 16 and 22, 1952.

75. Larson, October 6, 2009, Dohrer, September 2, 2009, to author; *CCR*, November 12, 1953, October 21 and November 18, 1954.

76. *CCR*, October 21, 1948, September 18, 1952, November 11, 1954, November 27, 1957; Participation calculated from *Shadows 1954–1959*.

77. *CCR*, March 14 and 21, 1946, March 22 and 29, 1951, March 24 and April 28, 1955, March 15 and 29, November 22, 1956, February 21, 1957; *CCS Tatler*, February 13, 1959; *Shadows 1955–1959*.

78. *CCR*, May 31, 1945, April 2, 1953, November 29, 1956; *Shadows 1954–1959*.

79. *CCR*, September 3, 1941, May 13, 1954, April 14, 1955; Niemeyer to author,

August 3, 2009. Participation and female percentages compiled from *Shadows 1956–1959*.

80. *CCR*, June 26, 1947, January 12, 1950, May 28 and December 17, 1953, October 14, 1954, November 17, 1955, September 13 and October 11, 1956.

81. Kramer to author, October 1, 2009; *CCR*, July 8, 1954; *Shadows 1956–1958*; Niemeyer to author, August 3, 2009.

82. *CCR*, January 16, 1947, February 16, 1956, March 14, 1957, February 20 and March 6, 1958.

83. Participation and female percentages of females calculated from *Shadows 1955–1959*.

84. Hamilton, November 9, 2009, Kramer, October 1, 2009, to author; *CCS Tatler*, March 31, 1959.

85. *CCR*, March 21, 1957, April 3, 1958, April 2 and May 28, 1959; *Shadows '59*.

86. *CCR*, October 8, 1953; *CCS Tatler*, May 8, 1959; staff numbers and percentages calculated from *Shadows 1955–1959*.

87. Percentages calculated from *Shadows 1955–1959*.

88. *Shadows 1956–1959*; *CCS Tatler*, May 28, 1959; *CCR*, September 6, 1951.

89. Percentages calculated from *Shadows 1955, 1957–1959*.

90. *CCR*, May 17, 1956, May 16, 1957, May 22, 1958, May 21 and 28, June 4, 1959.

91. Graebner, *Coming of Age*, 107; *CCS Tatler*, November 24, 1958, October 1959; *CCR*, September 27, 1956.

92. Davies, *Main Street Blues*, 139, and 153; Hassebrock, *Rural Reminiscences*, 215; Keleher, June 19, 2007, Huebner, June 19, 2007, Larson, October 6, 2009, Dohrer, September 2, 2009, Niemeyer, August 3, 2009, Boultinghouse, August 15, 2009, to author.

93. *Memories*; Breines, *Young, White, and Miserable*, 68, 75; Kramer, October 1, 2009; Bossard, December 10, 2009, to author; Kalish, *Little Heathens*, 209–210; Ravitch, *The Troubled Crusade*, 183–184.

94. *CCR*, April 9, 1959; Harnack, *Gone Away*, 176.

95. *Memories*.

96. *Memories*.

97. *Memories*; Hoover, *A Good Day's Work*, 205.

CONCLUSION

1. John Steinbeck, *Travels with Charley*, 183; Brokaw, *Long Way*, 3, 23.

2. Hudson, *Making the Corn Belt*, 208; Hoover, *A Good Day's Work*, 191, 193, 199, 206; Keleher to author, June 19, 2007.

3. Davies, Amato, and Pichaske, "Introduction," 9; Elkader Chamber of Commerce, *Elkader, Iowa*, 1, 12. "Elkader, Iowa," March 15, 2010.

4. *Olson, Look,* 89; "Elkader's Revival," *Des Moines Register*; Wood, *Survival,* 118–119.

5. Olson, *Look,* 90–91.

6. "Elkader's Revival"; Esperdy, *Modernizing Main Street,* 243–244.

7. *Main Street Elkader; Iowa's Elkader – Life Can Be This Good!*

8. "Elkader on the map again!" CCR, July 6, 1977; Olson, *Look,* 92–93; "Historic Sites in Elkader Iowa," March 31, 2010.

9. Lamberto, "How Iowans Live" 12; "Recreation in and around Elkader, Iowa," March 31, 2010.

10. Wood, *Survival,* 110, 118; Pat McTaggart, "Grand ol' Opera," *Cedar Rapids Gazette*; Olson, *Look,* 104.

11. "Johnson Industrial Park," June 21, 2011.

12. Davies, *Main Street Blues,* 182; Elkader Chamber of Commerce, *Elkader, Iowa,* 5–6; City of Elkader Visitor's Guide and Street Map of Elkader, Iowa.

13. Osha Gray Davidson, "Decline and Denial from *Broken Heartland*," 386–387; "Elkader, Iowa," March 15, 2010; Steve Gravelle, "Iowa's County–Seat Towns Not Immune to Demographics"; Wood, *Survival,* 130, 187, 189.

14. Wood, *Survival,* 43; Keleher to author, June 19, 2007.

15. Harstad, September 26, 2009, Kramer, October 1, 2009, Lenhart, April 6, 2010, to author; *Memories.*

16. Thomas Wolfe, *You Can't Go Home Again,* 262.

BIBLIOGRAPHY

Ahlstrom, Sydney E. *A Religious History of the American People*. New Haven: Yale University Press, 1972.

Allen, Frederick Lewis. *Only Yesterday: An Informal History of the Nineteen–Twenties*. New York: Harper Brothers, 1931.

Amato, Joseph A. *Jacob's Well: A Case for Rethinking Family History*. St. Paul: Minnesota Historical Society Press, 2008.

———. *Rethinking Home: A Case for Writing Local History*. Berkeley: University of California Press, 2002.

"Arthur Godfrey." June 6, 2009. http://en.wikipedia.org/wiki/Arthur_Godfrey

Artley, Bob. *Memories of a Former Kid*. Ames: Iowa State University Press, 1978.

Atherton, Lewis. *Main Street on the Middle Border*. Chicago: Quadrangle Paperback, 1966.

"Babar the Elephant." October 19, 2009. http://en.wikipedia.org/wiki/Babar_the_Elephant

"Bachelor Father." June 1, 2009. http://en.wikipedia.org/wiki/Bachelor_Father_(U.S._TV_series)

Bailey, Beth L. *From Front Porch to Back Seat: Courtship in Twentieth-Century America*. Baltimore: Johns Hopkins University Press, 1988.

Barnouw, Eric. *Tube of Plenty: The Evolution of American Television*. Revised edition; New York: Oxford University Press, 1982.

"Bobbsey Twins." September 13, 2009. http://en.wikipedia.org/wiki/Bobbsey_Twins

Breines, Wini. *Young, White, and Miserable: Growing Up Female in the Fifties*. Chicago: University of Chicago Press, 1992.

Brokaw, Tom. *A Long Way From Home: Growing Up in the American Heartland in the Forties and Fifties*. New York: Random House Trade Paperbacks, 2003.

Buenker, John D. "Growing Up Iowan—Sort Of." *Annals of Iowa* 67 (Spring/Summer 2008): 147–164.

Cameron, Ardis. "Open Secrets: Rereading Peyton Place." In *Peyton Place* by Grace Metalious, vii–xxx. Boston: Northeastern University Press, 1999.

CCS (Central Community School) Tatler. 1957–1959.

"Church [and] Neillsville UCC Winnebago Indian Mission." July 27, 2002. www.usgennet.org/

Church Records of Baptism and Membership. Peace United Church of Christ. Elkader, Iowa.

City of Elkader Visitor's Guide and Street Map of Elkader, Iowa. Brochure. September 24, 2009.

Clayton County Genealogical Society. *1984 History of Clayton County Iowa.* Elkader: Griffith Press, 1984.

Clayton County Land Deed Records. Recorder's Office. Elkader, Iowa.

Clayton County Register. June 11 and 14, 2008, March 31, 2010. http://www.claytoncountyregister.com

Clayton County Register. 1941–1959.

Cremin, Lawrence A. *The Transformation of the School: Progressivism in American Education, 1876–1957.* New York: Vintage Books, 1961.

Cronon, William. *Nature's Metropolis: Chicago and the Great West.* New York: W. W. Norton & Company, 1991.

Danbom, David B. *Born in the Country: A History of Rural America.* Baltimore: Johns Hopkins University Press, 1995.

Davidson, Osha Gray. "Decline and Denial from *Broken Heartland.*" In *A Place Called Home: Writings on the Midwestern Small Town,* ed. Richard O. Davies, Joseph A. Amato, and David R. Pichaske, 381–389. St. Paul: Minnesota Historical Society Press, 2003.

Davies, Richard O. *Main Street Blues: The Decline of Small–Town America.* Columbus: Ohio State University Press, 1998.

———, Joseph A. Amato, and David R. Pichaske. "Introduction: Small Towns of Thee We Sing." In *A Place Called Home: Writings on the Midwestern Small Town,* ed. Richard O. Davies, Joseph A. Amato, and David R. Pichaske, 3–9. St. Paul: Minnesota Historical Society Press, 2003.

Dillard, Annie. *An American Childhood.* New York: Harper and Row, 1987.

Dinnerstein, Leonard and Reimers, David M. *Ethnic Americans: A History of Immigration.* 3rd edition; New York: Harper and Row, 1988.

Douglas, Susan J. *Listening In: Radio and the American Imagination.* New York: Times Books/Random House, 1999.

Elkader Chamber of Commerce. *Elkader, Iowa: "Scenery Capital of the Midwest."* Elkader: Griffith Press, Inc., [1970].

"Elkader, Iowa." March 15, 2010. http://en.wikipedia.org/wiki/Elkader,_Iowa

"Elkader on the map again!—Nine Structures on National Register of Historic Places." *Clayton County Register*, July 6, 1977.

"Elkader's Revival: Volunteers' efforts earn Main Street Award." *Des Moines Register*, April 2, 2001, 7A.

Encyclopedia of American History, ed. Richard B. Morris. Revised and enlarged edition. New York: Harper and Brothers, 1961.

Engelhardt, Carroll. "Citizenship Training and Community Civics in Iowa Schools: Modern Methods for Traditional Ends." *Mid-America: An Historical Journal* 65 (April–July 1983): 55–69.

———. "The Common School and the Ideal Citizen: Iowa, 1876–1921." PhD diss., University of Iowa, 1969.

———. "Looking Back." *ccs Tatler*, May 28, 1959.

———. "Religion, Morality, and Citizenship in the Public Schools: Iowa, 1858–1930." In *Ideas in America's Cultures: From Republic to Mass Society*, ed. Hamilton Cravens, 45–57. Ames: Iowa State University Press, 1982.

"Engelhardt, Curtis Obituary." *Clayton County Register*, May 2, 1979.

"Engelhardt, Ella (Faber) Obituary." *Clayton County Register*, October 18, 1962.

"Engelhardt, Marie (Schmidt) Obituary." *Clayton County Register*, April 10, 1930.

"Engelhardt, Robert Obituary." *Clayton County Register*, May 8, 1958.

"Engelhardt, Ruby (Olson) Obituary." *Clayton County Register*, July 9, 1997.

"Engelhardt, Rudolph Obituary." *Elkader Register*, September 14, 1893.

Esperdy, Gabrielle M. *Modernizing Main Street: Architecture and Consumer Culture*. Chicago: University of Chicago Press, 2008.

"Faber, Isabelle (Hulverson) Obituary." *Clayton County Register*, March 2, 1922.

"Faber, John G. Obituary." *Clayton County Register*, March 13, 1940.

"Father Knows Best." July 28, 2009. http://en.wikipedia.org/wiki/Father _Knows_Best

Federal Writers' Project. *Iowa, A Guide to the Hawkeye State*. New York: The Viking Press, 1938.

Fink, Deborah. *Open Country Iowa: Rural Women, Tradition and Change*. Albany: State University of New York Press, 1986.

Freeman, Susan K. *Sex Goes to School: Girls and Sex Education before the 1960s*. Chicago: University of Illinois Press, 2008.

French, Linda in *Memories, 1959–2009*. 50th Reunion Booklet; cchs Class of 1959.

Gaustad, Edwin, and Leigh Schmidt. *Religious History of America: The Heart of the American Story from Colonial Times to Today*. Revised edition; Harper San Francisco, 2002.

Gilbert, James. *A Cycle of Outrage: American's Reaction to the Juvenile Delin-
quent in the 1950s*. New York: Oxford University Press, 1986.

Gjerde, Jon. *From Peasants to Farmers: The Migration from Balestrand Norway
to the Upper Middlewest*. New York: Cambridge University Press, 1985.

Goldman, Eric. *The Crucial Decade—And After, 1945–1960*. New York: Vintage Books, 1960.

Goodwin, Doris Kearns. *No Ordinary Time—Franklin and Eleanor Roosevelt:
The Home Front in World War II*. New York: Simon and Schuster, 1994.

Graebner, William. *The Age of Doubt: American Thought and Culture in the
1940s*. Boston: Twayne Publishers, 1991.

———. *Coming of Age in Buffalo: Youth and Authority in the Postwar Era*.
Philadelphia: Temple University Press, 1990.

Grant, H. Roger. "An Albia Childhood." *Annals of Iowa* 67 (Spring/Summer
2008): 131–146.

Gravelle, Steve. "Iowa's County–Seat Towns Not Immune to Demographics."
February 20, 2011. http://easterniowagovernment.com/

Halberstam, David. *The Fifties*. New York: Villard Books, 1993.

"The Hardy Boys." July 8, 2009. http://en.wikipedia.org/wiki/The_Hardy
_Boys

Harnack, Curtis. *We Have All Gone Away*. Garden City: Doubleday and
Company, Inc., 1973.

Harris, Jay S. ed. *TV Guide: The First Twenty–Five Years*. New York: Simon
and Schuster, 1978.

Hartman, Andrew. *Education and the Cold War: The Battle for the American
School*. New York: Macmillan, 2008.

Hassebrock, Kenneth. *Rural Reminiscences: The Agony of Survival*. Ames:
Iowa State University Press, 1990.

Hayes, John H. *Introduction to the Bible*. Philadelphia: The Westminster
Press, 1971.

Hearst, James. "Young Poet on the Land." In *Growing Up in Iowa: Reminiscences of 14 Iowa Authors*, ed. Clarence A. Andrews, 39–59. Ames: Iowa
State University Press, 1978.

Heer, Jeet, and Kent Worcester, eds. *Arguing Comics: Literary Masters in a
Popular Medium*. Jackson: University Press of Mississippi, 2004.

Henry, Lyell D., Jr. *Was This Heaven? A Self-Portrait of Iowa On Early Post-
cards*. Iowa City: University of Iowa Press, 1995.

Hilmes, Michele. *Hollywood and Broadcasting From Radio to Cable*. Urbana:
University of Illinois Press, 1990.

———. *Radio Voices: American Broadcasting, 1922–1952*. New York: Times
Books/Random House, 1999.

"Historic Sites in Elkader Iowa." March 31, 2010. http://elkader–iowa.com/
Historic-Sites.html

Historic Tour of Scenic Elkader. Brochure: September 24, 2009.

"History of Peace United Church of Christ—Elkader, Iowa, 1905–2005,
in Celebration of Our 100th Anniversary." Typed manuscript, 2005.

Hoffbeck, Steven R. *The Haymakers: A Chronicle of Five Farm Families.*
St. Paul: Minnesota Historical Society Press, 2000.

Hofstadter, Richard. *The Age of Reform: From Bryan to F.D.R.* New York:
Vintage Books, 1955.

Hokanson, Drake. *Reflecting A Prairie Town: A Year in Peterson.* Iowa City:
University of Iowa Press, 1994.

Hoover, Dwight. *A Good Day's Work: An Iowa Farm in the Great Depression.*
Chicago: Ivan R. Dee, 2007.

Hudson, John C. *Making the Corn Belt: A Geographical History of Middle–
Western Agriculture.* Bloomington: Indiana University Press, 1994.

Hudson, Winthrop S. *Religion in America.* New York: Charles Scribner's
Sons, 1965.

Iowa's Elkader—Life Can Be This Good! Brochure: September 24, 2009.

Jacobson, Lisa. *Raising Consumers: Children and the American Mass Market in
the Early Twentieth Century.* New York: Columbia University Press, 2004.

"Johnson Industrial Park." June 21, 2011. http://www.elkader–iowa.com/
Industrial-Park.html

Josefsberg, Milt. *The Jack Benny Show: The Life and Times of America's Best-
Loved Entertainer.* New Rochelle: Arlington House Publishers, 1977.

Kalish, Mildred Armstrong. *Little Heathens: Hard Times and High Spirits on
An Iowa Farm During the Great Depression.* New York: Bantam Dell, 2007.

Kimble, James J. *Mobilizing the Home Front: War Bonds and Domestic Propaganda.* College Station: Texas A&M University Press, 2006.

Kirk, Robert Wm. *Earning Their Stripes: The Mobilization of American Children in the Second World War.* New York: Peter Lang, 1994.

Kline, Ronald P. *Consumers in the Country: Technology and Social Change in
Rural America.* Baltimore: Johns Hopkins University Press, 2000.

Lamberto, Nick. "How Iowans Live A Gracious Life in One Small Town."
Des Moines Sunday Register, November 21, 1965, 12.

Leonard Maltin's 2003 Movie and Video Guide. New York: Plume, 2002.

Lerch, Larry and Anne. "Building a Railroad: The Chicago, Milwaukee and
St. Paul in Clayton County, Iowa." *The Milwaukee Railroader* 19 (September 1989): 5–15.

"Let's Pretend." November 29, 2008. http://en.wikipedia.org/wiki/Let's
_Pretend

Levine, Susan. *School Lunch Politics: The Surprising History of America's Favorite Welfare Program*. Princeton: Princeton University Press, 2008.

Lindenmeyer, Kriste. *The Greatest Generation Grows Up: American Childhood in the 1930s*. Chicago: Ivan R. Dee, 2005.

Lovoll, Odd S. *The Promise of America: A History of the Norwegian-American People*. Minneapolis: University of Minnesota Press, 1984.

"The Lutheran Hour." March 27, 2010. http://en.wikipedia.org/wiki/Lutheran _Hour_Ministries

Main Street Elkader. Pamphlet examined by author September 17, 2009.

Marty, Martin E. *Pilgrims in Their Own Land: 500 Years of Religion in America*. Boston: Little, Brown and Company, 1984.

———. *Righteous Empire: The Protestant Experience in America*. New York: Dial Press, 1970.

McJimsey, George. "Naturalized Iowan." *Annals of Iowa* 67 (Spring/Summer 2008): 181–195.

McTaggart, Pat. "Grand ol' Opera." *Cedar Rapids Gazette*, November 25, 2003.

Memories, 1959–2009. 50th Reunion Booklet; CCHS Class of 1959.

"The Mercer Boys." November 16, 2011. http://series/Mercer/index.html

Meyers, Kent. *The Witness of Combines*. Minneapolis: University of Minnesota Press, 1998.

"Mr. and Mrs. North." July 16, 2009. http://en.wikipedia.org/wiki/Mr._Mrs. _North

"Mr. Keen, Tracer of Lost Persons." May 15, 2009. http://en.wikipedia.org/ wiki/Mr._Keen_Tracer_of_Lost_Persons

Murray, Gail Schmunk. *American Children's Literature and the Construction of Childhood*. New York: Twayne Publishers, 1998.

My Confirmation: A Guide to Confirmation Instruction. Philadelphia: The Christian Education Press, 1954.

Nachman, Gerald. *Raised on Radio*. New York: Pantheon Books, 1998.

Nelson, Herman L. "The Beautiful Land." In *A History of Iowa* by Leland L. Sage, 3–22. Ames: Iowa State University Press, 1974.

Norris, Kathleen. *Dakota: A Spiritual Geography*. New York: Ticknor and Fields, 1993.

Nyberg, Amy Kiste. *Seal of Approval: The History of the Comics Code*. Jackson: University Press of Mississippi, 1991.

Nye, Russel. *The Unembarrassed Muse: The Popular Arts in America*. New York: Dial Press, 1970.

"Olson, Adolph Obituary." *Clayton County Register*, August 5, 1970.

Olson, Edward W. *Look What You Started Mr. Davis . . . Elkader, Iowa.* Elkader: Privately printed, 2010.

Olson Family History. Mimeographed booklet, n.d.

"Olson, Kenneth Obituary." *Clayton County Register*, July 18, 1984.

"Olson, Rachel (Halstenson) Obituary." *Clayton County Register*, December 1, 1932.

"Olson, Ruth (Wold) Obituary." *Clayton County Register*, November 30, 1950.

"The Open Road for Boys." May 23, 2009. http://www.en.wikipedia.org/wiki/The_Open_Road_for_Boys

"Oral Roberts." July 27, 2010. http://en.wikipedia.org/wiki/Oral_Roberts

Oshinsky, David M. *Polio: An American Story.* New York: Oxford University Press, 2006.

Ossian, Lisa L. *The Home Fronts of Iowa.* Columbia: University of Missouri Press, 2009.

Perrett, Geoffrey. *Days of Sadness, Years of Triumph: The American People, 1939–1945.* Baltimore: Penguin Books, 1973.

Polenberg, Richard. *War and Society: The United States, 1941–1945.* Philadelphia: J. B. Lippincott Company, 1972.

Price, Realto E., ed. *History of Clayton County Iowa from the Earliest Times Down to the Present.* 2 vols. Chicago: Robert O. Law Company, 1916.

Putnam, Robert D. *Bowling Alone: The Collapse and Revival of American Community.* New York: Simon and Schuster, 2000.

Qualey, Carlton C. and Gjerde, Jon A. "The Norwegians." In *They Chose Minnesota: A Survey of the State's Ethnic Groups*, ed. June Drenning Holmquist, 220–280. St. Paul: Minnesota State Historical Society Press, 1981.

Quick, Herbert. *One Man's Life: An Autobiography.* Indianapolis: The Bobbs–Merrill Company, 1925.

Ravitch, Diane. *The Troubled Crusade: American Education, 1945–1980.* New York: Basic Books, 1983.

"Recreation in and around Elkader, Iowa." March 31, 2010. http://www.elkader–iowa.com/recreation.htm

Reidelbach, Maria. *Completely Mad: A History of the Comic Book and Magazine.* Boston: Little, Brown and Company 1991.

Rikoon, Sanford J. *Threshing in the Midwest: A Study of Traditional Culture and Technological Change.* Bloomington: Indiana University Press, 1988.

Riney-Kehrberg, Pamela. *Childhood on the Farm: Work, Play and Coming of Age in the Midwest.* Lawrence: University Press of Kansas, 2005.

Rivers, Caryl. *Aphrodite at Mid-Century: Growing Up Catholic and Female in Post-War America.* Garden City: Doubleday, 1973.

"Robert Sidney Bowen." May 22, 2009. http://en.wikipedia.org/wiki/Robert_Sidney_Bowen

Sage, Leland L. *A History of Iowa*. Ames: Iowa State University Press, 1974.

Sammond, Nicholas. *Babes in Tomorrowland: Walt Disney and the Making of the American Child, 1930–1960*. Durham: Duke University Press, 2005.

Schwartz, Delmore. "Masterpieces as Cartoons." In *Arguing Comics: Literary Masters on a Popular Medium*, ed. Jeet Heer and Kent Worcester, 52–62. Jackson: University Press of Mississippi, 2004.

Schwieder, Dorothy. *Growing Up with the Town: Family and Community on the Great Plains*. Iowa City: University of Iowa Press, 2002.

———. *Iowa: The Middle Land*. Ames: Iowa State University Press, 1996.

Scot, Barbara J. *Prairie Reunion*. New York: Farrar, Straus, and Giroux, 1995.

Shadows, 1954–1959 (school annuals).

Shortridge, James R. *The Middle West: Its Meaning in American Culture*. Lawrence: University Press of Kansas, 1989.

Shover, John L. *First Majority—Last Minority: The Transformation of Rural Life in America*. DeKalb: Northern Illinois University Press, 1976.

Steinbeck, John. *Travels with Charley: In Search of America*. New York: Viking Press, 1962.

"Steve Allen." July 20, 2009. http://en.wikipedia.org/wiki/Steve_Allen

Stock, Catherine McNicol. *Main Street in Crisis: The Great Depression and the Old Middle Class on the Northern Plains*. Chapel Hill: University of North Carolina Press, 1992.

Sunquist, James L. *Dynamics of the Party System: Alignment and Realignment of Political Parties in the United States*. Washington D.C.: Brookings Institution, 1983.

Svendsbye, Lloyd A. *"I Paid All My Debts": A Norwegian Immigrant Saga of Life on the Prairie of North Dakota*. Minneapolis: Lutheran University Press, 2009.

Toth, Susan Allen. *Blooming: A Small-Town Girlhood*. Boston: Little, Brown and Company, 1978.

TV Guide Film and Video Companion. New York: Friedman/Fairfax Book, 2002.

Vidich, Arthur J., and Joseph Bensman. *Small Town in Mass Society: Class, Power, and Religion in a Rural Community*. Garden City, NY: Anchor Books, 1960.

U.S. Bureau of the Census, *Census of Population: 1960*, Volume 1, *Characteristics of the Population*, Part 1, *U.S. Summary*. Washington, D.C.: U.S. Government Printing Office, 1964.

Wall, Joseph Frazier. *Iowa: A Bicentennial History.* New York: W. W. Norton and Co., 1976.

"What's My Line?" August 2, 2009. http://en.wikipedia.org/wiki/What's _My_Line%3F

Whitfield, Stephen J. *The Culture of the Cold War.* Baltimore: Johns Hopkins University Press, 1991.

Wills, Garry. *John Wayne's American: The Politics of Celebrity.* New York: Simon and Schuster, 1997.

"Wisconsin Historical Images: Winnebago Indian Mission School of the Evangelical and Reformed Church at Neillsville, Wisconsin." 1940 Postcard image issued by the Wisconsin Historical Society. www.wisconsin history.org/whi/ fullRecord.asp?id.42064&qstring

"Wold, Ole A. Obituary." *Clayton County Register,* March 10, 1937.

Wolfe, Thomas. *You Can't Go Home Again.* New York: Dell Publishing Co., Inc., 1965.

Wood, Michael. *America in the Movies or "Santa Maria It Had Slipped My Mind!"* New York: Delta Book, 1976.

Wood, Richard E. *Survival of Rural America: Small Victories and Bitter Harvests.* Lawrence: University Press of Kansas, 2008.

INDEX

OTHER BUR OAK BOOKS OF INTEREST

The Biographical Dictionary of Iowa
Edited by David Hudson, Marvin
Bergman, and Loren Horton

A Bountiful Harvest:
The Midwestern Farm Photographs
of Pete Wettach, 1925–1965
By Leslie A. Loveless

Central Standard:
A Time, a Place, a Family
By Patrick Irelan

Christmas on the Great Plains
Edited by Kenneth Robbins and
Dorothy Robbins

A Country So Full of Game:
The Story of Wildlife in Iowa
By James J. Dinsmore

Deep Nature:
Photographs from Iowa
Photographs by Linda Scarth and
Robert Scarth, essay by John Pearson

The Elemental Prairie:
Sixty Tallgrass Plants
Paintings by George Olson,
essay by John Madson

The Emerald Horizon:
The History of Nature in Iowa
By Cornelia F. Mutel

Enchanted by Prairie
Photographs by Bill Witt,
essay by Osha Gray Davidson

The Folks
By Ruth Suckow

Harker's Barns:
Visions of an American Icon
Photographs by Michael P. Harker,
text by Jim Heynen

Harker's One-Room Schoolhouses:
Visions of an Iowa Icon
Photographs by Michael P. Harker,
essay by Paul Theobald

The Indians of Iowa
By Lance Foster

An Iowa Album:
A Photographic History, 1860–1920
By Mary Bennett

The Iowa Nature Calendar
By Jean C. Prior and James Sandrock,
illustrated by Claudia McGehee

Iowa's Archaeological Past
By Lynn M. Alex

An Iowa Schoolma'am:
Letters of Elizabeth "Bess" Corey,
1904–1908
Edited by Philip L. Gerber and
Charlotte Wright